# ULTIMATE COMICS
# SPIDER-MAN

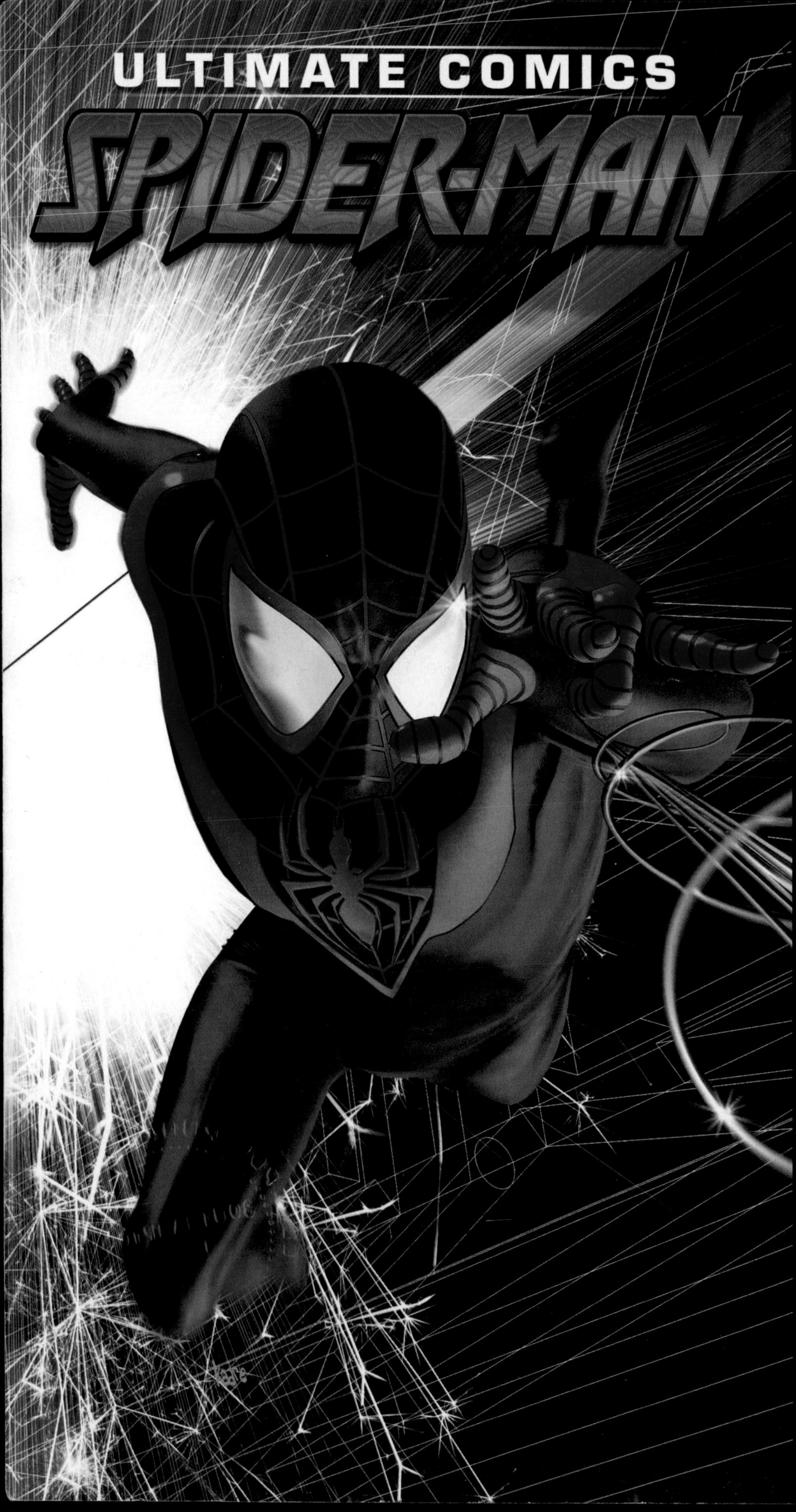
ULTIMATE COMICS
SPIDER-MAN

WRITER: **BRIAN MICHAEL BENDIS**

ARTIST: **SARA PICHELLI**

FINISHES, ISSUE #5: **DAVID MESSINA**

COLORIST: **JUSTIN PONSOR**

LETTERER: **VC'S CORY PETIT**

COVER ART: **KAARE ANDREWS**

## ULTIMATE COMICS FALLOUT #4

REED RICHARDS

    WRITER: **JONATHAN HICKMAN**

    ARTIST: **SALVADOR LARROCA**

    COLORIST: **FRANK D'ARMATA**

VALERIE COOPER

    WRITER: **NICK SPENCER**

    ARTIST: **CLAYTON CRAIN**

LETTERERS: **VC'S CORY PETIT & CLAYTON COWLES**

COVER ART: **MARK BAGLEY, ANDY LANNING & JUSTIN PONSOR**

ASSISTANT EDITOR: **JON MOISAN**

ASSOCIATE EDITOR: **SANA AMANAT**

SENIOR EDITOR: **MARK PANICCIA**

COLLECTION EDITOR: **JENNIFER GRÜNWALD**

ASSISTANT EDITORS: **ALEX STARBUCK & NELSON RIBEIRO**

EDITOR, SPECIAL PROJECTS: **MARK D. BEAZLEY**

SENIOR EDITOR, SPECIAL PROJECTS: **JEFF YOUNGQUIST**

SVP OF PRINT & DIGITAL PUBLISHING SALES: **DAVID GABRIEL**

EDITOR IN CHIEF: **AXEL ALONSO**

CHIEF CREATIVE OFFICER: **JOE QUESADA**

PUBLISHER: **DAN BUCKLEY**

EXECUTIVE PRODUCER: **ALAN FINE**

SPIDER-MAN BY BRIAN MICHAEL BENDIS VOL. 1. Contains material originally published in magazine form as ULTIMATE COMICS SPIDER-MAN #1-5 and ULTIMATE COMICS FALLOUT #4. Second 978-0-7851-5713-7. Published by MARVEL WORLDWIDE, INC., a subsidiary of MARVEL ENTERTAINMENT, LLC. OFFICE OF PUBLICATION: 135 West 50th Street, New York, NY 10020. Copyright Marvel Characters, Inc. All rights reserved. All characters featured in this issue and the distinctive names and likenesses thereof, and all related indicia are trademarks of Marvel Characters, Inc. n any of the names, characters, persons, and/or institutions in this magazine with those of any living or dead person or institution is intended, and any such similarity which may exist is purely in the U.S.A. ALAN FINE, EVP - Office of the President, Marvel Worldwide, Inc. and EVP & CMO Marvel Characters B.V.; DAN BUCKLEY, Publisher & President - Print, Animation & Digital Divisions; Creative Officer; TOM BREVOORT, SVP of Publishing; DAVID BOGART, SVP of Operations & Procurement, Publishing; C.B. CEBULSKI, SVP of Creator & Content Development; DAVID GABRIEL, Publishing Sales; JIM O'KEEFE, VP of Operations & Logistics; DAN CARR, Executive Director of Publishing Technology; SUSAN CRESPI, Editorial Operations Manager; ALEX MORALES, Publishing STAN LEE, Chairman Emeritus. For information regarding advertising in Marvel Comics or on Marvel.com, please contact Niza Disla, Director of Marvel Partnerships, at ndisla@marvel.com. For inquiries, please call 800-217-9158. **Manufactured between 6/19/2013 and 7/22/2013 by R.R. DONNELLEY, INC., SALEM, VA, USA.**

# 1

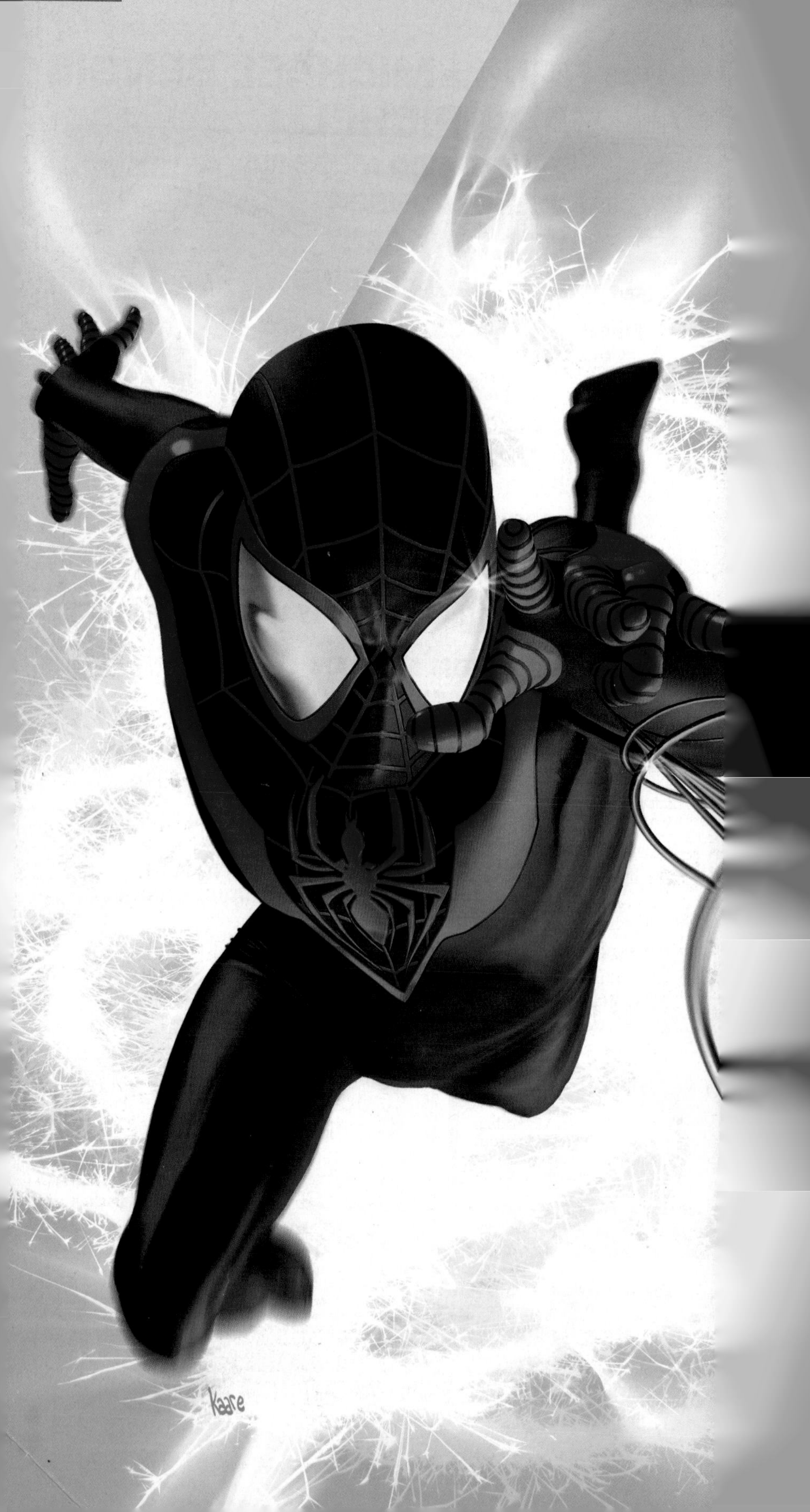
Kaare

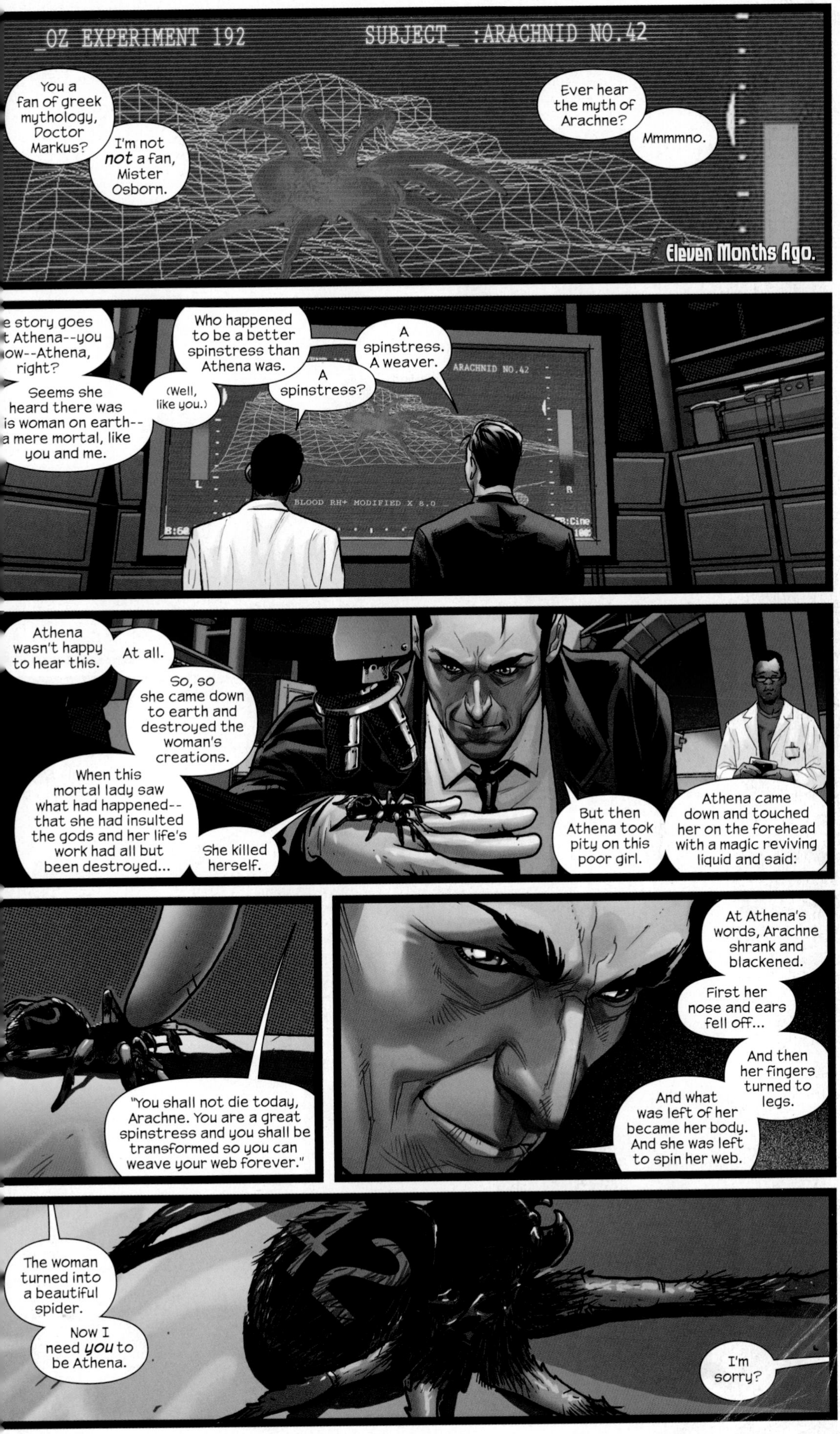
_OZ EXPERIMENT 192
SUBJECT_ :ARACHNID NO.42
You a fan of greek mythology, Doctor Markus?
I'm not *not* a fan, Mister Osborn.
Ever hear the myth of Arachne?
Mmmmno.
Eleven Months Ago.
e story goes t Athena--you ow--Athena, right?
Who happened to be a better spinstress than Athena was.
A spinstress. A weaver.
Seems she heard there was is woman on earth-- a mere mortal, like you and me.
(Well, like you.)
A spinstress?
ARACHNID NO.42
BLOOD RH+ MODIFIED X 8.0
Athena wasn't happy to hear this.
At all.
So, so she came down to earth and destroyed the woman's creations.
When this mortal lady saw what had happened-- that she had insulted the gods and her life's work had all but been destroyed...
She killed herself.
But then Athena took pity on this poor girl.
Athena came down and touched her on the forehead with a magic reviving liquid and said:
"You shall not die today, Arachne. You are a great spinstress and you shall be transformed so you can weave your web forever."
At Athena's words, Arachne shrank and blackened.
First her nose and ears fell off...
And then her fingers turned to legs.
And what was left of her became her body. And she was left to spin her web.
The woman turned into a beautiful spider.
Now I need *you* to be Athena.
I'm sorry?

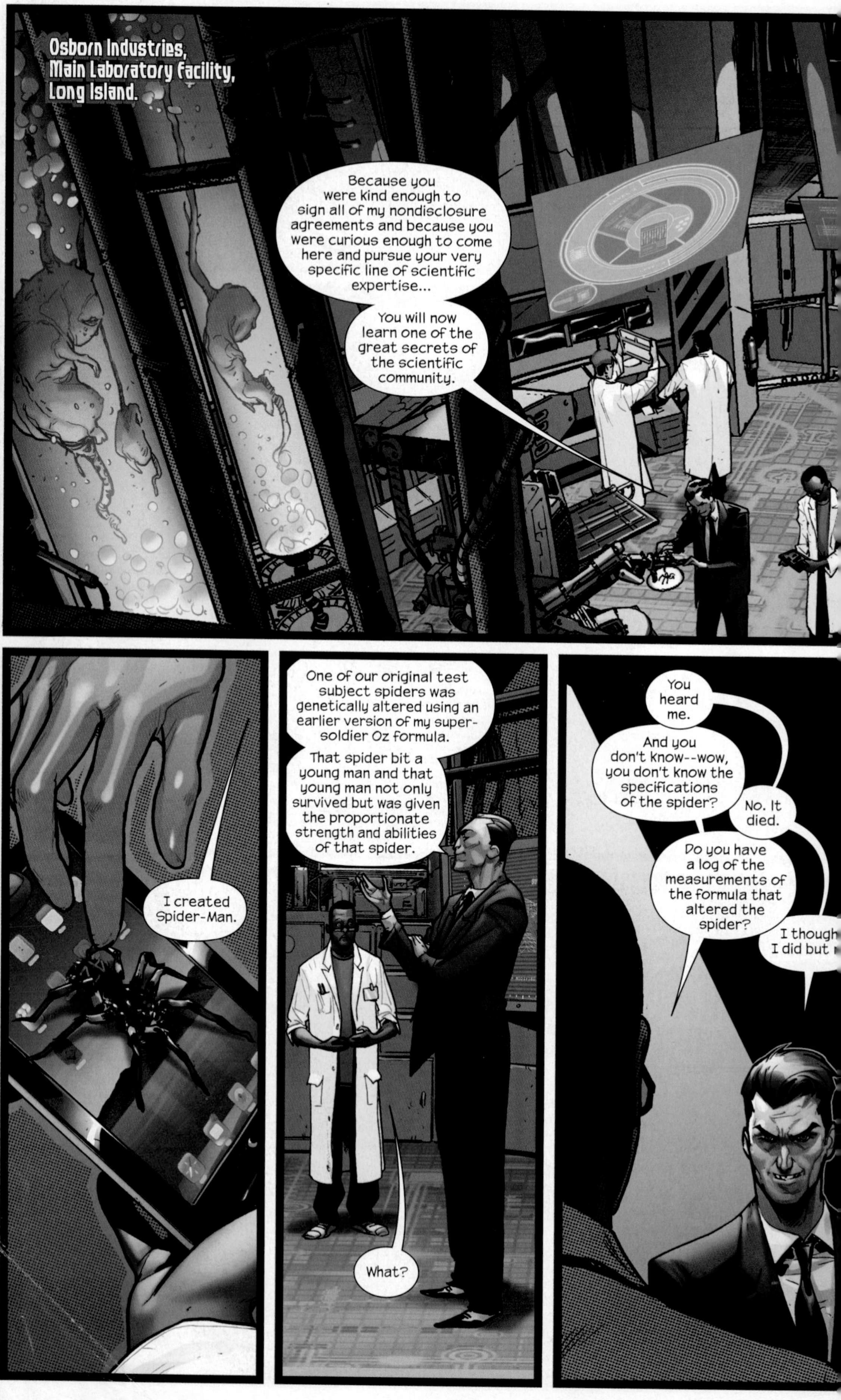
Osborn Industries, Main Laboratory Facility, Long Island.
Because you were kind enough to sign all of my nondisclosure agreements and because you were curious enough to come here and pursue your very specific line of scientific expertise...
You will now learn one of the great secrets of the scientific community.
I created Spider-Man.
One of our original test subject spiders was genetically altered using an earlier version of my super-soldier Oz formula.
That spider bit a young man and that young man not only survived but was given the proportionate strength and abilities of that spider.
What?
You heard me.
And you don't know--wow, you don't know the specifications of the spider?
No. It died.
Do you have a log of the measurements of the formula that altered the spider?

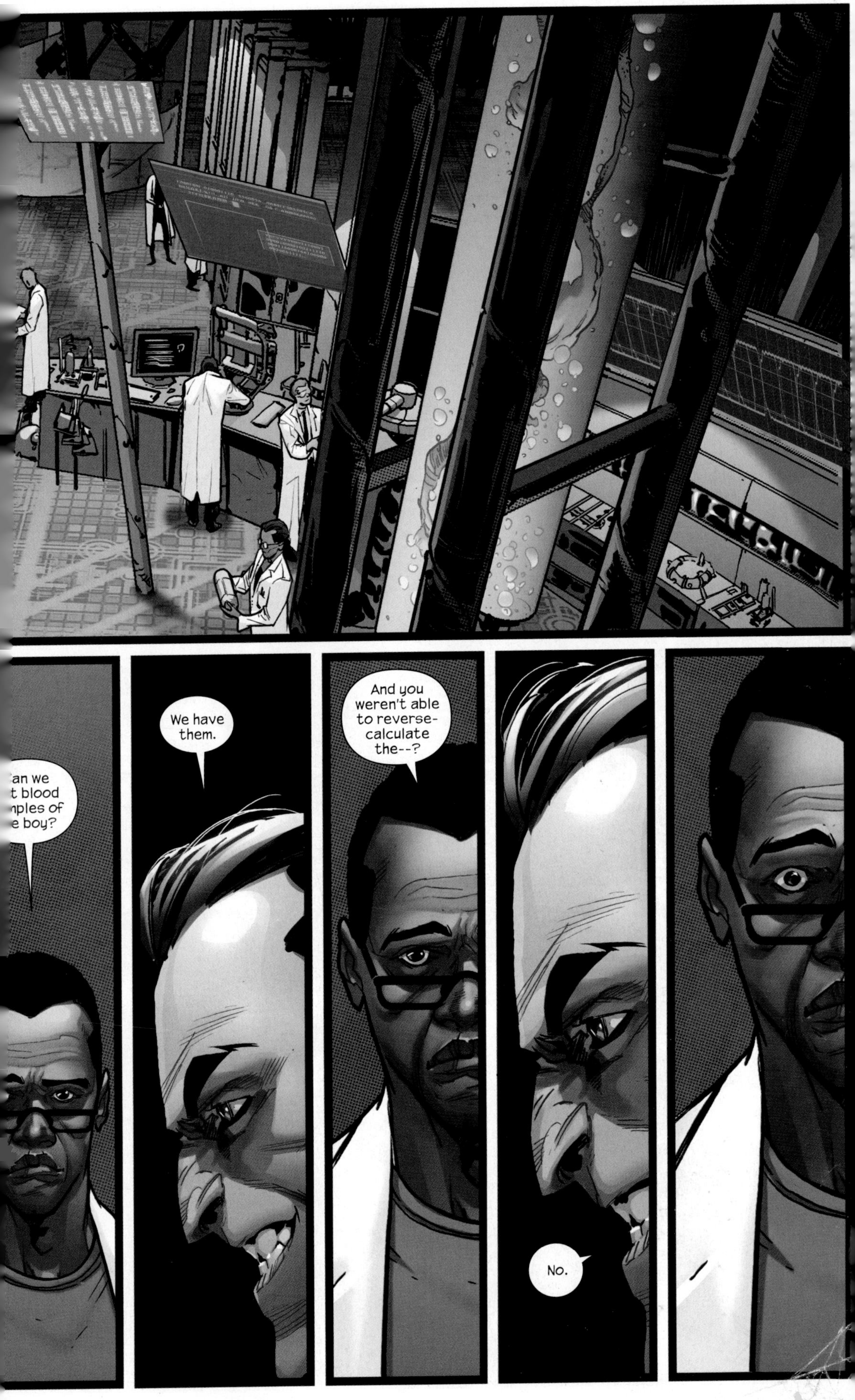

an we
t blood
nples of
e boy?
We have them.
And you weren't able to reverse-calculate the--?
No.

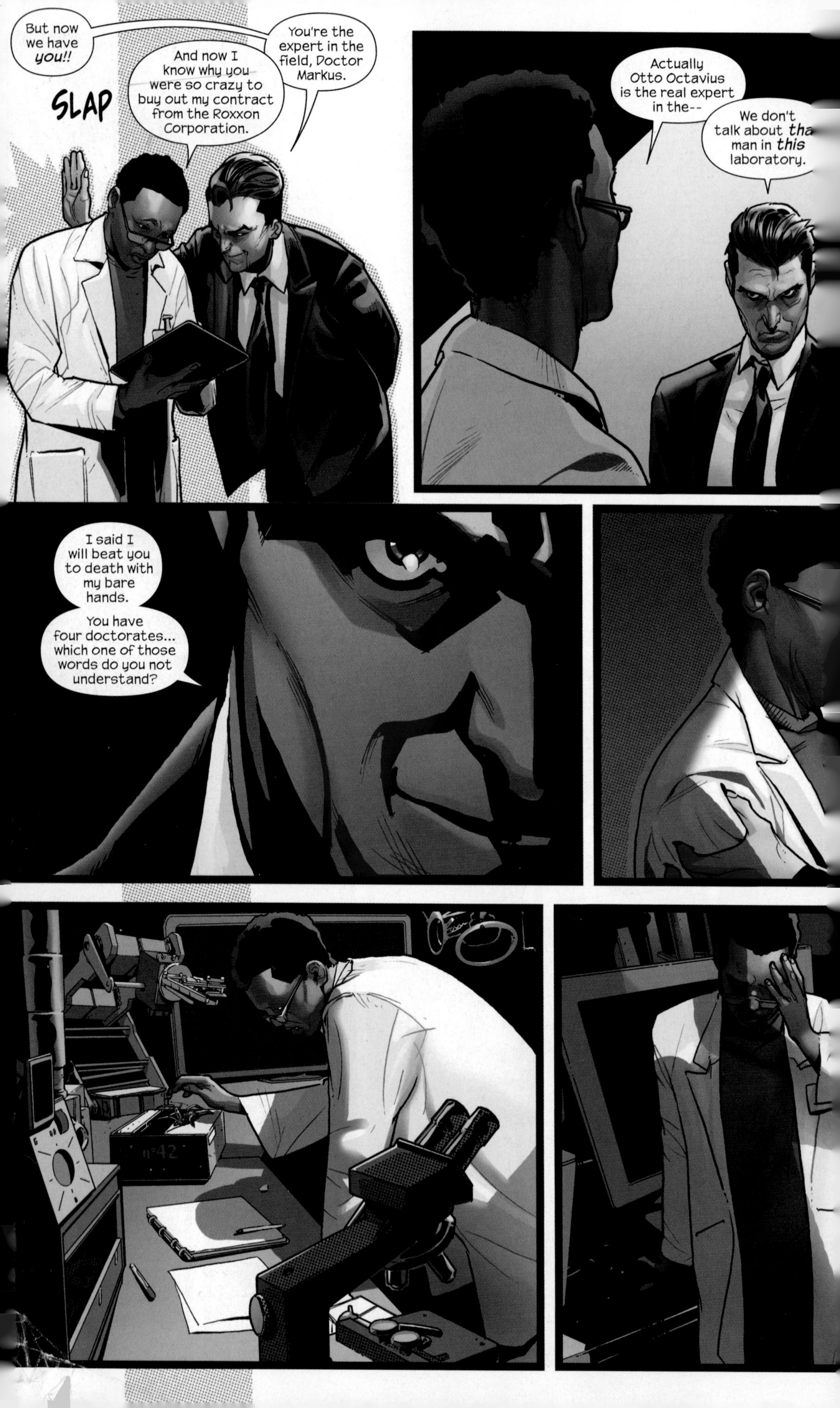

But now we have *you!!*
You're the expert in the field, Doctor Markus.
And now I know why you were so crazy to buy out my contract from the Roxxon Corporation.
SLAP
Actually Otto Octavius is the real expert in the--
We don't talk about *tha* man in *this* laboratory.
I said I will beat you to death with my bare hands.
You have four doctorates... which one of those words do you not understand?

You created Spider-Man.

And I hope you understand that if this information leaves this building I will *kill* you.

Excuse me?

But if you solve this problem for me I will reward you to the point where I reinvent your life on every conceivable level.

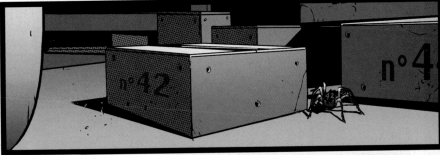

74° • LOG IN • REGISTER • ARCH

# DAILY BUGLE

| LOCAL | INTERNATIONAL | ARTS & ENTERTAINMENT | OPINION | SPO

# NORMAN OSBORN I
# THE GREEN GOBLIN!

**CONTROVERSIAL INDUSTRIALIST IS REVEALED TO BE GENETICALLY ALTER MONSTER NOW IN T CUSTODY OF S.H.I.E.**

*Reporting by Frederick Fosswell*

Agents of the world peacekeeping task forc S.H.I.E.L.D. have confirmed to the Daily Bu that controversial indu trialist Norman Osbor had infected his own b with one of his experiments altering himself into what one of our S.H.I.E.L.D. sources are referring to as the Green Goblin.

Sources also confirm t this Green Goblin is the same one that attacked Midtown High School a few mont ago, shutting the school down for weeks. It is also referred to as the public debut o the mystery man called Spider-Man. Whether or not there is a connection betwee Spider-Man and Norman Osborn's double life has yet to be revealed.

Speculation continues as to why Norman Osborn would break one of the cardinal rules of science by experimenting on himself. Sources close to Norman say that certain pressures to create a workable version of his experimental "super-soldier" formula led him to use the formula on himself.

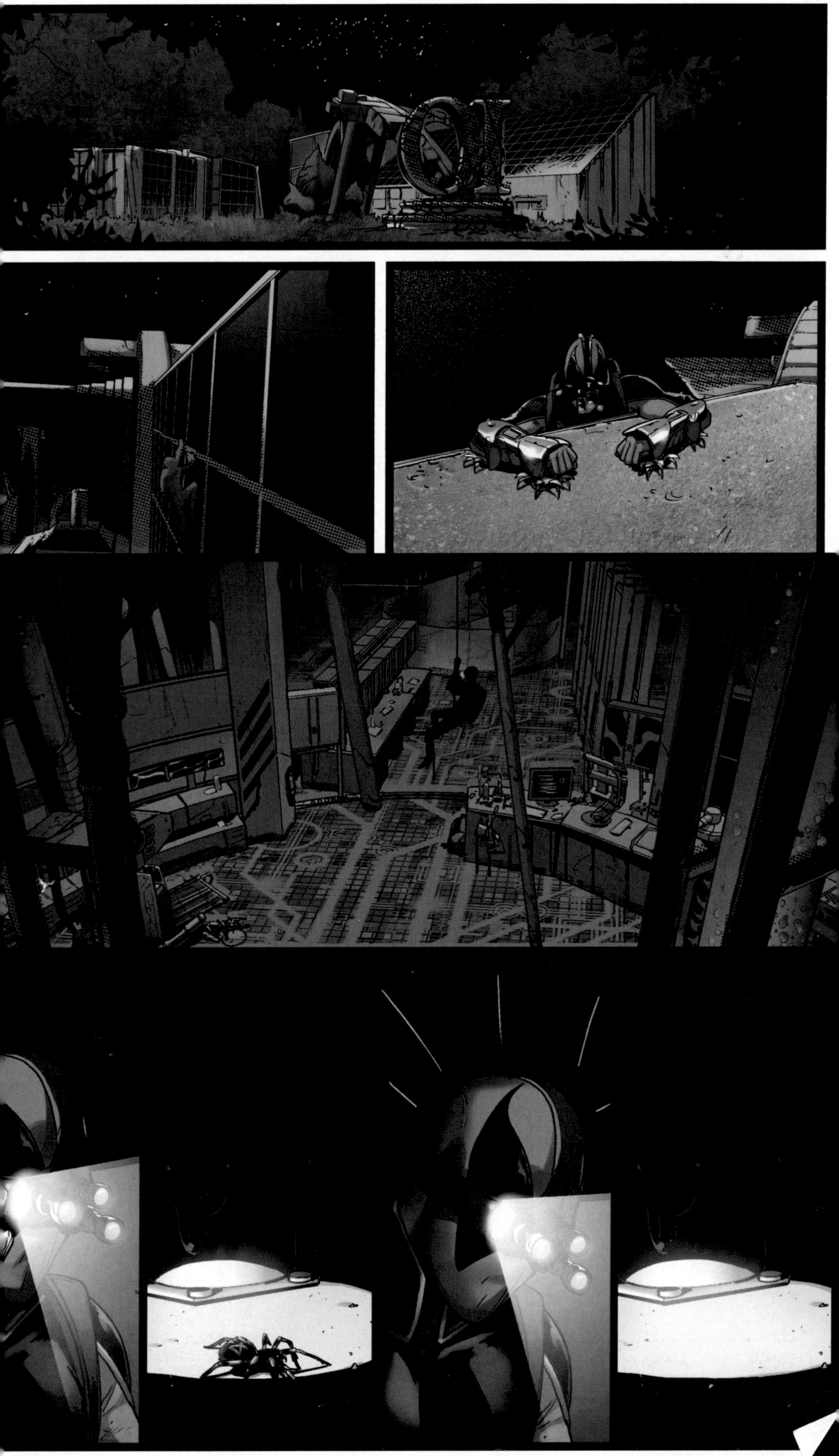

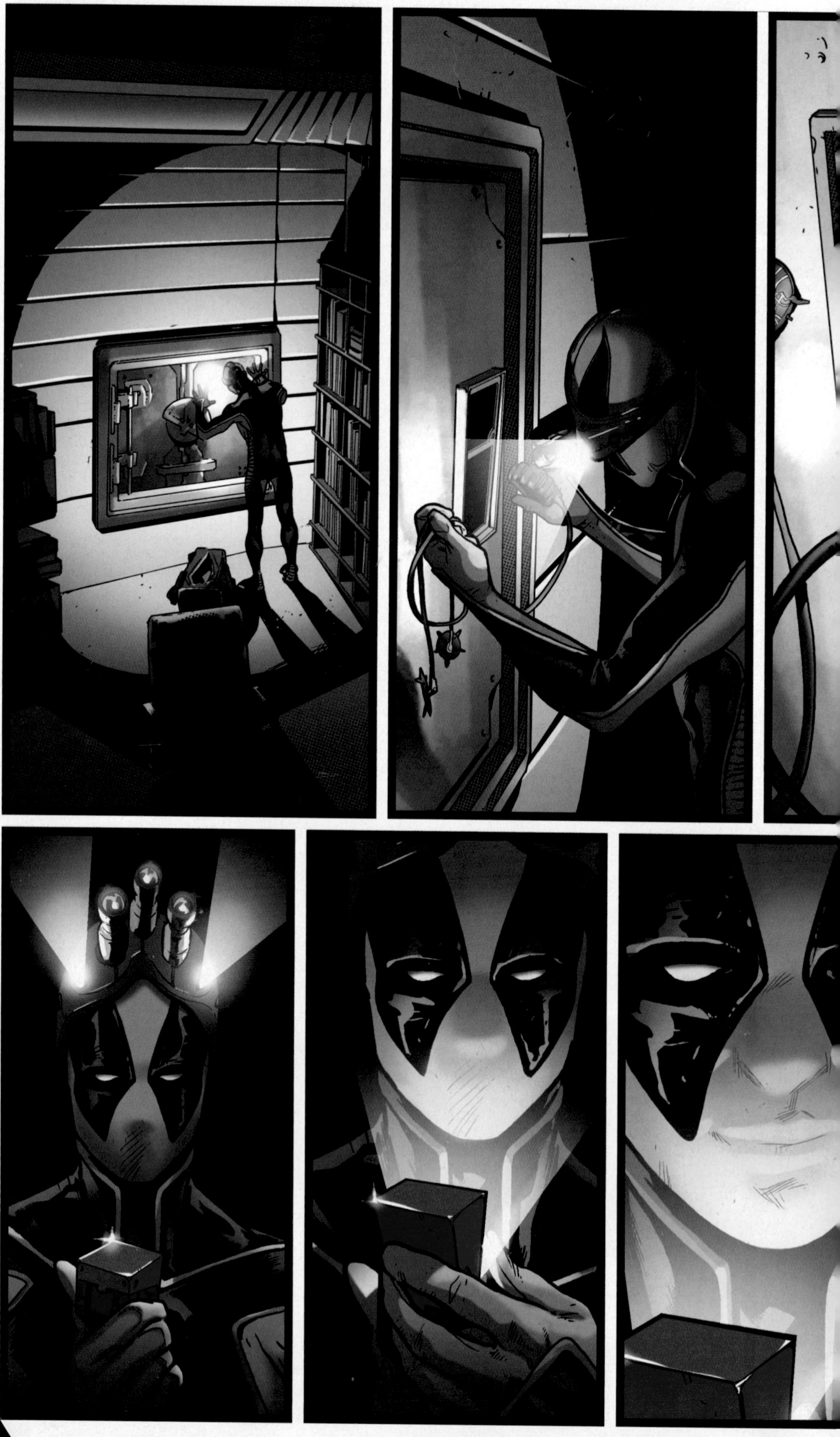

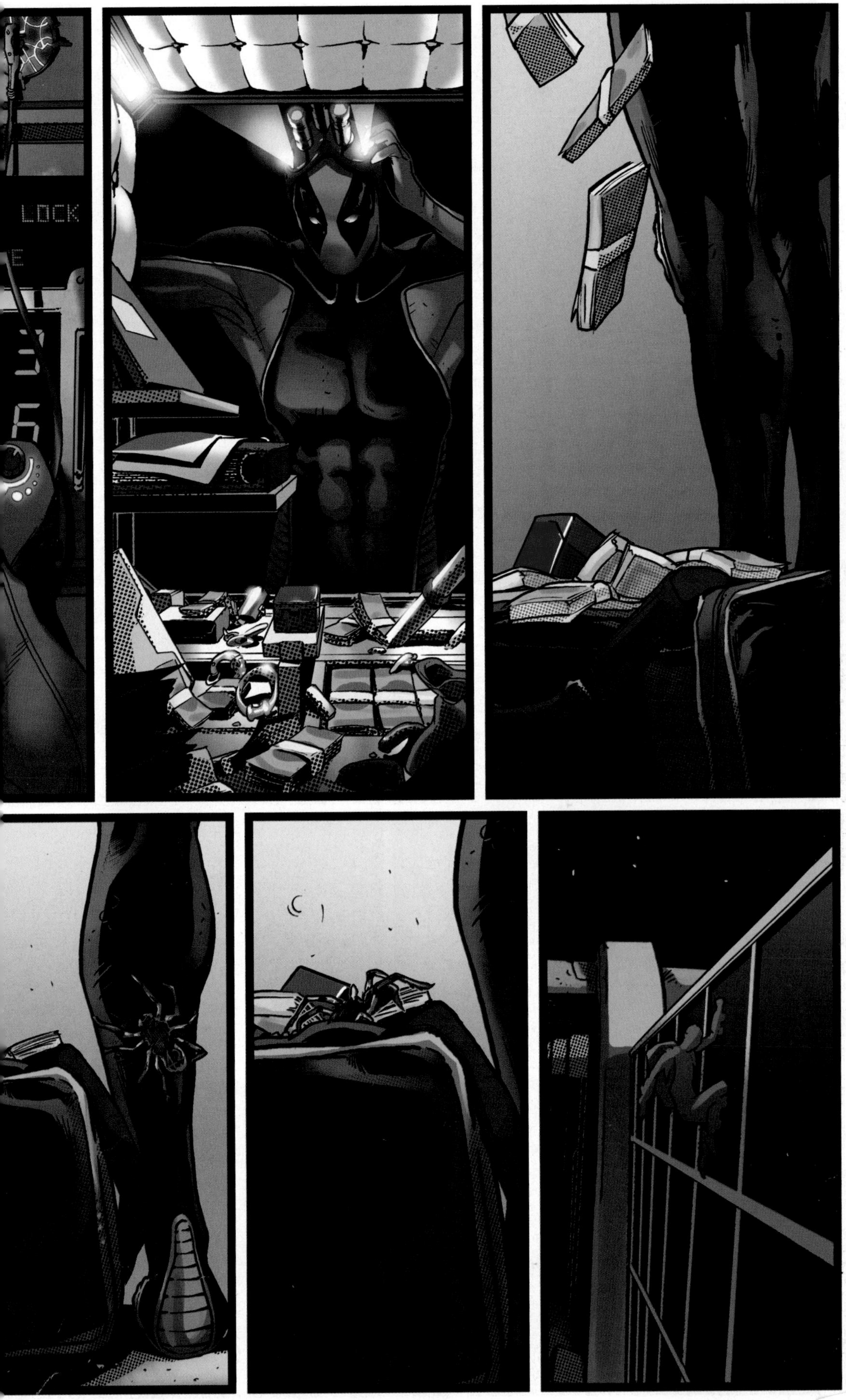

LOCK

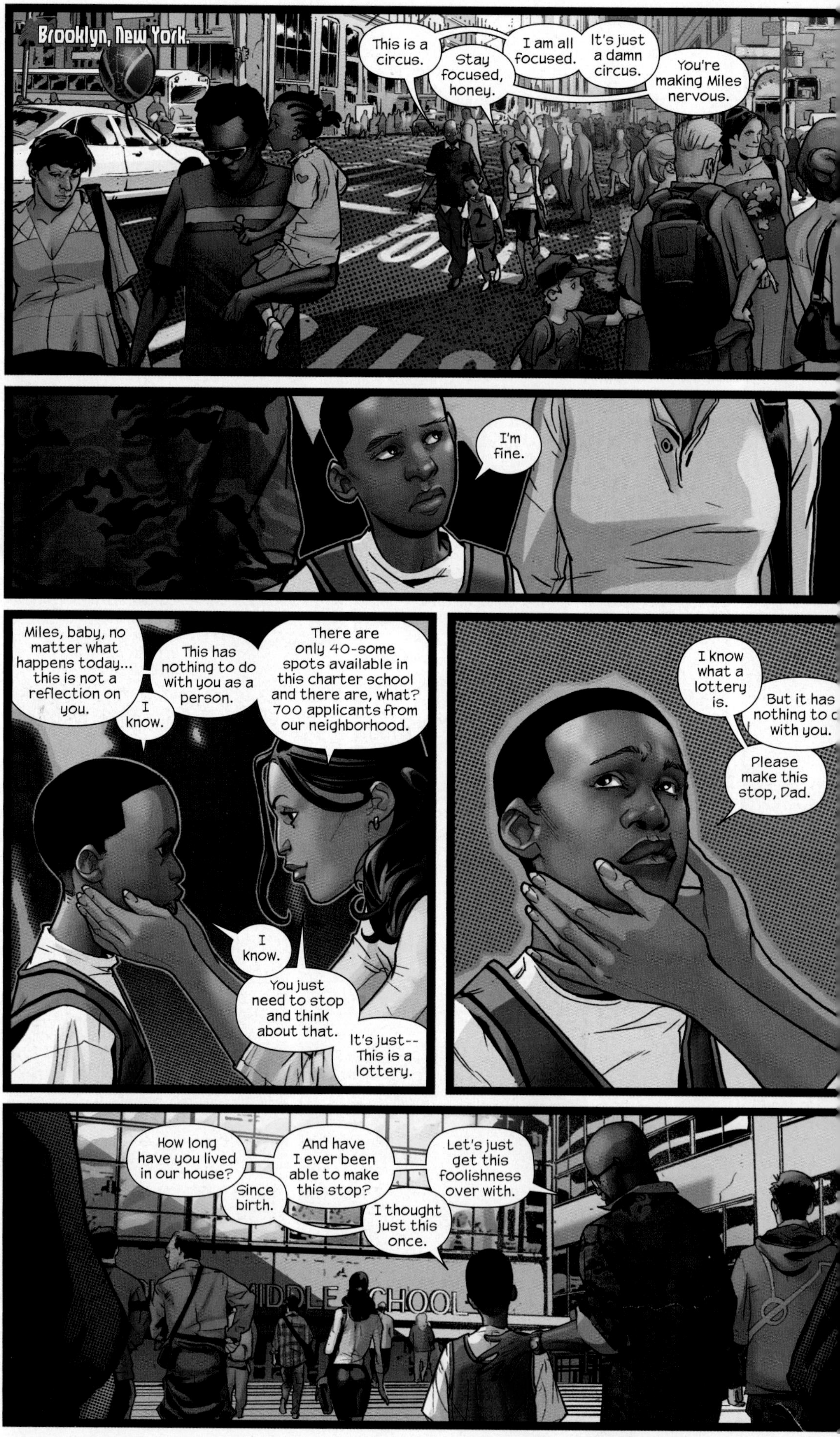
Brooklyn, New York.
This is a circus.
Stay focused, honey.
I am all focused.
It's just a damn circus.
You're making Miles nervous.
I'm fine.
Miles, baby, no matter what happens today... this is not a reflection on you.
I know.
This has nothing to do with you as a person.
There are only 40-some spots available in this charter school and there are, what? 700 applicants from our neighborhood.
I know.
You just need to stop and think about that.
It's just-- This is a lottery.
I know what a lottery is.
But it has nothing to do with you.
Please make this stop, Dad.
How long have you lived in our house?
Since birth.
And have I ever been able to make this stop?
I thought just this once.
Let's just get this foolishness over with.
MIDDLE SCHOOL

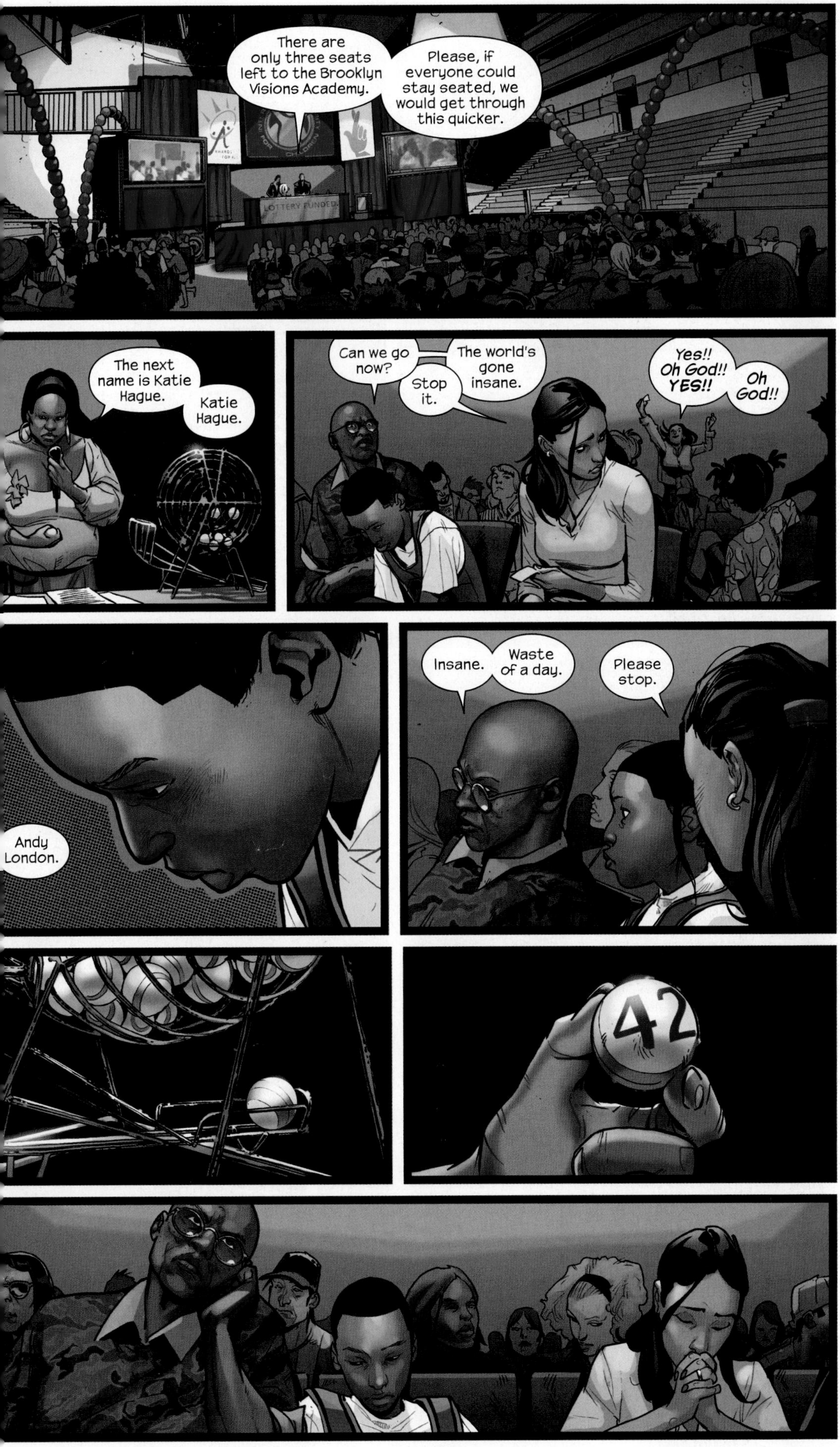

There are only three seats left to the Brooklyn Visions Academy.
Please, if everyone could stay seated, we would get through this quicker.
LOTTERY FUNDED
The next name is Katie Hague.
Katie Hague.
Can we go now?
The world's gone insane.
Stop it.
Yes!! Oh God!! YES!!
Oh God!!
Andy London.
Insane.
Waste of a day.
Please stop.
42

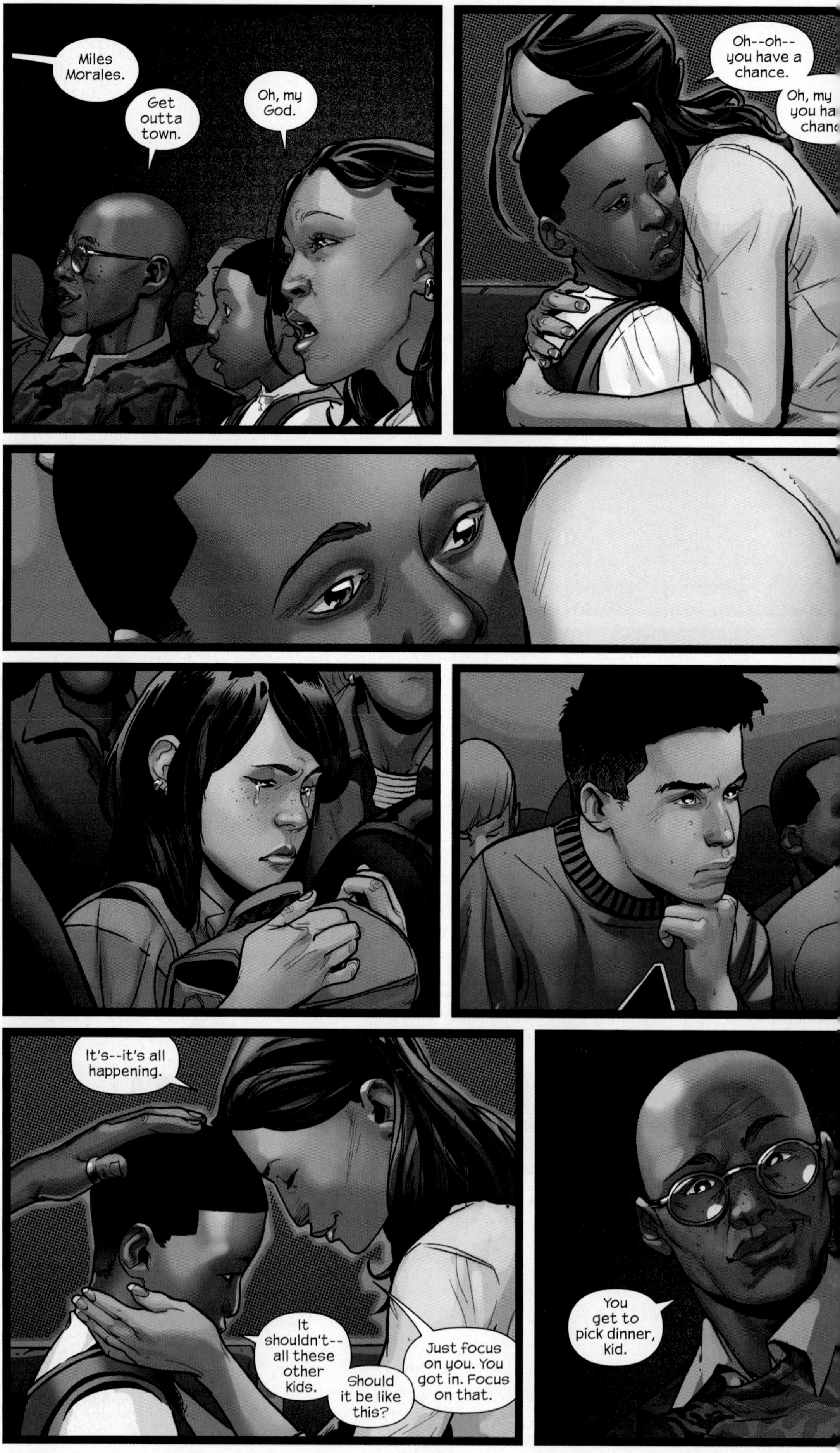
Miles Morales.
Get outta town.
Oh, my God.
Oh--oh-- you have a chance.
Oh, my you ha chanc
It's--it's all happening.
It shouldn't-- all these other kids.
Should it be like this?
Just focus on you. You got in. Focus on that.
You get to pick dinner, kid.

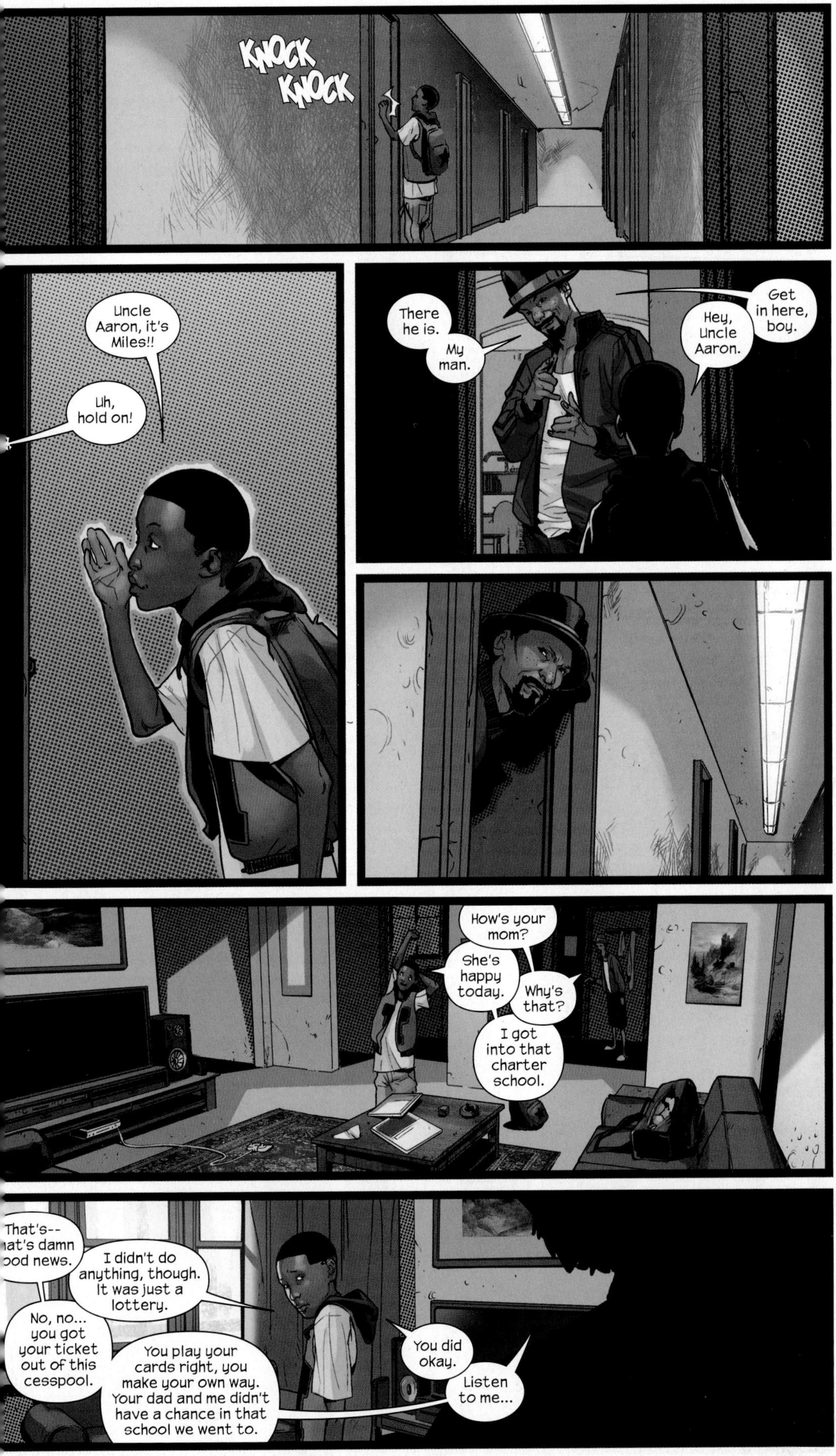
KNOCK KNOCK
Uncle Aaron, it's Miles!!
Uh, hold on!
There he is.
My man.
Get in here, boy.
Hey, Uncle Aaron.
How's your mom?
She's happy today.
Why's that?
I got into that charter school.
That's-- ...at's damn ...ood news.
I didn't do anything, though. It was just a lottery.
No, no... you got your ticket out of this cesspool.
You play your cards right, you make your own way. Your dad and me didn't have a chance in that school we went to.
You did okay.
Listen to me...

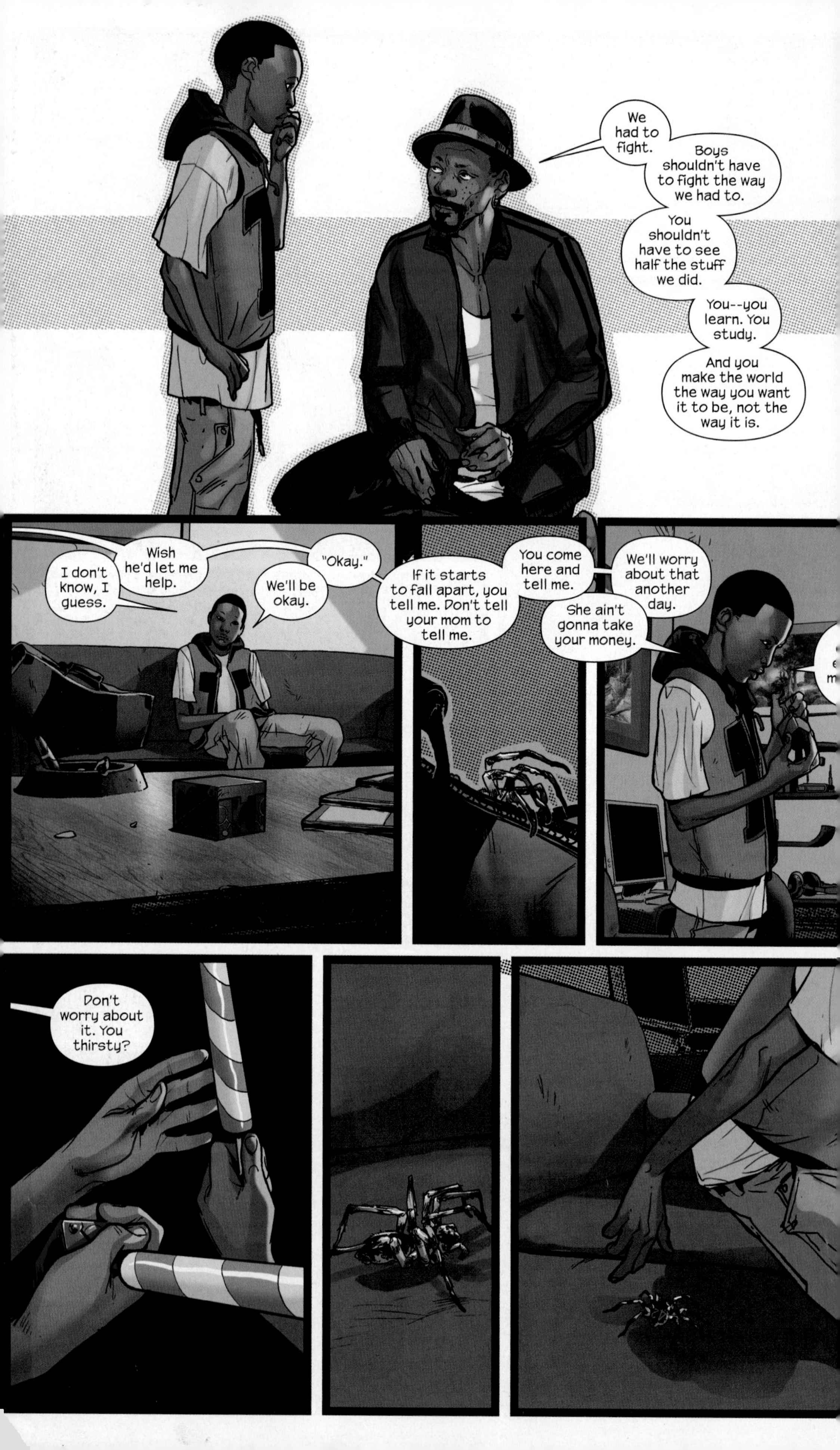
We had to fight.
Boys shouldn't have to fight the way we had to.
You shouldn't have to see half the stuff we did.
You--you learn. You study.
And you make the world the way you want it to be, not the way it is.
I don't know, I guess.
Wish he'd let me help.
We'll be okay.
"Okay."
If it starts to fall apart, you tell me. Don't tell your mom to tell me.
You come here and tell me.
She ain't gonna take your money.
We'll worry about that another day.
Don't worry about it. You thirsty?

This is a good thing. This-- this calls for popsicles.

Right?

Yeah.

Your daddy gonna be able to pay for it?

You make it.

Don't let people make it for you.

What's this?

Oh hey no. That is something else--that is something for work.

What is it?

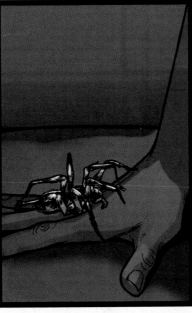

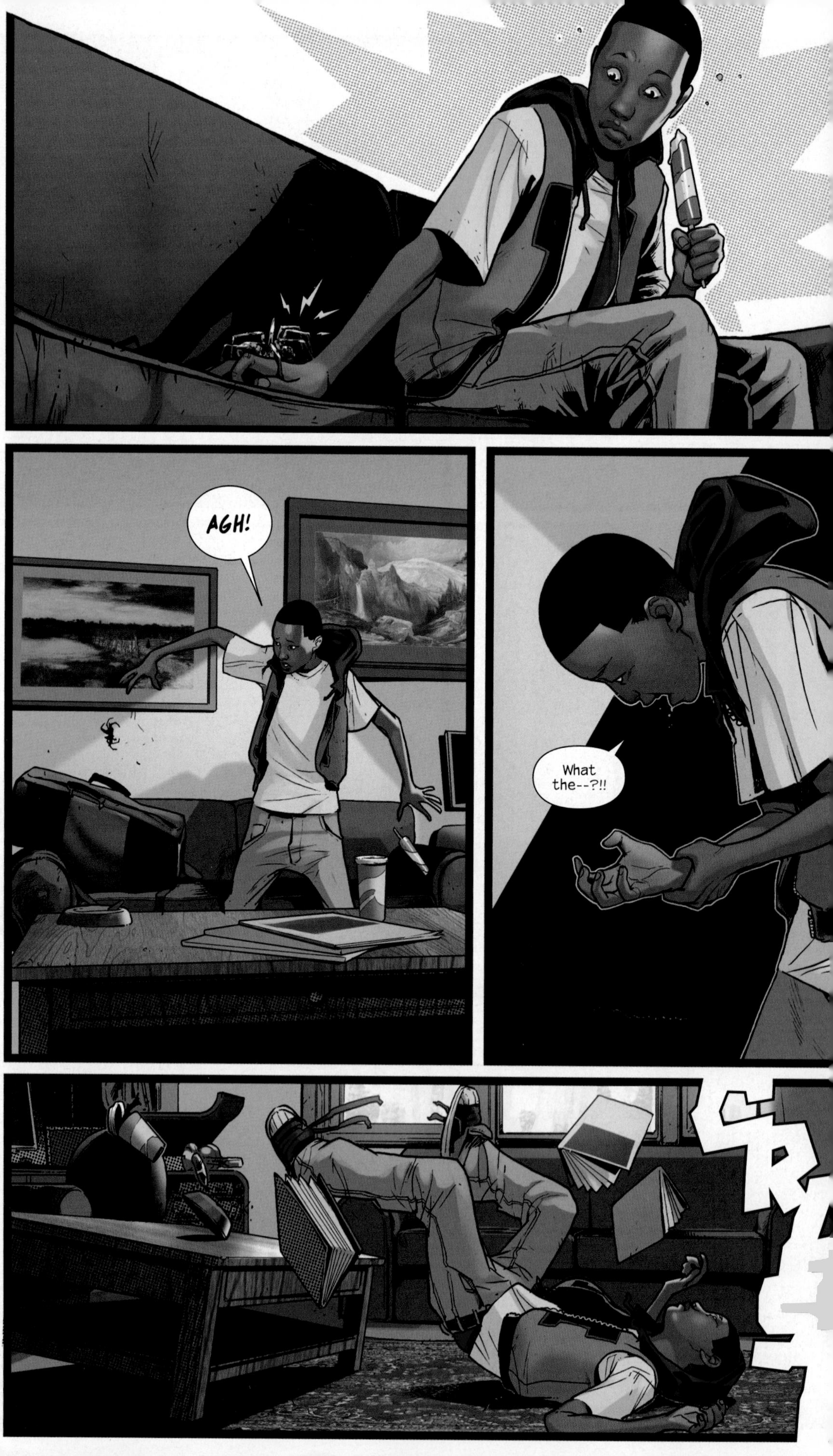
AGH!
What the--?!!

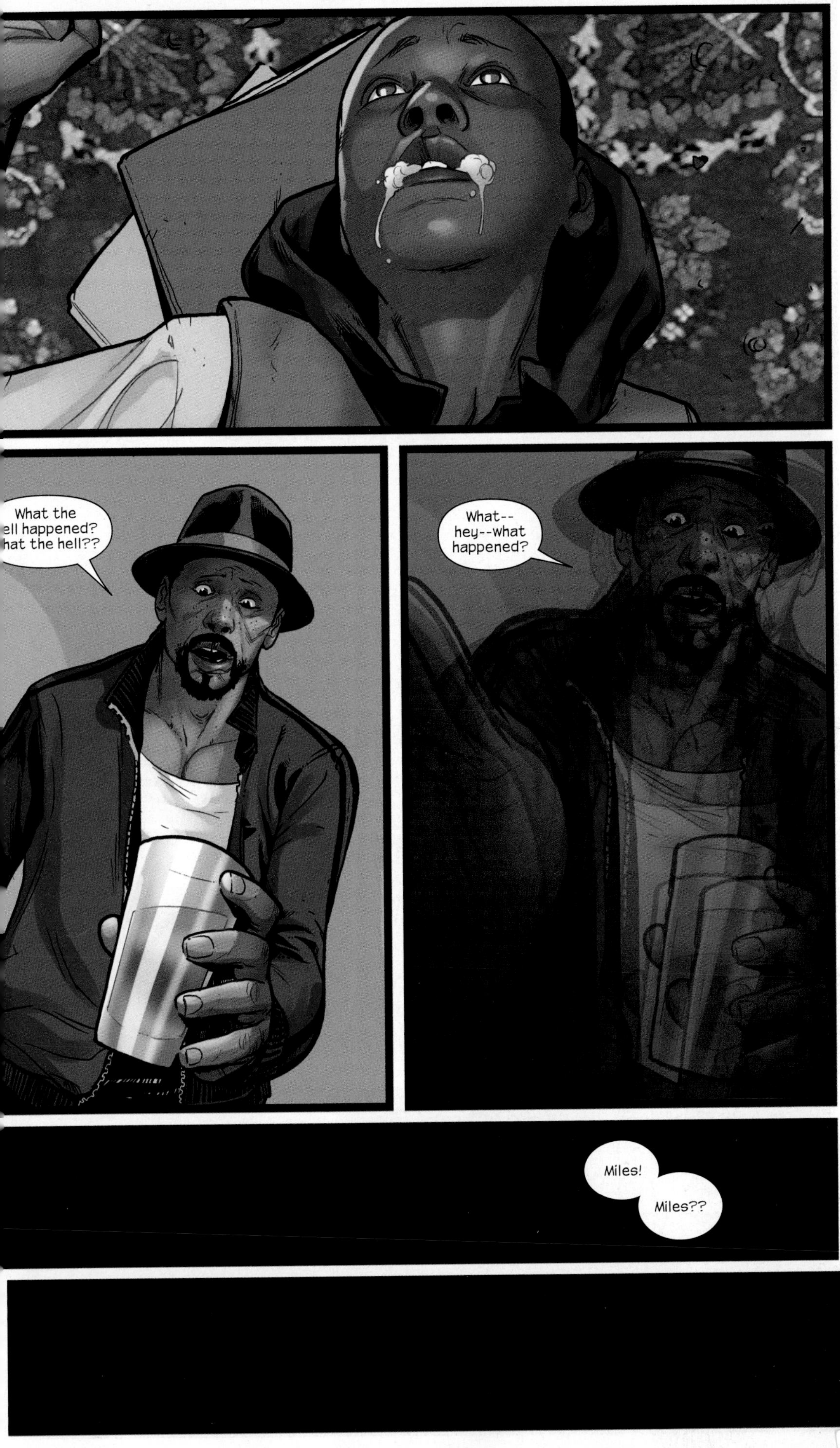
What the
ell happened?
hat the hell??
What--
hey--what
happened?
Miles!
Miles??

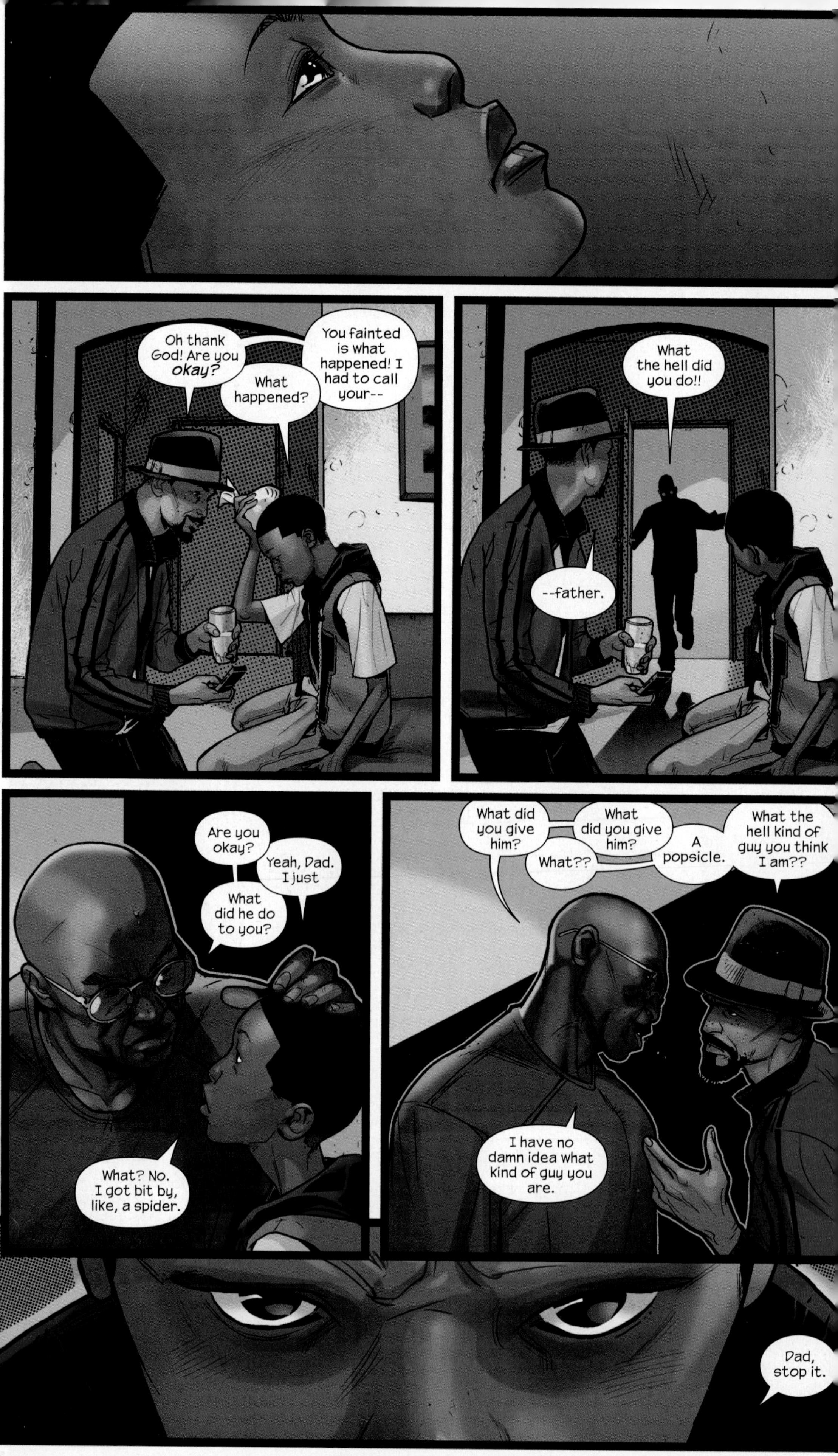

Oh thank God! Are you *okay?*
What happened?
You fainted is what happened! I had to call your--
What the hell did you do!!
--father.
Are you okay?
Yeah, Dad. I just
What did he do to you?
What? No. I got bit by, like, a spider.
What did you give him?
What did you give him?
What??
A popsicle.
What the hell kind of guy you think I am??
I have no damn idea what kind of guy you are.
Dad, stop it.

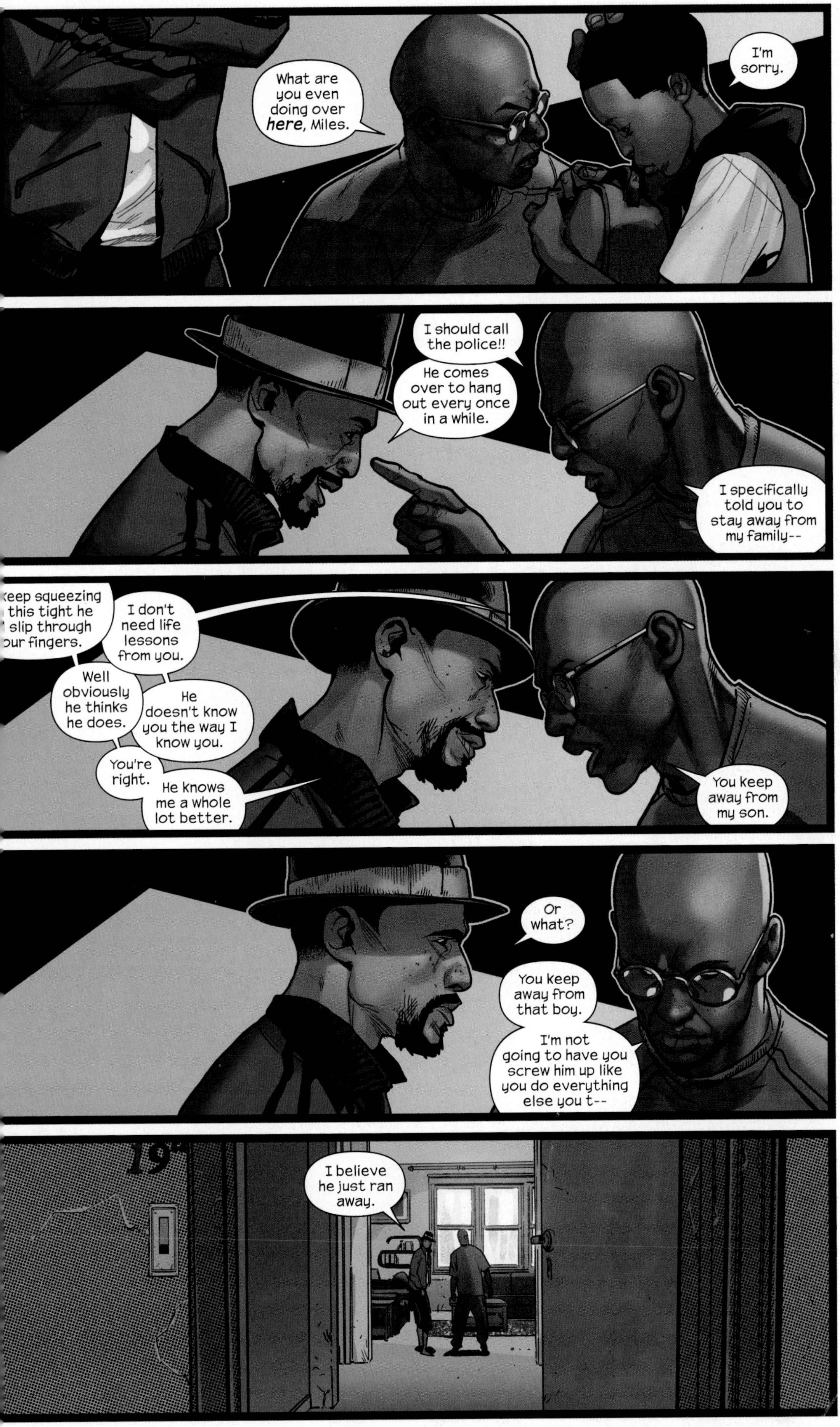
What are you even doing over *here*, Miles.
I'm sorry.
I should call the police!!
He comes over to hang out every once in a while.
I specifically told you to stay away from my family--
I don't need life lessons from you.
eep squeezing this tight he slip through our fingers.
Well obviously he thinks he does.
He doesn't know you the way I know you.
You're right.
He knows me a whole lot better.
You keep away from my son.
Or what?
You keep away from that boy.
I'm not going to have you screw him up like you do everything else you t--
I believe he just ran away.

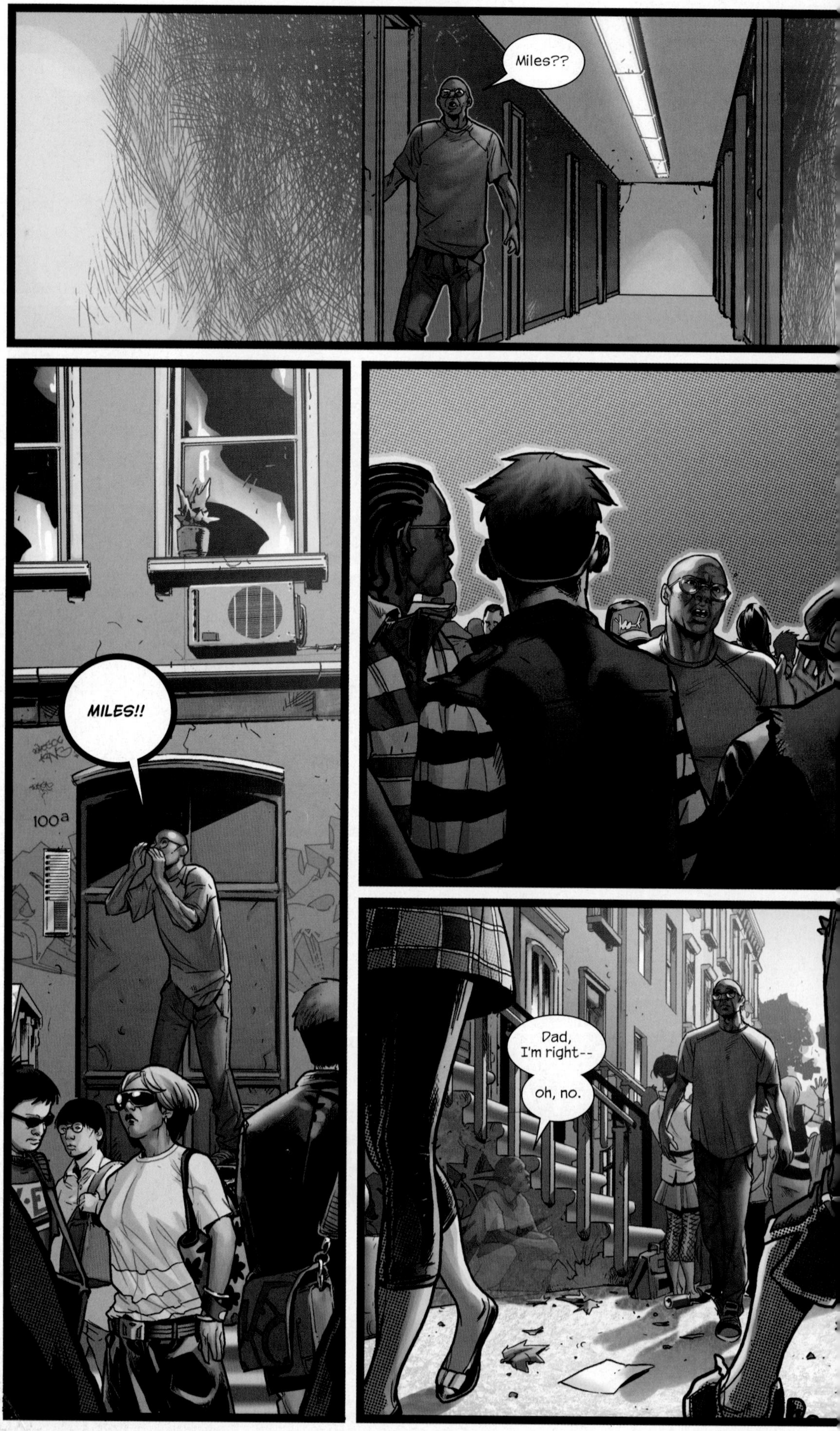
Miles??
MILES!!
100a
Dad, I'm right--
oh, no.

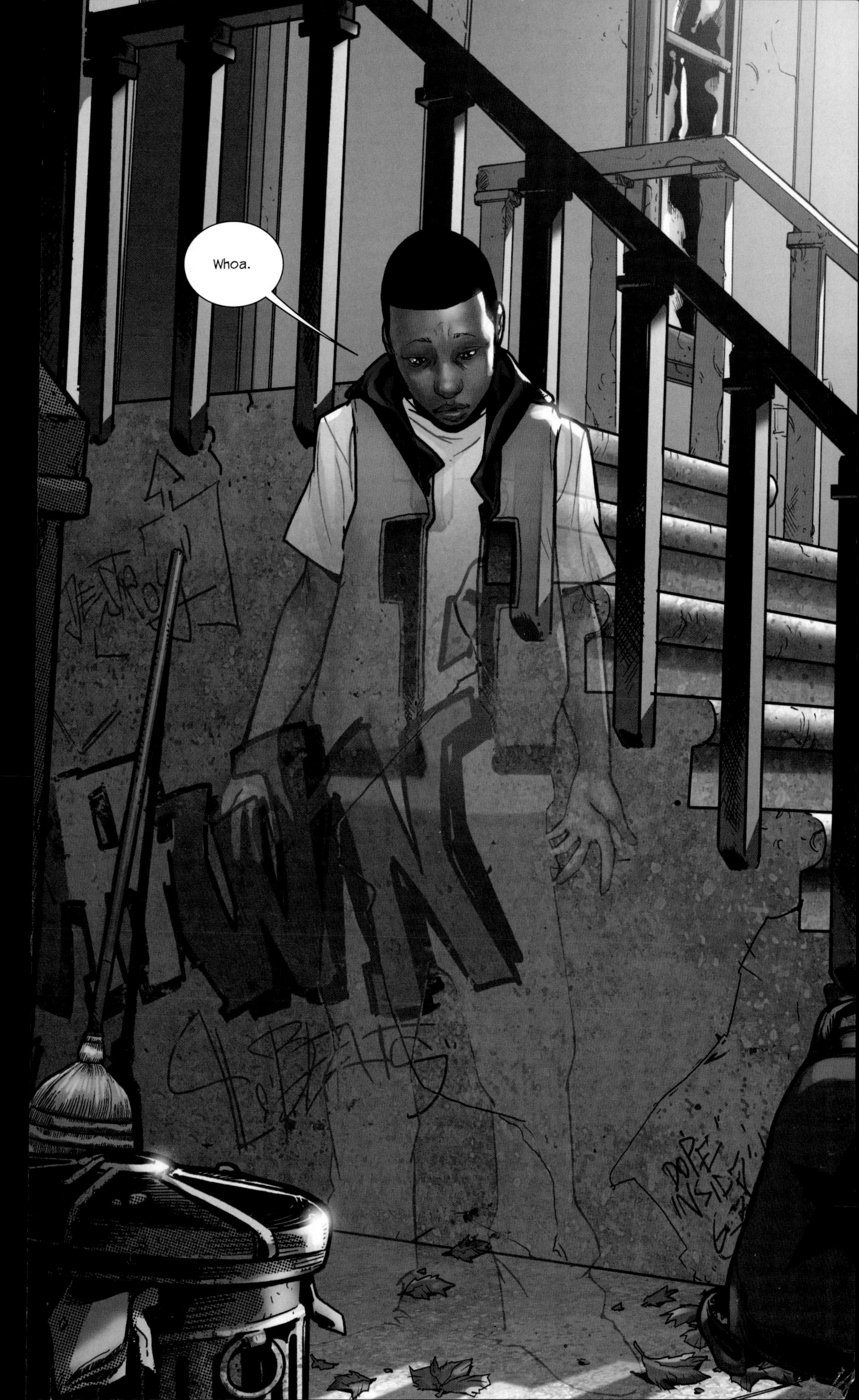
Whoa.

2

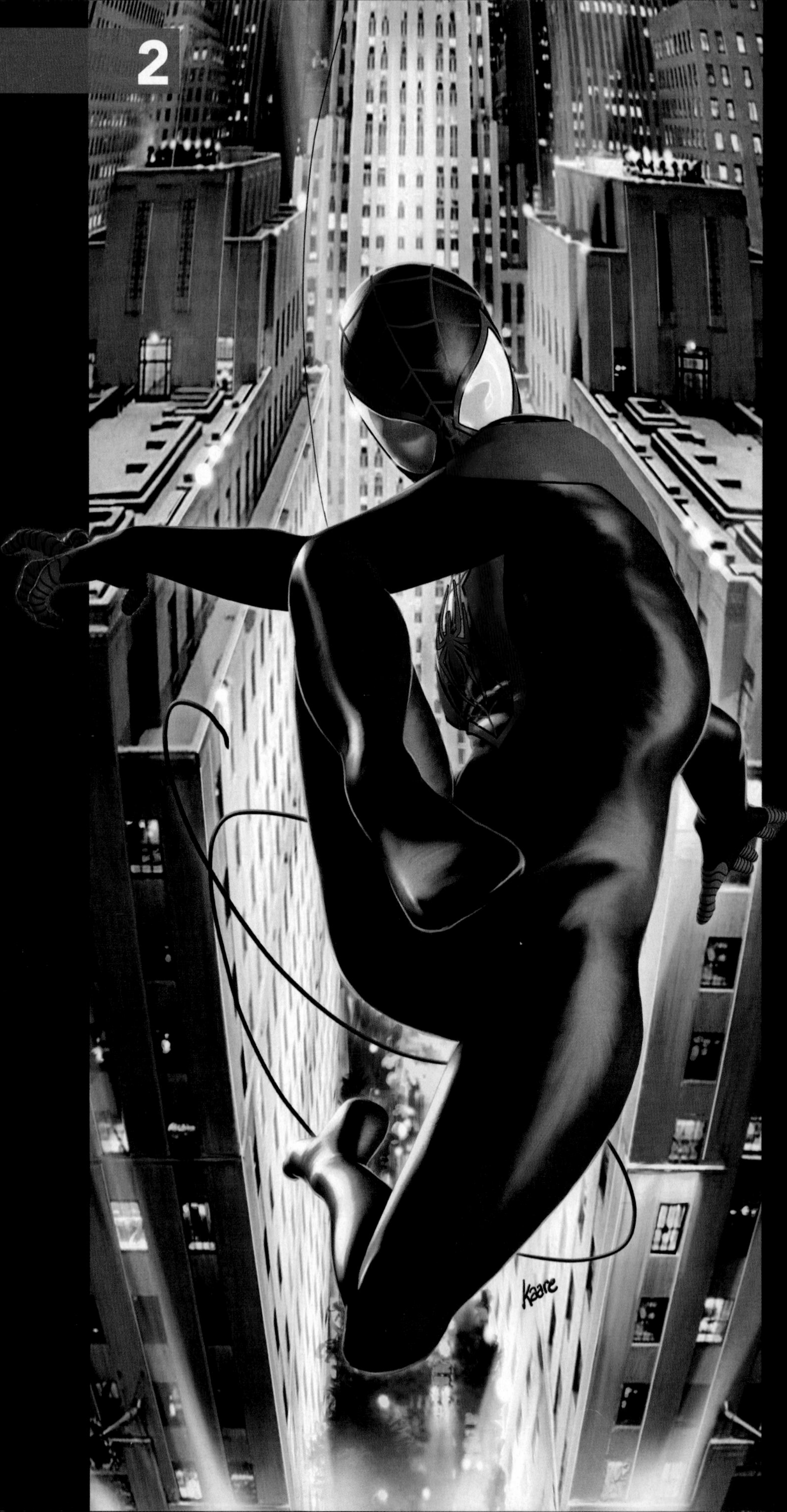
Kaare

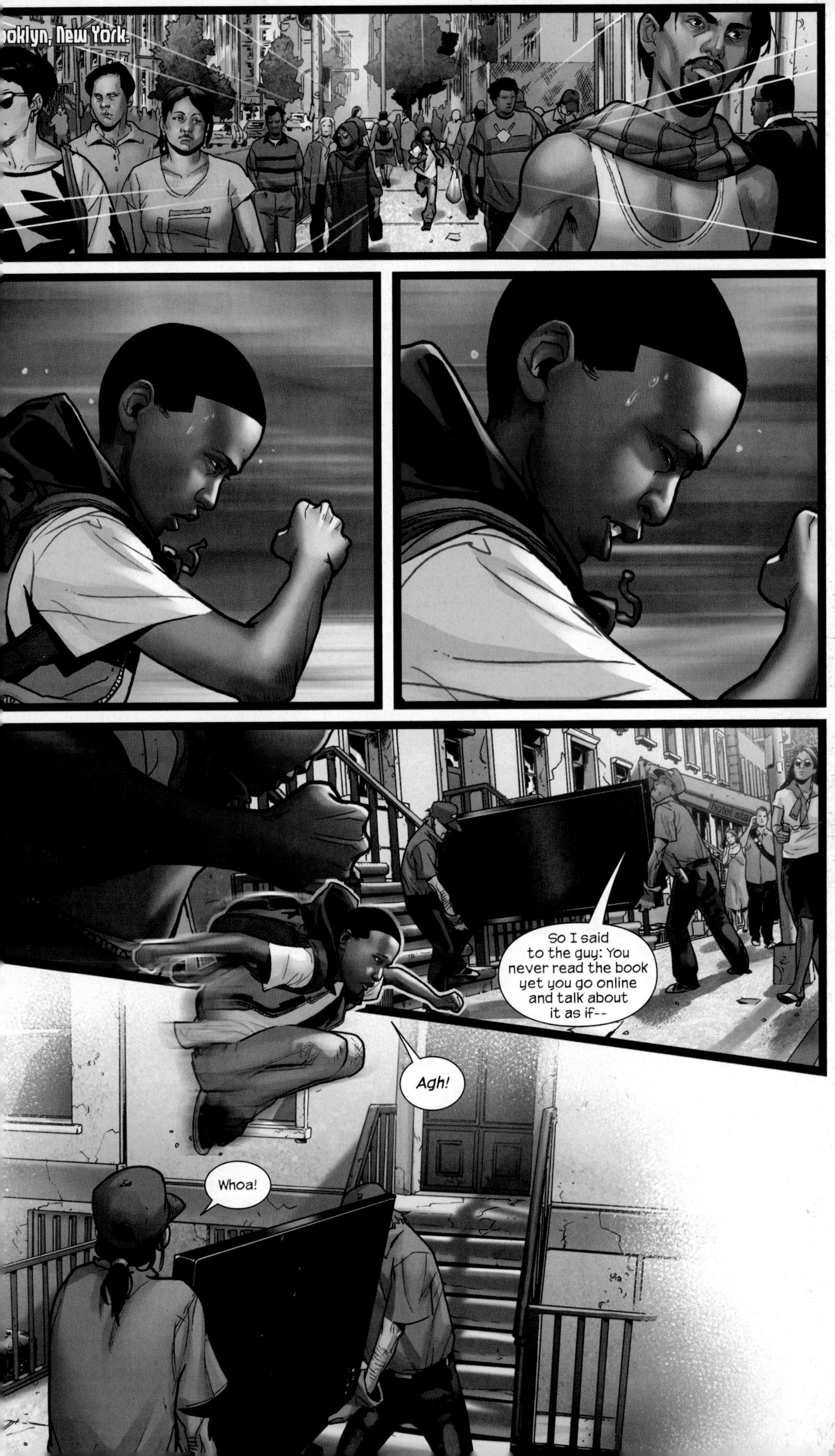

...ooklyn, New York.
So I said to the guy: You never read the book yet you go online and talk about it as if--
Agh!
Whoa!

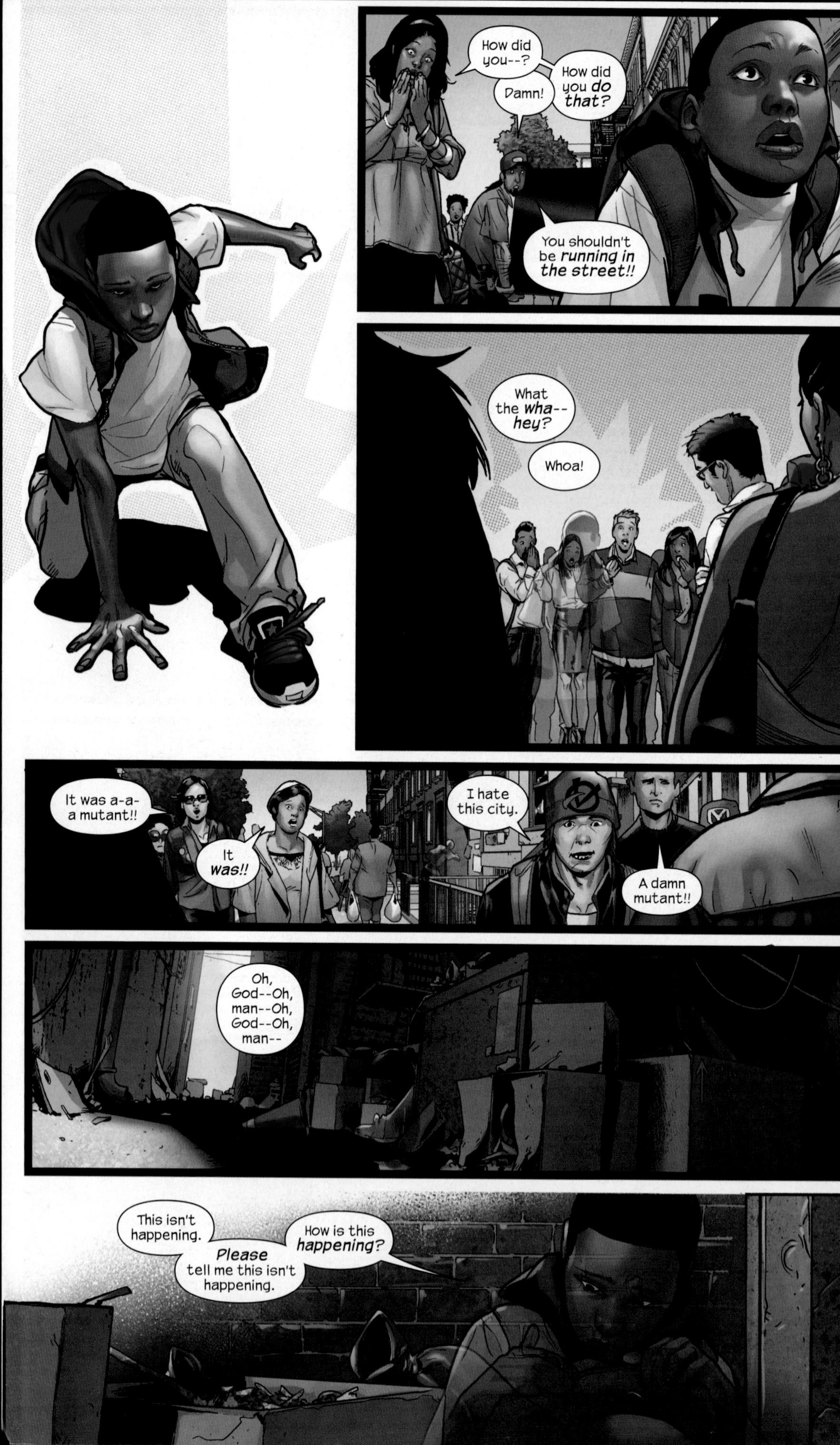
How did you--?
Damn!
How did you do that?
You shouldn't be running in the street!!
What the wha-- hey?
Whoa!
It was a-a-a mutant!!
It was!!
I hate this city.
A damn mutant!!
Oh, God--Oh, man--Oh, God--Oh, man--
This isn't happening.
Please tell me this isn't happening.
How is this happening?

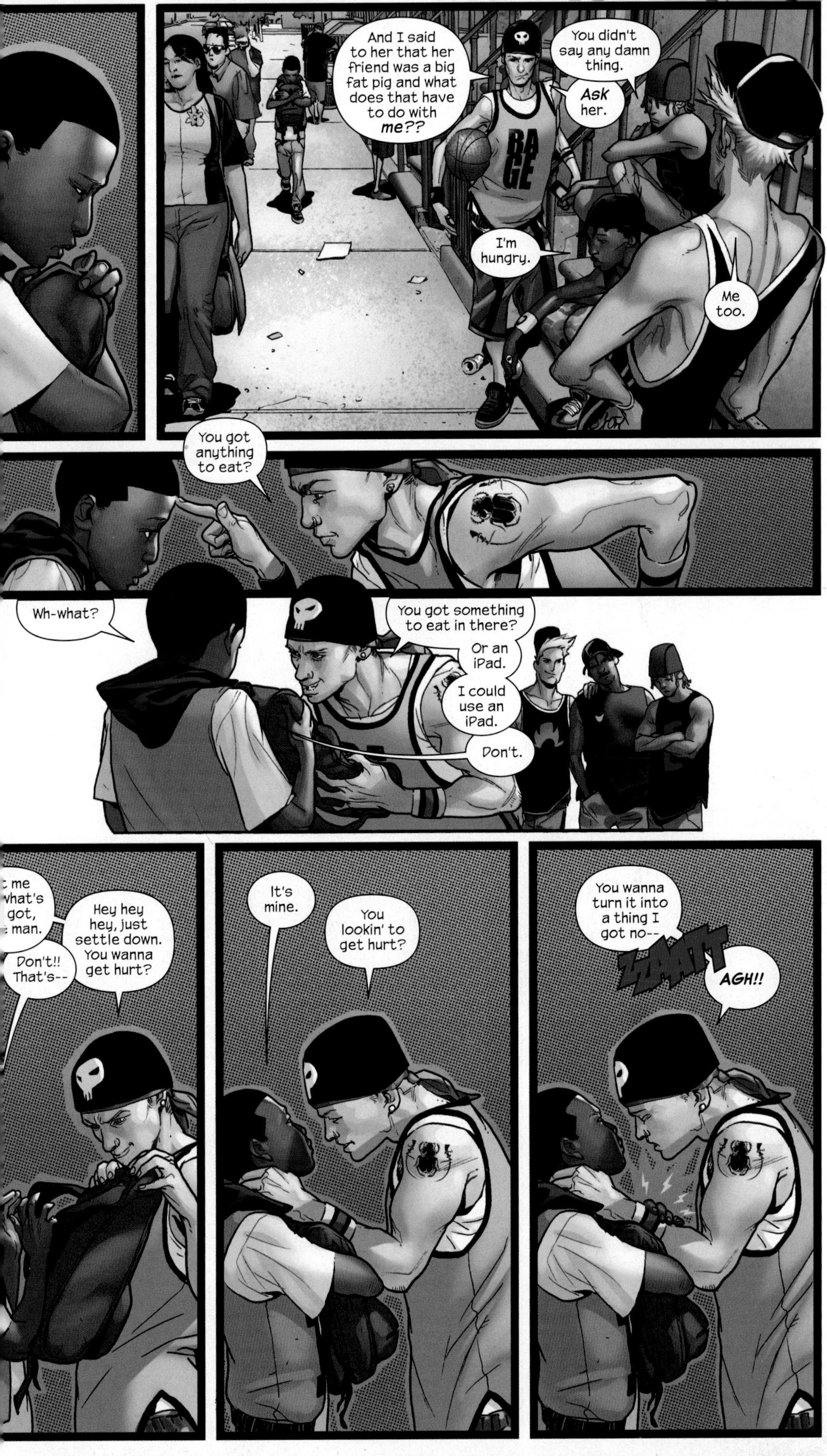
And I said to her that her friend was a big fat pig and what does that have to do with *me??*
You didn't say any damn thing.
*Ask* her.
I'm hungry.
Me too.
You got anything to eat?
Wh-what?
You got something to eat in there?
Or an iPad.
I could use an iPad.
Don't.
me what's got, man.
Hey hey hey, just settle down. You wanna get hurt?
Don't!! That's--
It's mine.
You lookin' to get hurt?
You wanna turn it into a thing I got no--
ZZAAT!
*AGH!!*

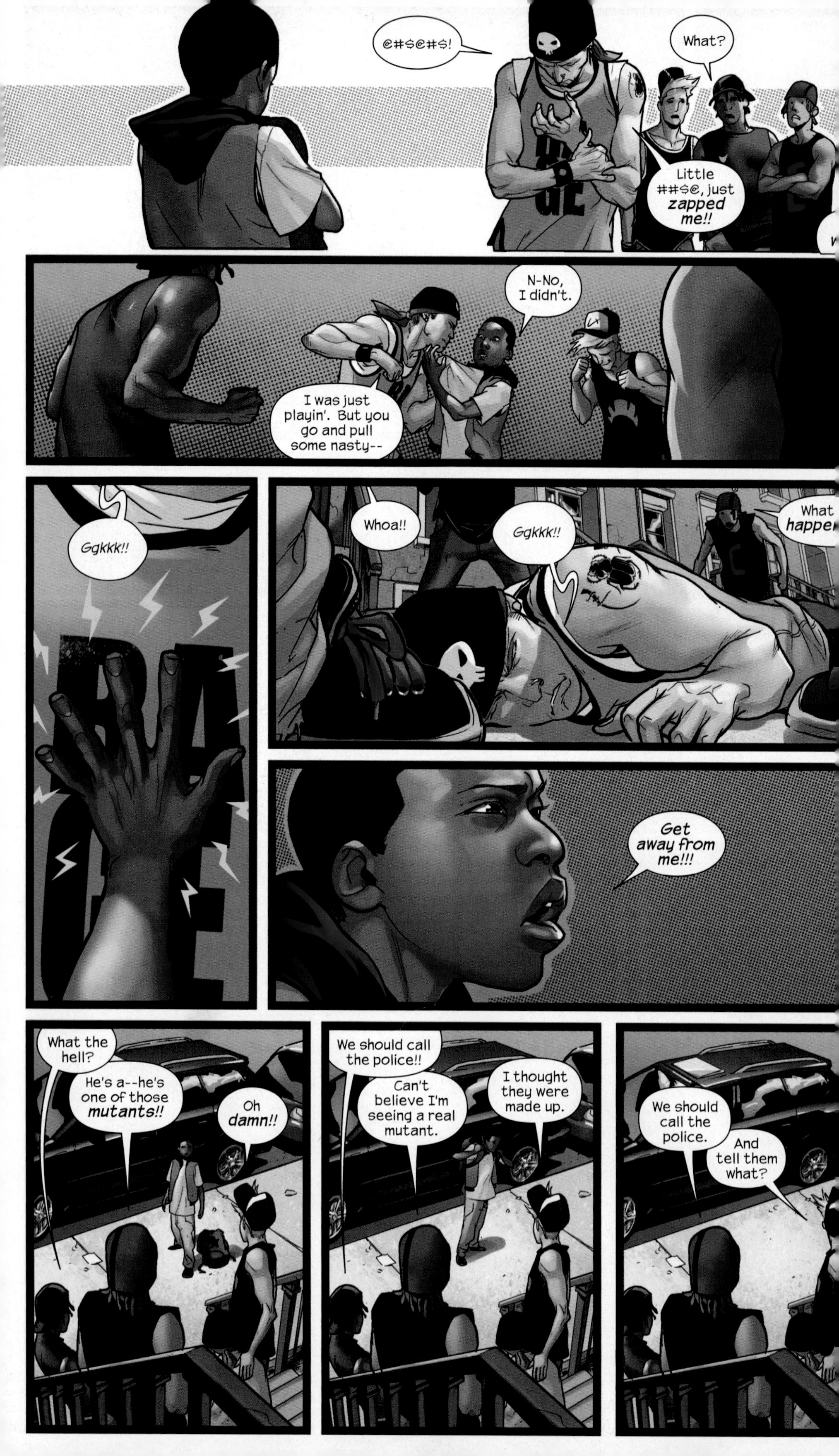
@#$@#$!
What?
Little ##$@, just zapped me!!
N-No, I didn't.
I was just playin'. But you go and pull some nasty--
Ggkkk!!
Whoa!!
Ggkkk!!
Get away from me!!!
What the hell?
He's a--he's one of those mutants!!
Oh damn!!
We should call the police!!
Can't believe I'm seeing a real mutant.
I thought they were made up.
We should call the police.
And tell them what?

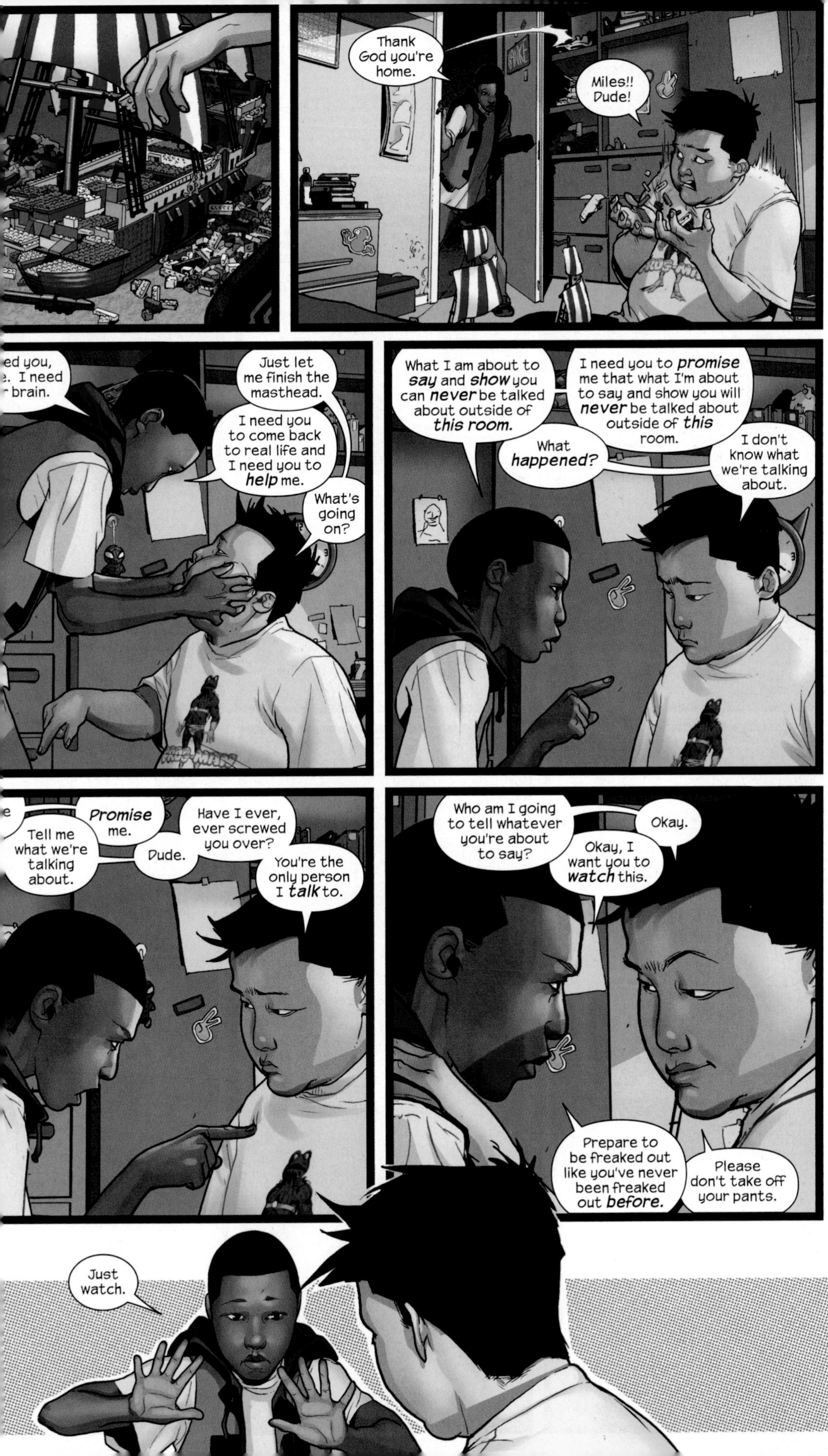
Thank God you're home.
Miles!! Dude!
...ed you, ...e. I need ...r brain.
Just let me finish the masthead.
I need you to come back to real life and I need you to *help* me.
What's going on?
What I am about to *say* and *show* you can *never* be talked about outside of *this room.*
I need you to *promise* me that what I'm about to say and show you will *never* be talked about outside of *this* room.
What *happened?*
I don't know what we're talking about.
*Promise* me.
Tell me what we're talking about.
Dude.
Have I ever, ever screwed you over?
You're the only person I *talk* to.
Who am I going to tell whatever you're about to say?
Okay.
Okay, I want you to *watch* this.
Prepare to be freaked out like you've never been freaked out *before.*
Please don't take off your pants.
Just watch.

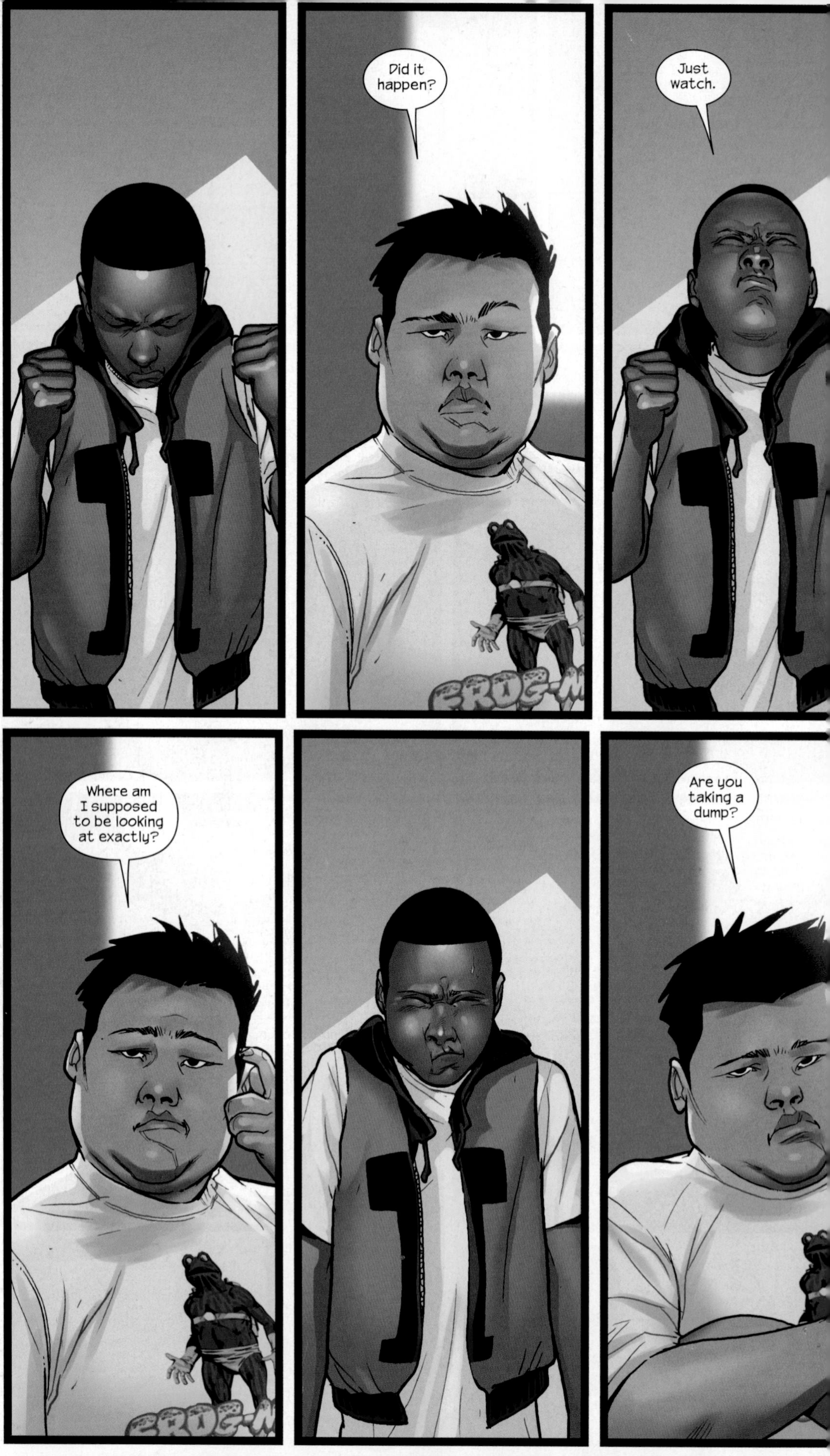

Did it happen?
Just watch.
Where am I supposed to be looking at exactly?
Are you taking a dump?

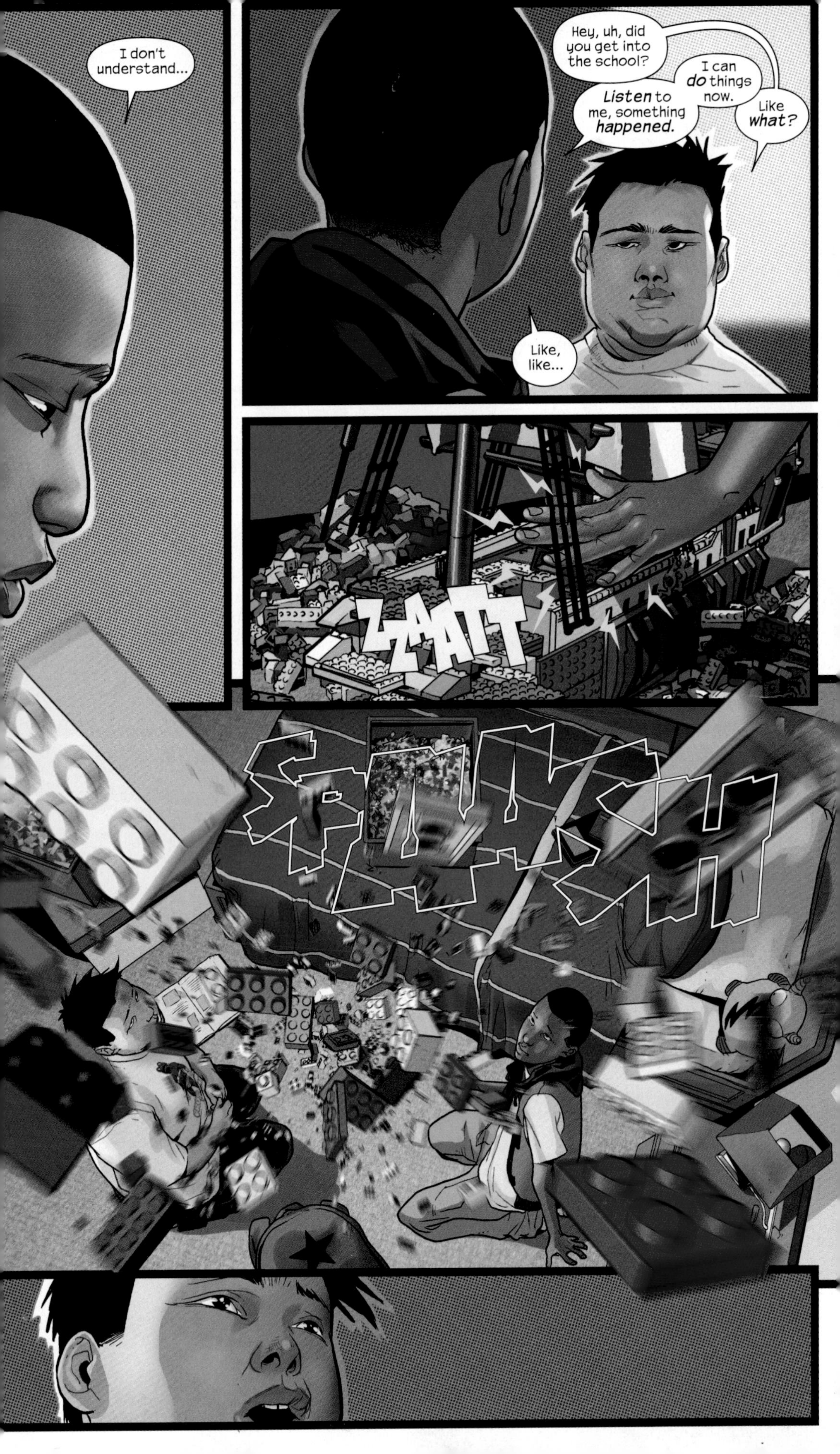
I don't understand...
Hey, uh, did you get into the school?
Listen to me, something happened.
I can do things now.
Like what?
Like, like...
ZZAATT
SPLASH

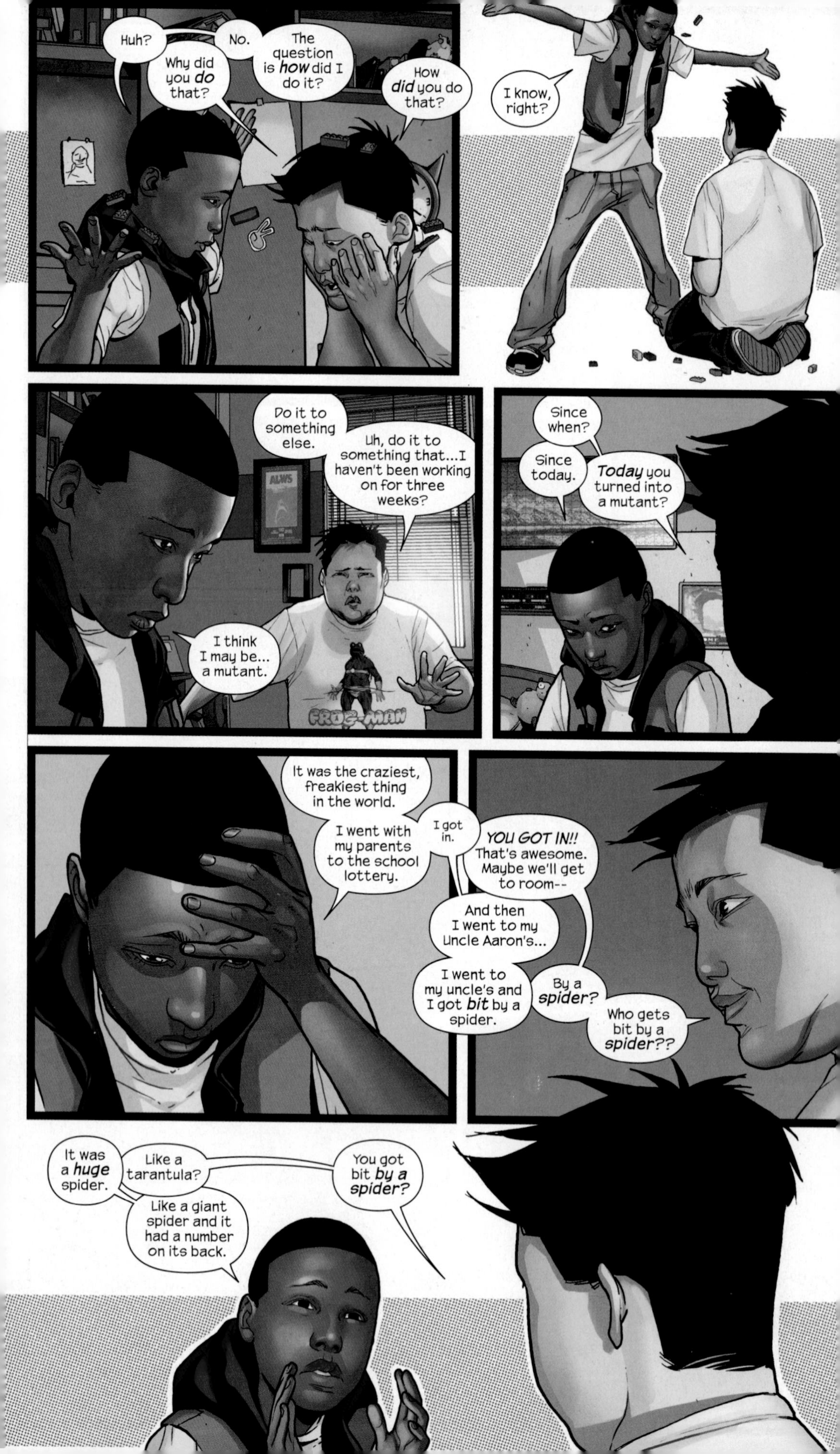
Huh?
Why did you do that?
No.
The question is how did I do it?
How did you do that?
I know, right?
Do it to something else.
Uh, do it to something that...I haven't been working on for three weeks?
I think I may be... a mutant.
ALWS
FROG-MAN
Since when?
Since today.
Today you turned into a mutant?
It was the craziest, freakiest thing in the world.
I went with my parents to the school lottery.
I got in.
YOU GOT IN!! That's awesome. Maybe we'll get to room--
And then I went to my Uncle Aaron's...
I went to my uncle's and I got bit by a spider.
By a spider?
Who gets bit by a spider??
You got bit by a spider?
It was a huge spider.
Like a tarantula?
Like a giant spider and it had a number on its back.

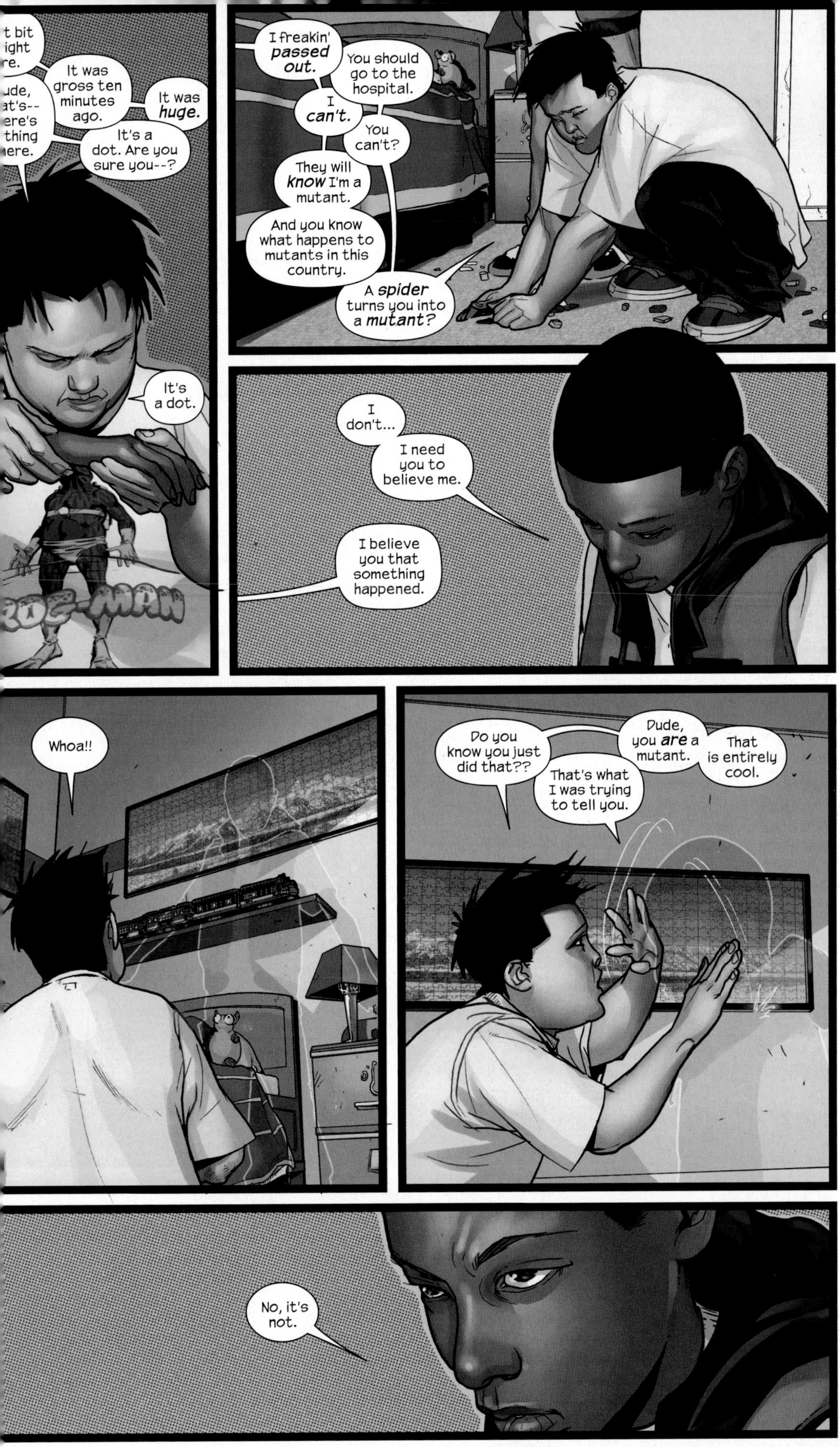

It was gross ten minutes ago.
It was huge.
It's a dot. Are you sure you--?
It's a dot.
I freakin' passed out.
You should go to the hospital.
I can't.
You can't?
They will know I'm a mutant.
And you know what happens to mutants in this country.
A spider turns you into a mutant?
I don't...
I need you to believe me.
I believe you that something happened.
Whoa!!
Do you know you just did that??
Dude, you are a mutant.
That is entirely cool.
That's what I was trying to tell you.
No, it's not.

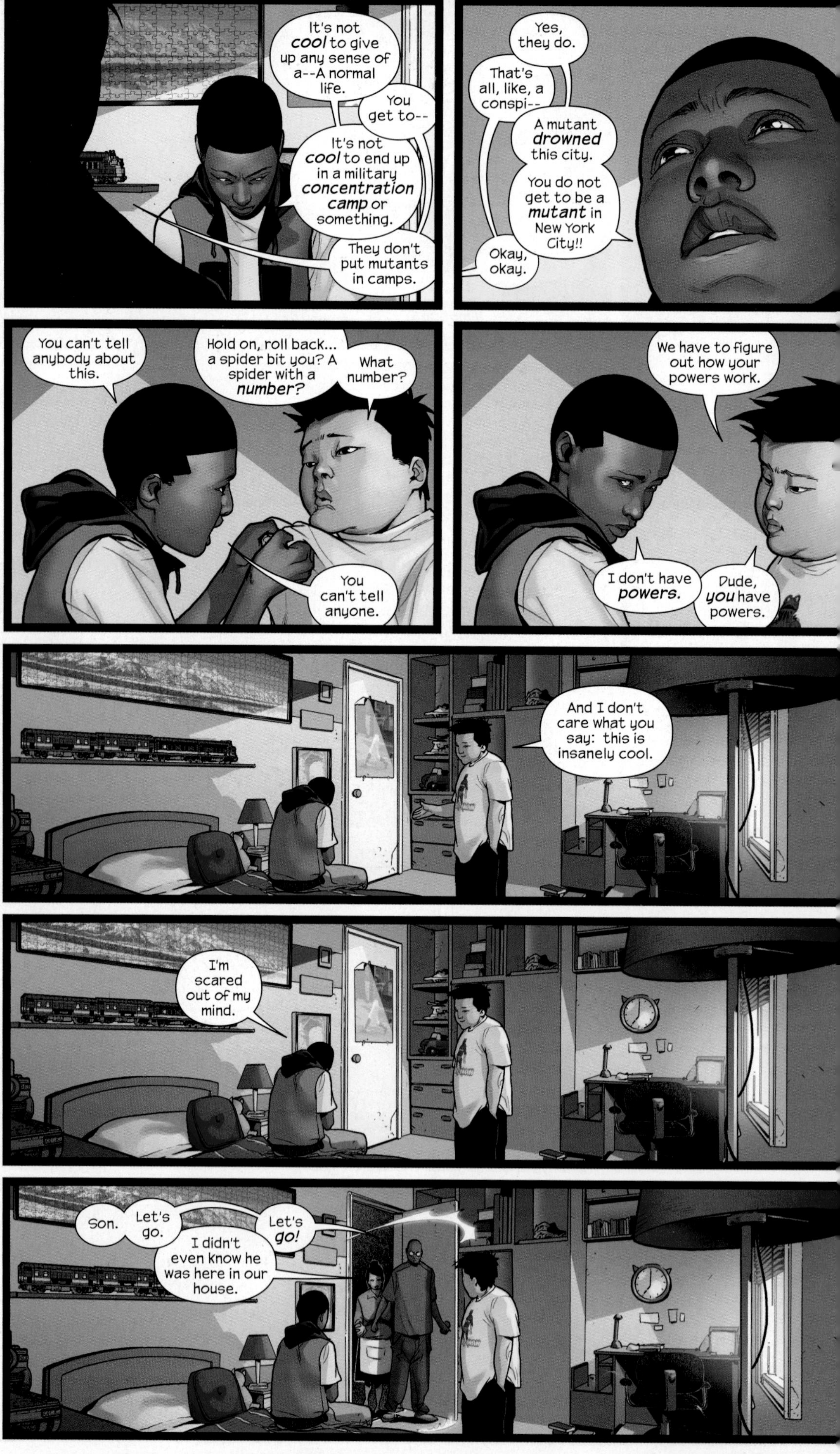
It's not cool to give up any sense of a--A normal life.
You get to--
It's not cool to end up in a military concentration camp or something.
They don't put mutants in camps.
Yes, they do.
That's all, like, a conspi--
A mutant drowned this city.
You do not get to be a mutant in New York City!!
Okay, okay.
You can't tell anybody about this.
Hold on, roll back... a spider bit you? A spider with a number?
What number?
You can't tell anyone.
We have to figure out how your powers work.
I don't have powers.
Dude, you have powers.
And I don't care what you say: this is insanely cool.
I'm scared out of my mind.
Son.
Let's go.
Let's go!
I didn't even know he was here in our house.

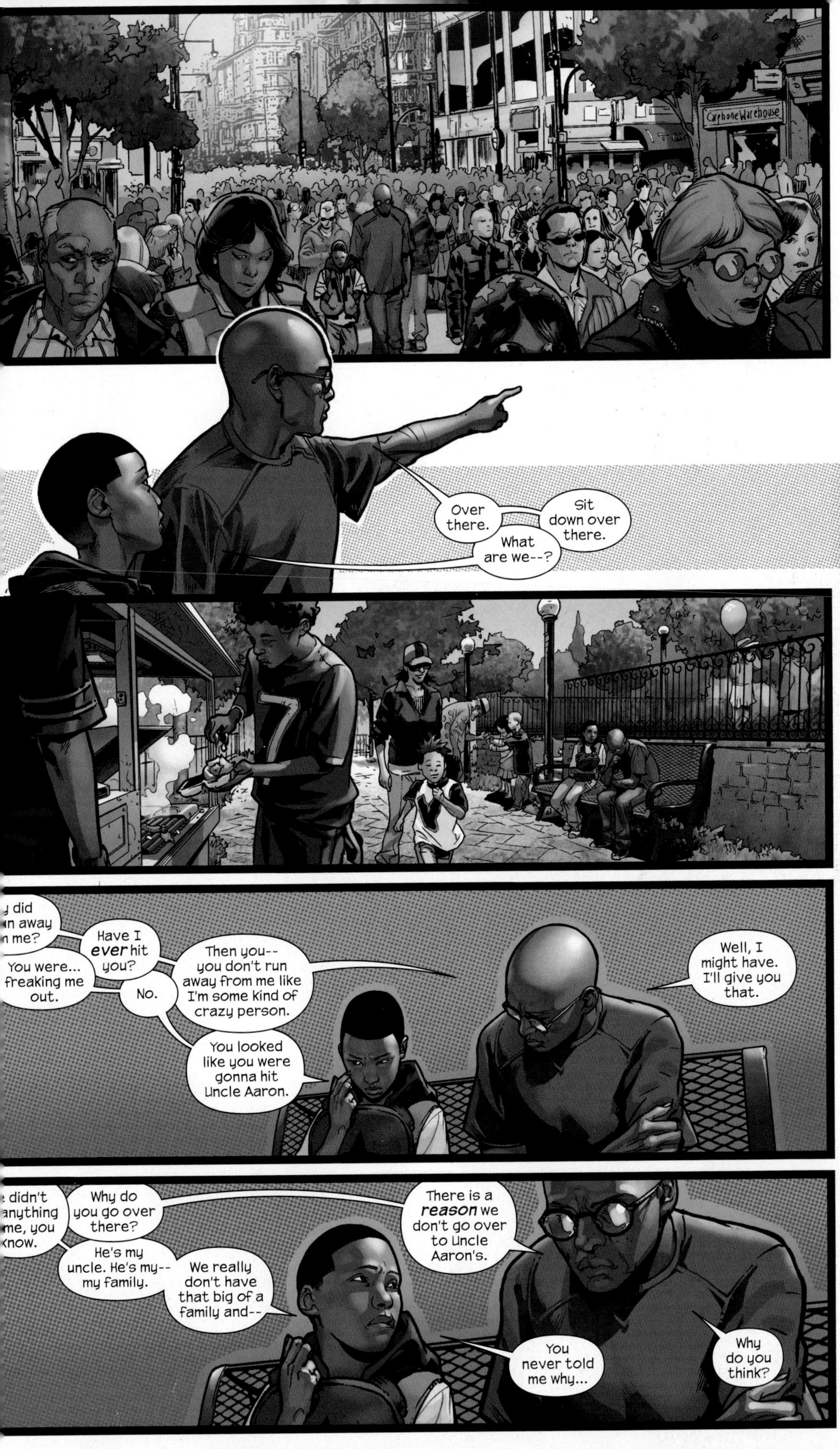

Carphone Warehouse
Over there.
What are we--?
Sit down over there.
Have I *ever* hit you?
You were... freaking me out.
No.
Then you-- you don't run away from me like I'm some kind of crazy person.
You looked like you were gonna hit Uncle Aaron.
Well, I might have. I'll give you that.
Why do you go over there?
He's my uncle. He's my-- my family.
We really don't have that big of a family and--
There is a *reason* we don't go over to Uncle Aaron's.
You never told me why...
Why do you think?

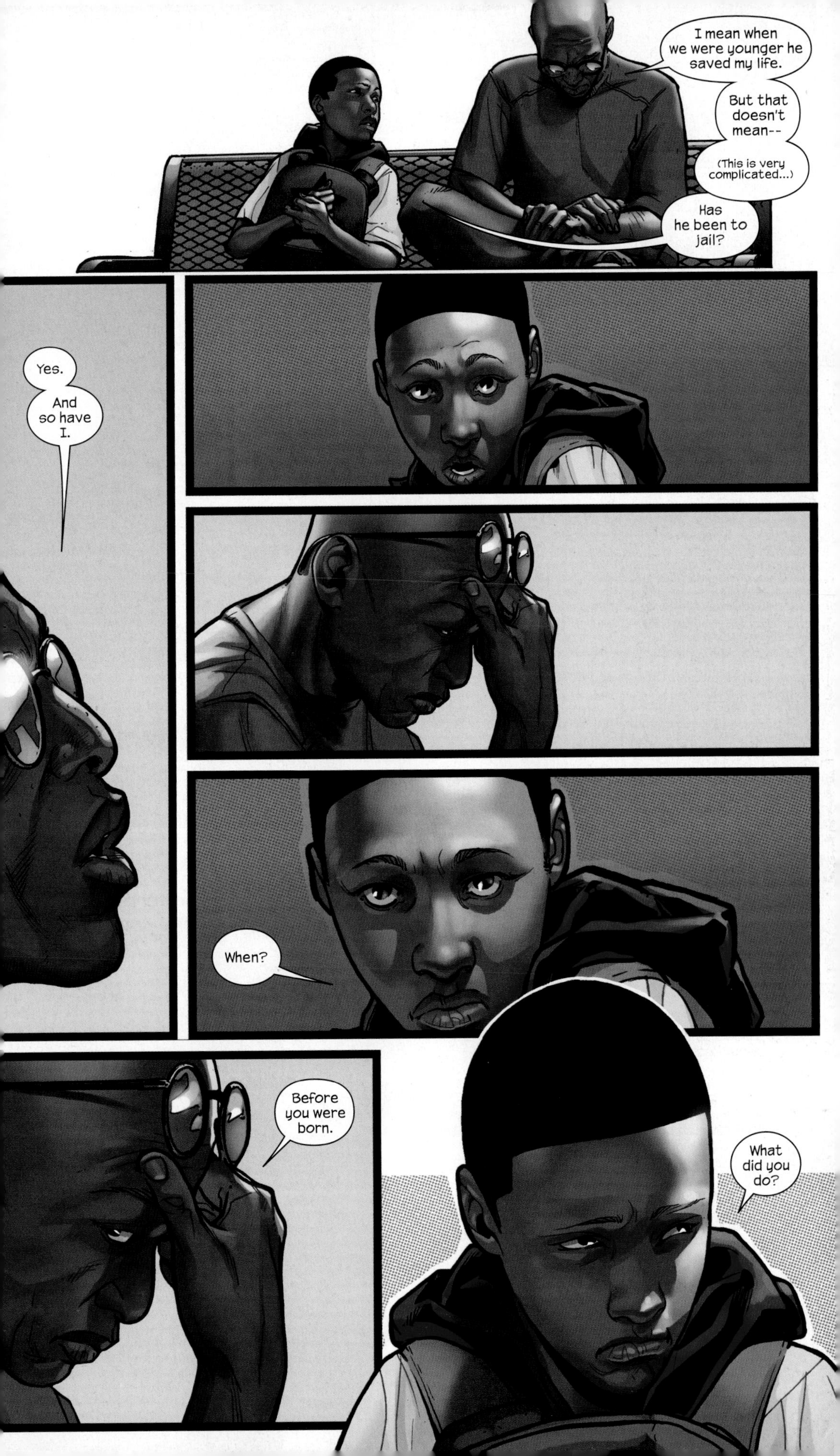
I mean when we were younger he saved my life.
But that doesn't mean--
(This is very complicated...)
Has he been to jail?
Yes.
And so have I.
When?
Before you were born.
What did you do?

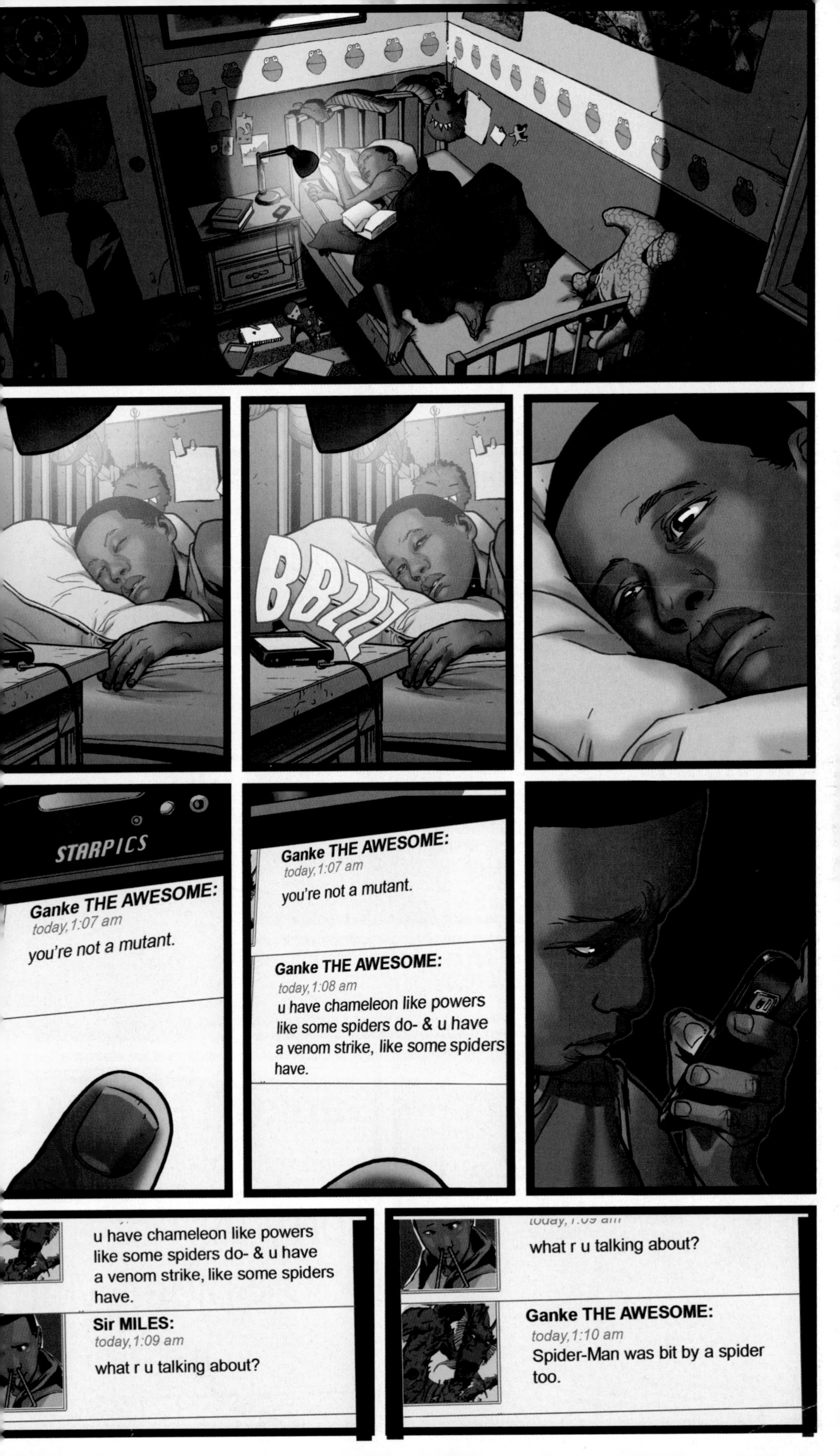

BBZZZ
STARPICS
Ganke THE AWESOME:
today, 1:07 am
you're not a mutant.
Ganke THE AWESOME:
today, 1:07 am
you're not a mutant.
Ganke THE AWESOME:
today, 1:08 am
u have chameleon like powers like some spiders do- & u have a venom strike, like some spiders have.
u have chameleon like powers like some spiders do- & u have a venom strike, like some spiders have.
Sir MILES:
today, 1:09 am
what r u talking about?
what r u talking about?
Ganke THE AWESOME:
today, 1:10 am
Spider-Man was bit by a spider too.

STARPICS
Z100

Spider-man was bit by a s
too.

**Ganke THE AWESOME:**
*today, 1:12 am*
Spider-Man myth busted
Ben Urich

**Ganke THE AWESOME:**
*today, 1:12 am*
S myth busted By

fresh with O | sign the... | States is in the World Cup... | sophisticated...
Gossip • Celeb Photos • PopWrap | Teams ▽ • High Schools ▽ • Scores ▽ | TV • Movies • Events • Travel
ocal ▽ | Business Opinion Columnists ▽ • Politics Metro US News World News Real Estate ▽ • Weird But True Crime Lottery

# HOW SPIDER-MAN BECAME SPIDER-MAN
By BEN URICH
Last Updated: 3:37 PM, July 13, 2011
Posted: 5:54 AM, July 13, 2011

picture by Peter Parker

👍 Like | 🖂 Send | 7,042 people like this. Be the first of your friends.
+1 | 35 | 586 | 🖂 🔢 ➕ More 🖨 Print

The dismembered body of a missing 6-year-old Hasidic boy was found early today at two locations in Brooklyn — with police arresting a suspect in the grisly slaying who had the child's severed feet in his freezer, authorities said.

Police made the gruesome discovery after raiding a Kensington home and arresting 35-year-old Levi Aron, who led them to parts of missing boy Leibby Kletzky's body, stuffed in a red suitcase.

though said with levity, Spider-Man told police officers
that he was bit by a spider that gave him
spider-powers.
Incredible reaction of the public and the guys from the

STARPICS
Z100

**Ganke THE AWESOME:**
*today, 1:10 am*
sorry u'r not a mutant but...
R U Spider-Man?!!

**Ganke THE AWE**
*today, 1:10 am*
sorry u'r not a mu
R U Spider-Man'

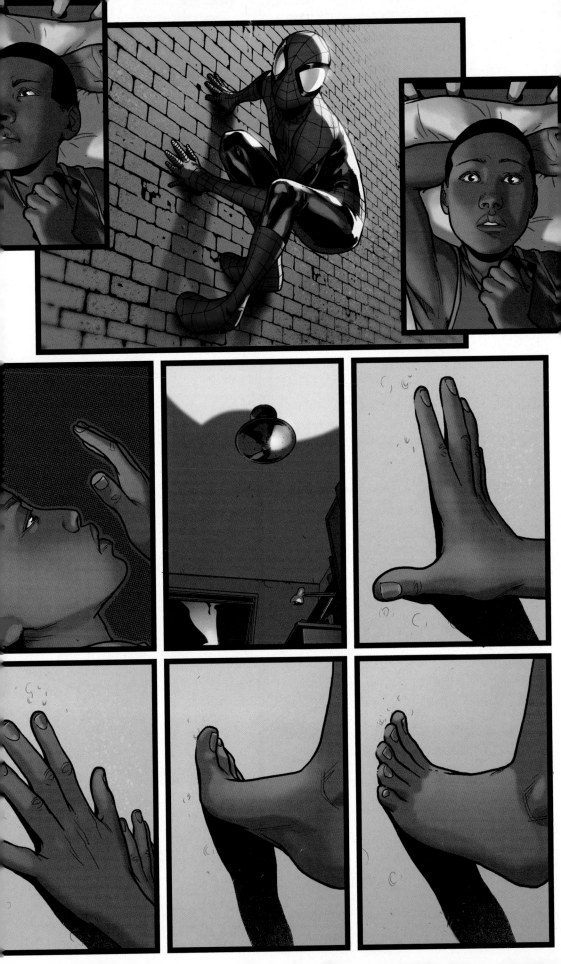

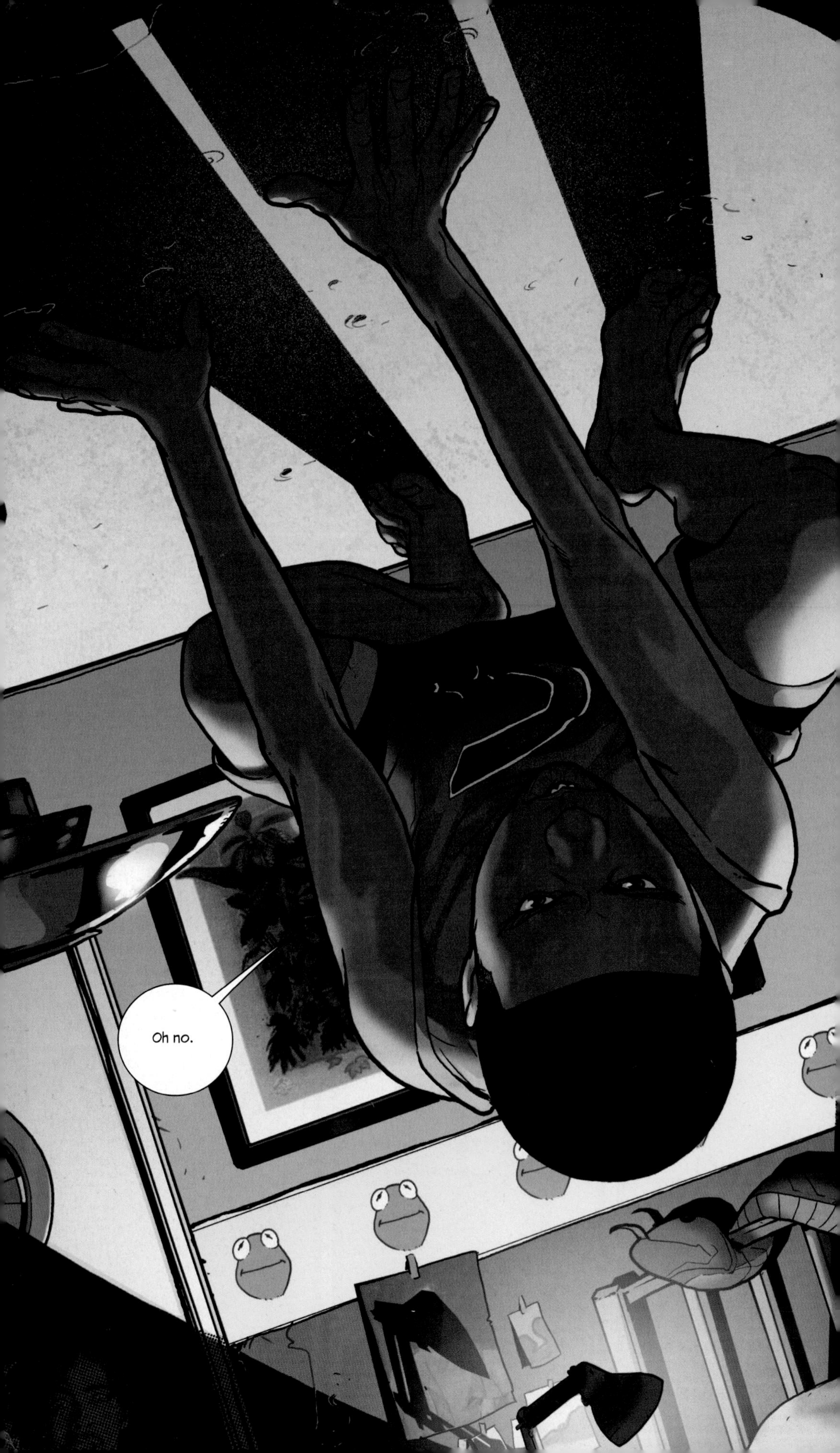
Oh no.

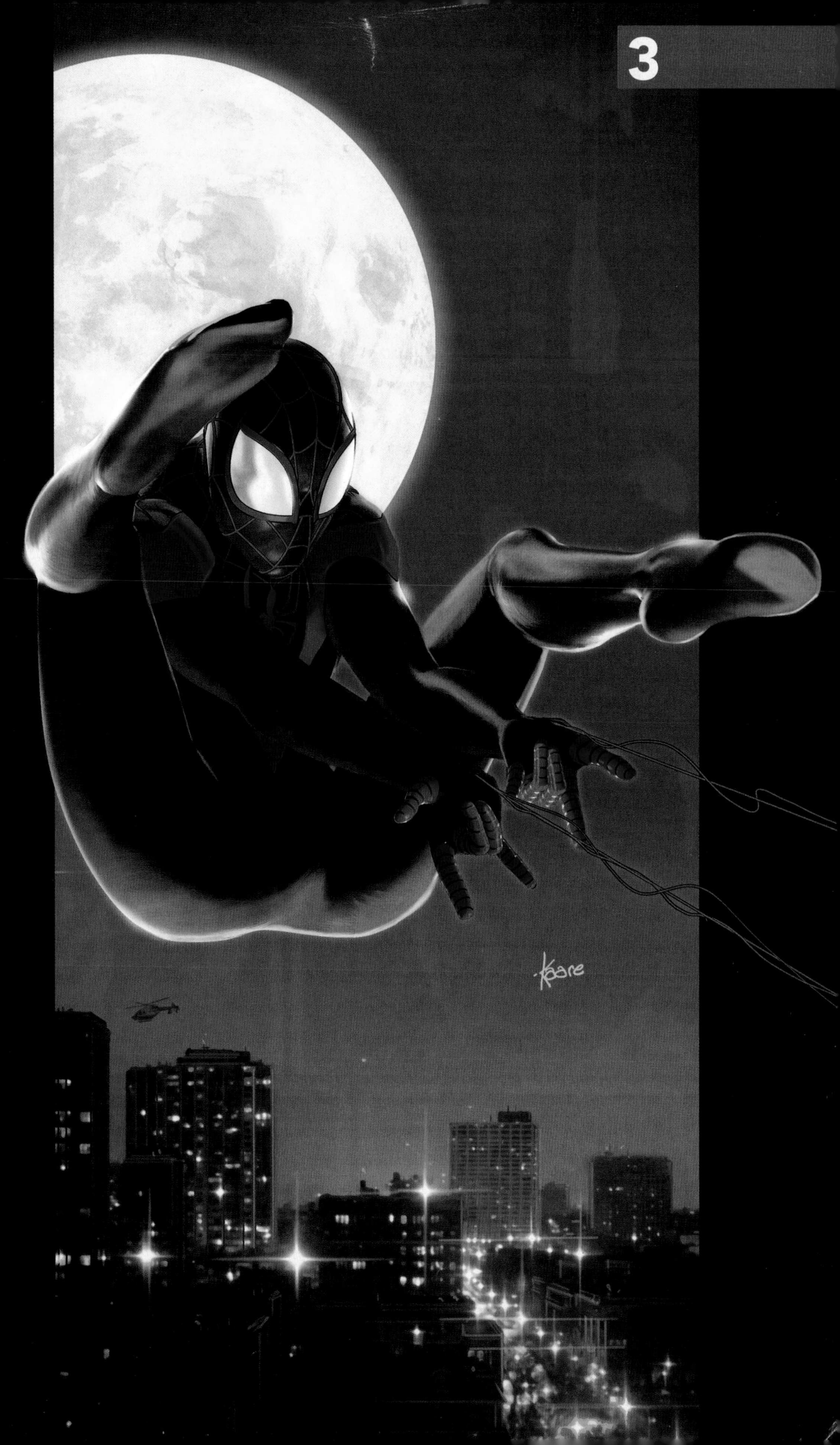
3
Kaare

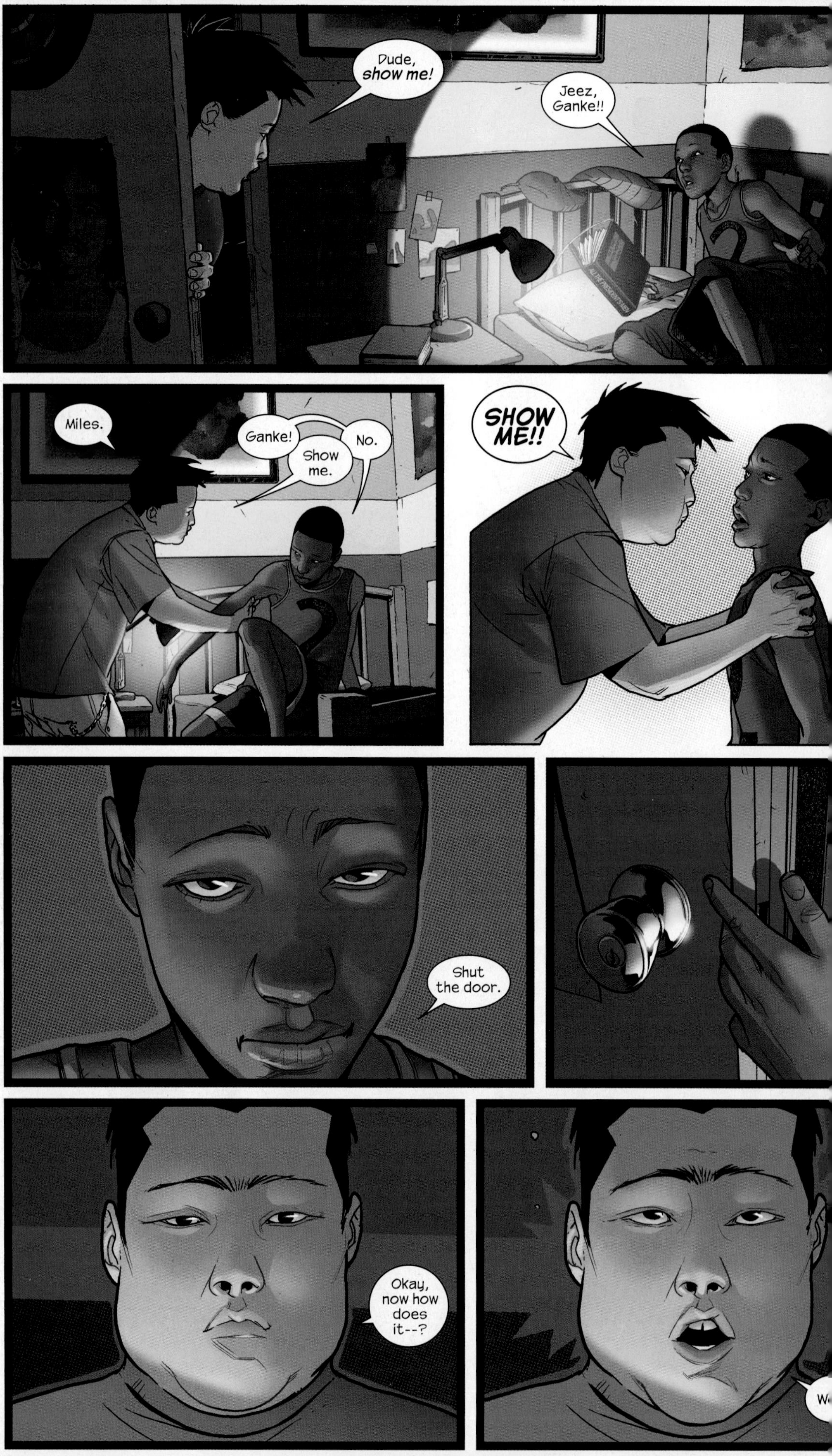
Dude, show me!
Jeez, Ganke!!
Miles.
Ganke!
No.
Show me.
SHOW ME!!
Shut the door.
Okay, now how does it--?

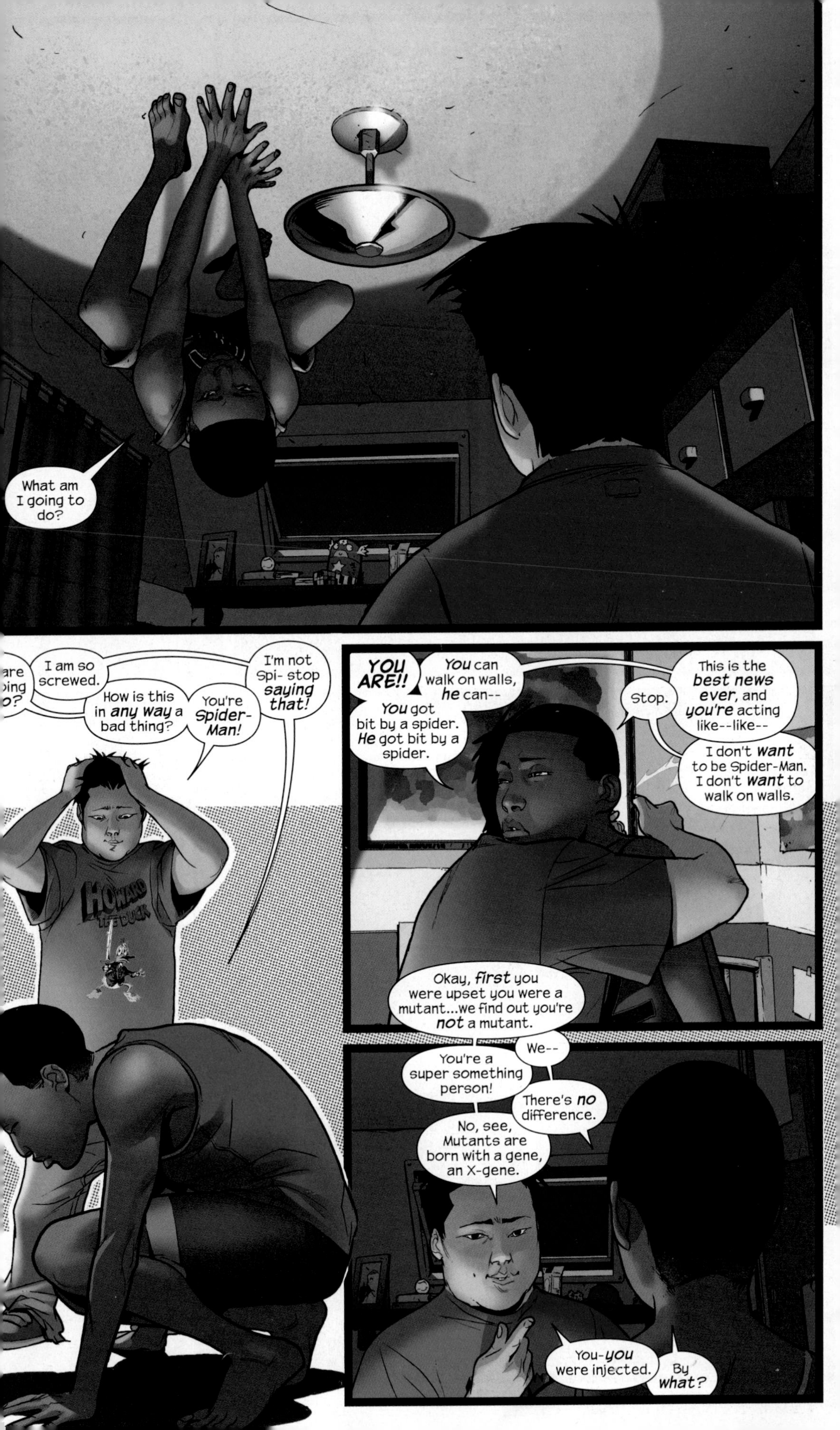
What am I going to do?
I am so screwed.
How is this in *any way* a bad thing?
You're *Spider-Man!*
I'm not Spi- stop *saying that!*
***YOU ARE!!***
*You* can walk on walls, *he* can--
*You* got bit by a spider. *He* got bit by a spider.
This is the *best news ever*, and *you're* acting like--like--
Stop.
I don't *want* to be Spider-Man. I don't *want* to walk on walls.
Okay, *first* you were upset you were a mutant...we find out you're *not* a mutant.
You're a super something person!
We--
There's *no* difference.
No, see, Mutants are born with a gene, an X-gene.
You-*you* were injected.
By *what?*

Well, fine. *I'll* go over there.

...r to ...e. ...st ...s can ...e and ...s and ...it.

Why are you so obsessed with girls all of a sudden?

All of a sudden?

You play with Legos all day.

I don't hey--not *all* day.

You don't get girls by playing with Legos.

I *sculpt* with Legos and like you know girls all of a sudden.

I just-- I want normal.

Normal what?

**NORMAL!**

I want to go to school. I want to go to college.

I've been killing myself to get into charter school.

I mean, we *have* to.

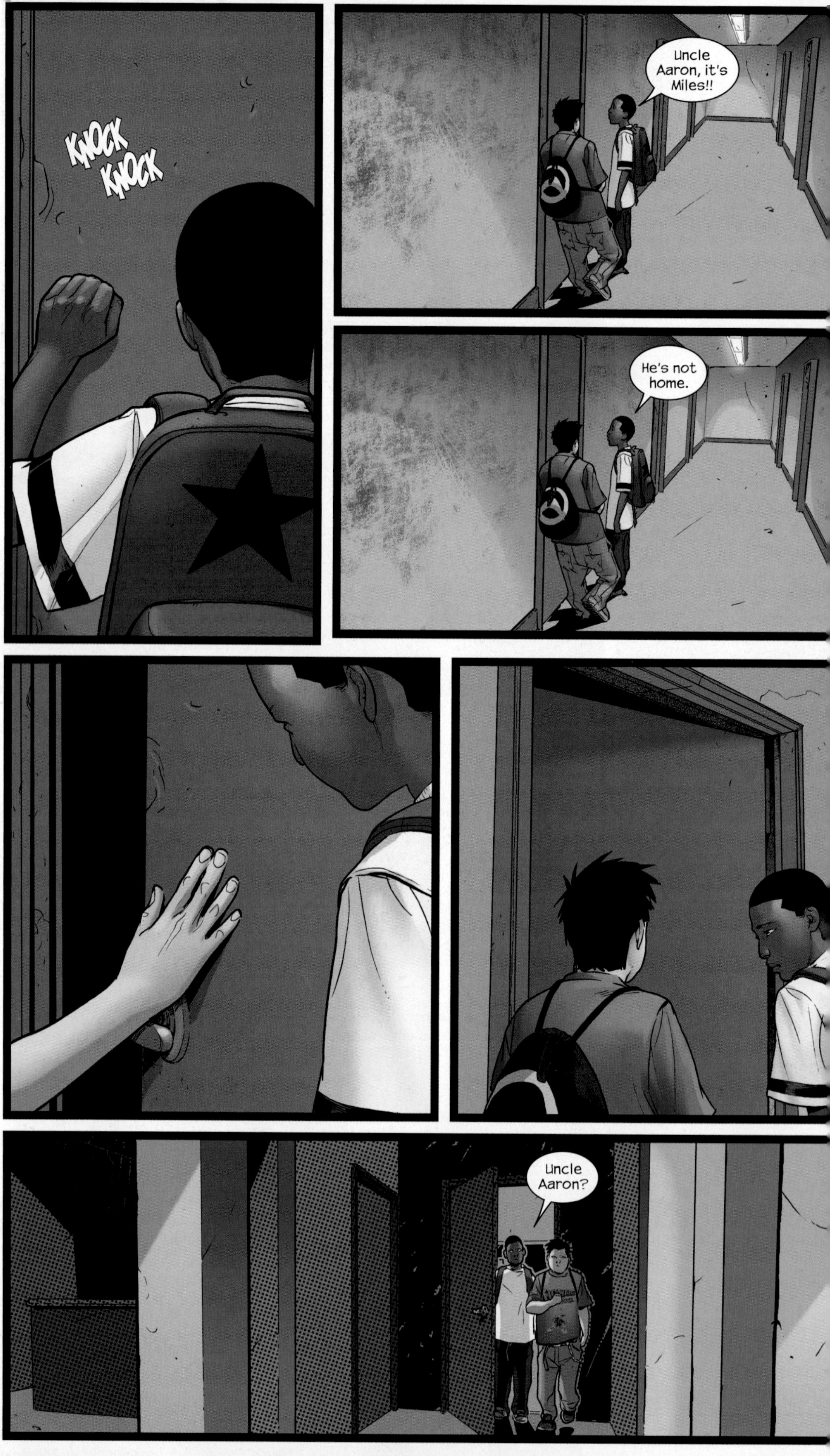
KNOCK KNOCK
Uncle Aaron, it's Miles!!
He's not home.
Uncle Aaron?

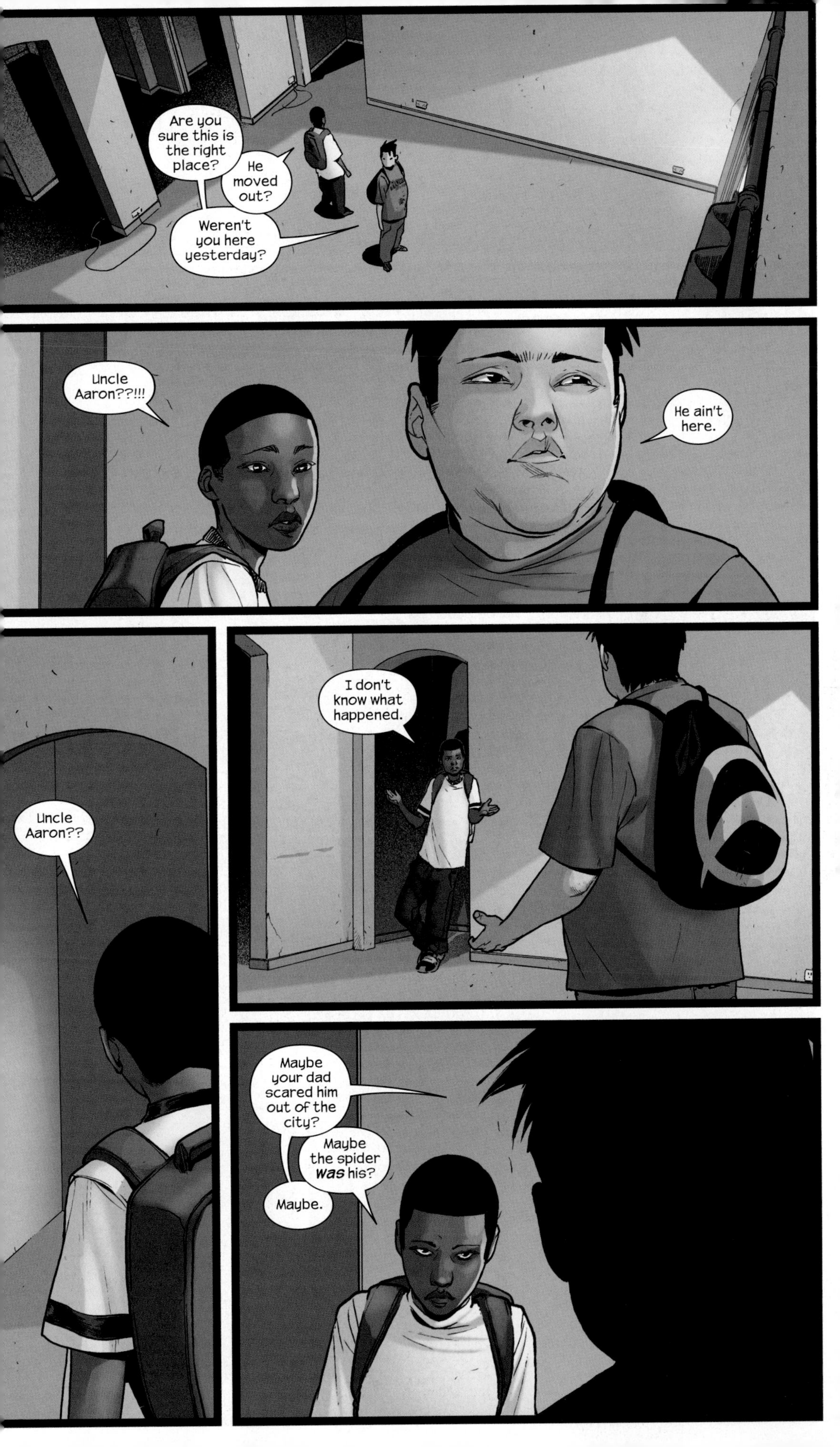

Are you sure this is the right place?
He moved out?
Weren't you here yesterday?
Uncle Aaron??!!!
He ain't here.
Uncle Aaron??
I don't know what happened.
Maybe your dad scared him out of the city?
Maybe the spider **was** his?
Maybe.

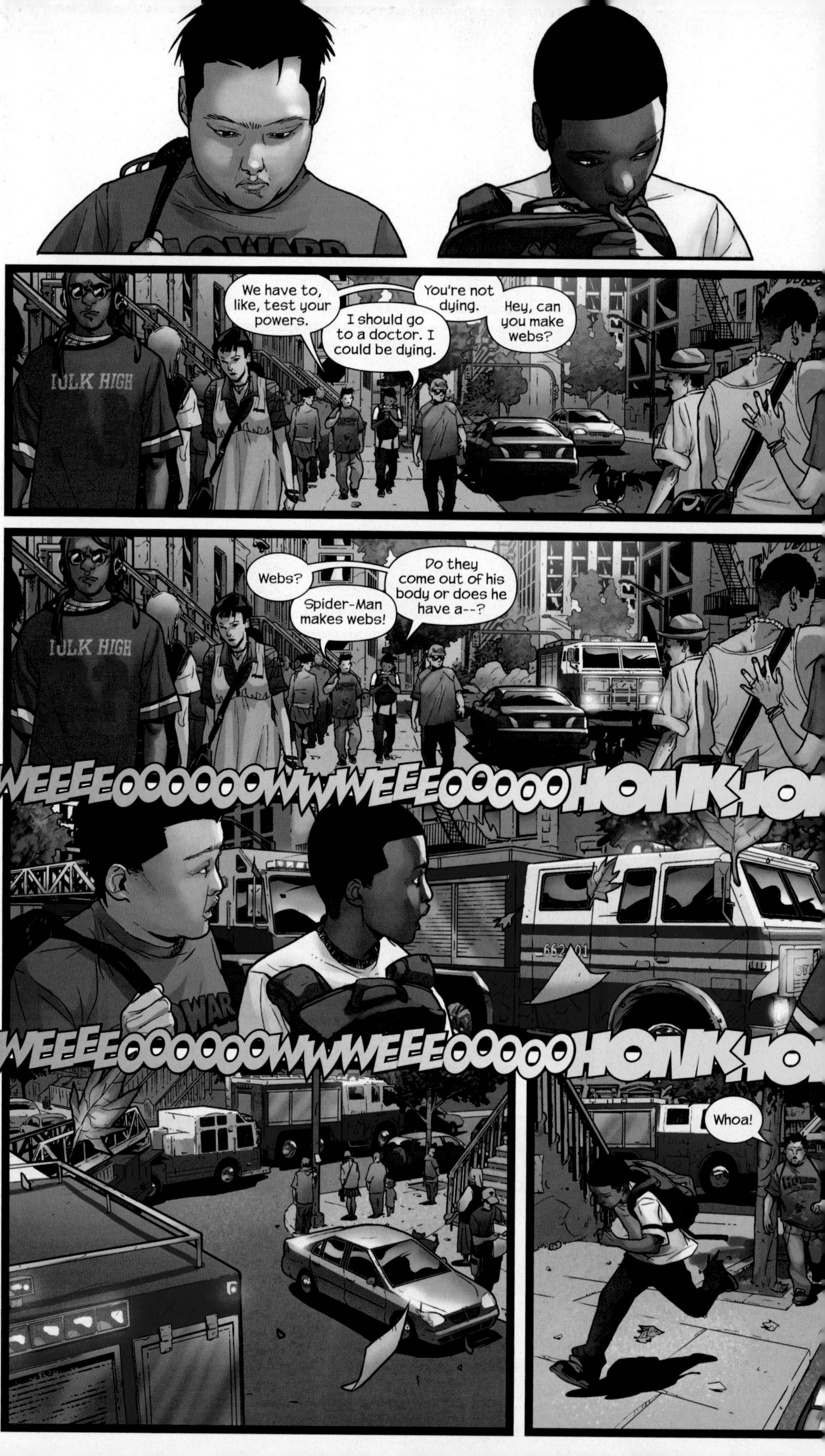

We have to, like, test your powers.
I should go to a doctor. I could be dying.
You're not dying.
Hey, can you make webs?
Webs?
Spider-Man makes webs!
Do they come out of his body or does he have a--?
WEEEEOOOOOOWWWEEEOOOOOHONKHON
WEEEEOOOOOOWWWEEEOOOOOHONKHON
Whoa!

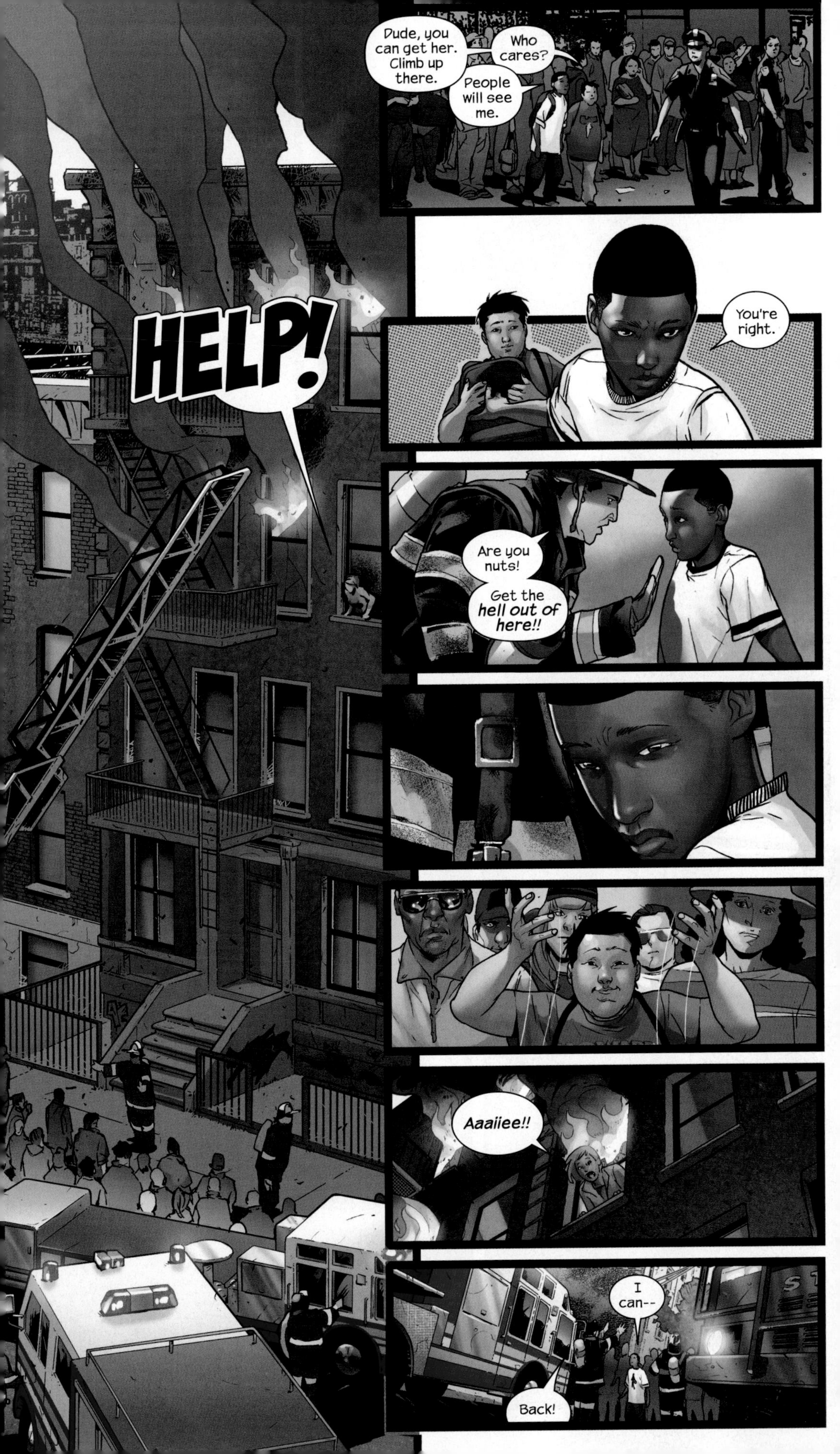
HELP!
Dude, you can get her. Climb up there.
Who cares?
People will see me.
You're right.
Are you nuts!
Get the *hell out of here!!*
*Aaaiiee!!*
I can--
Back!

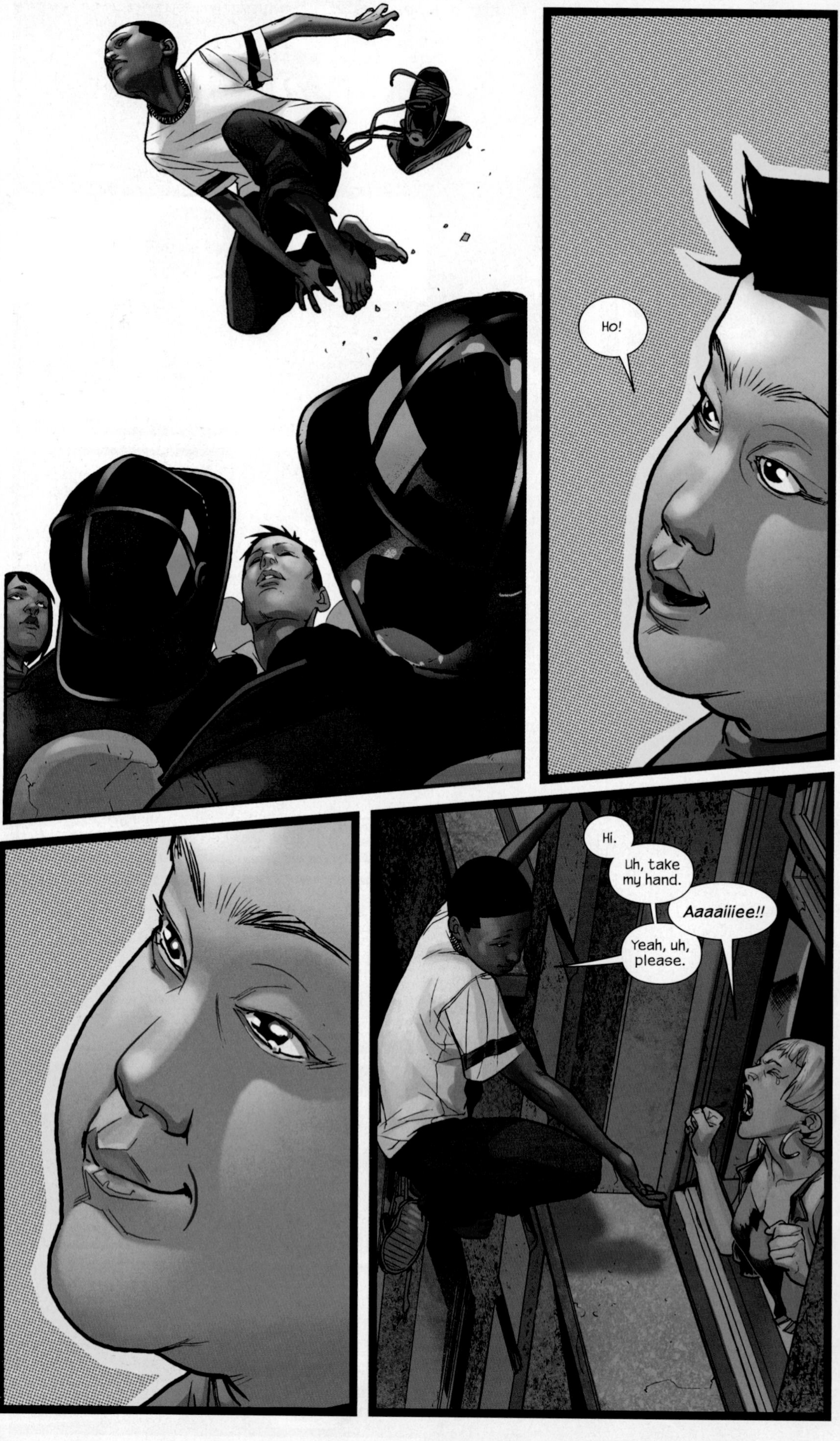
Ho!
Hi.
Uh, take my hand.
Aaaaiiiee!!
Yeah, uh, please.

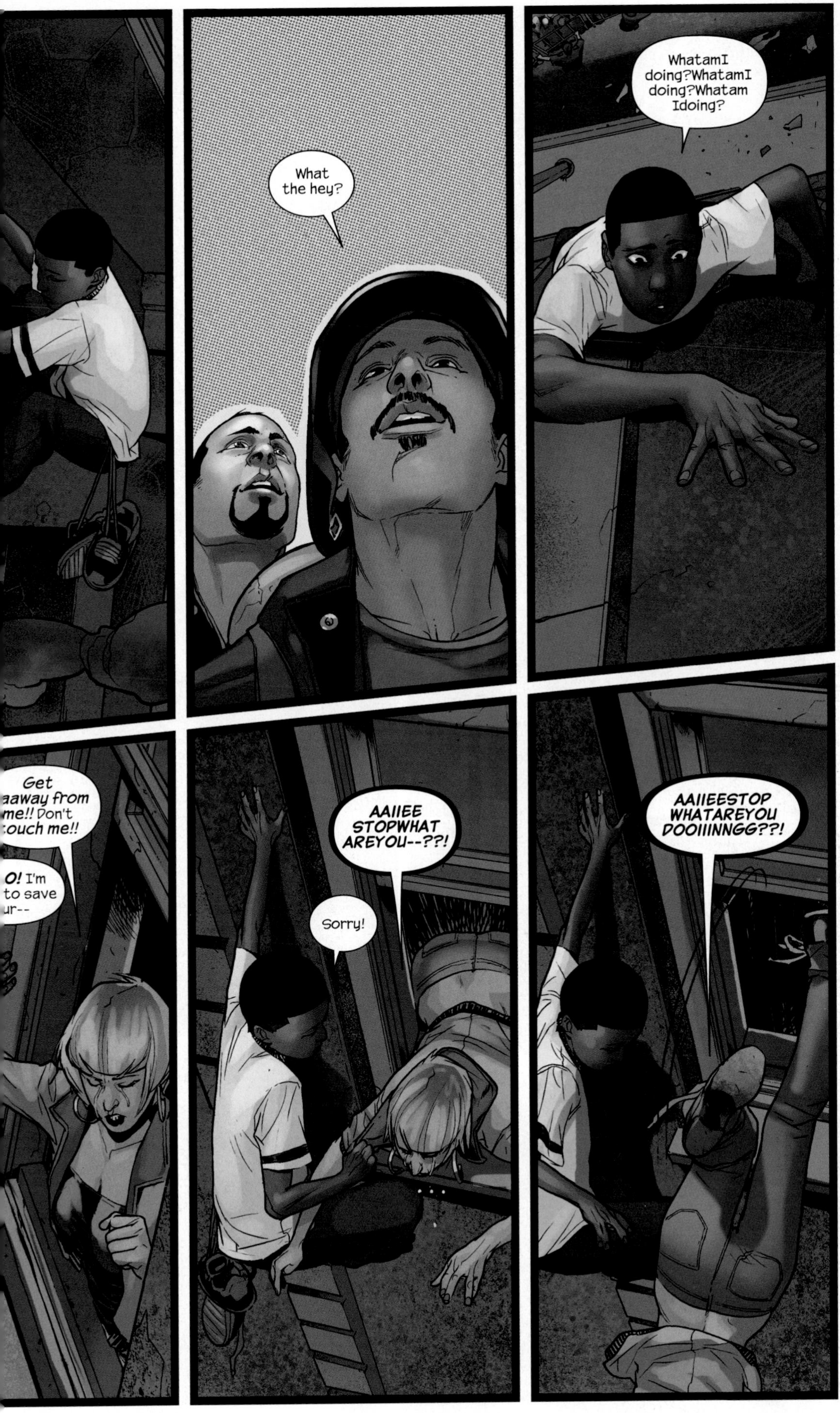
What the hey?
WhatamI doing?WhatamI doing?Whatam Idoing?
Get aaway from me!! Don't touch me!!
O! I'm to save ur--
AAIIEE STOPWHAT AREYOU--??!
Sorry!
AAIIEESTOP WHATAREYOU DOOIIINNGG??!

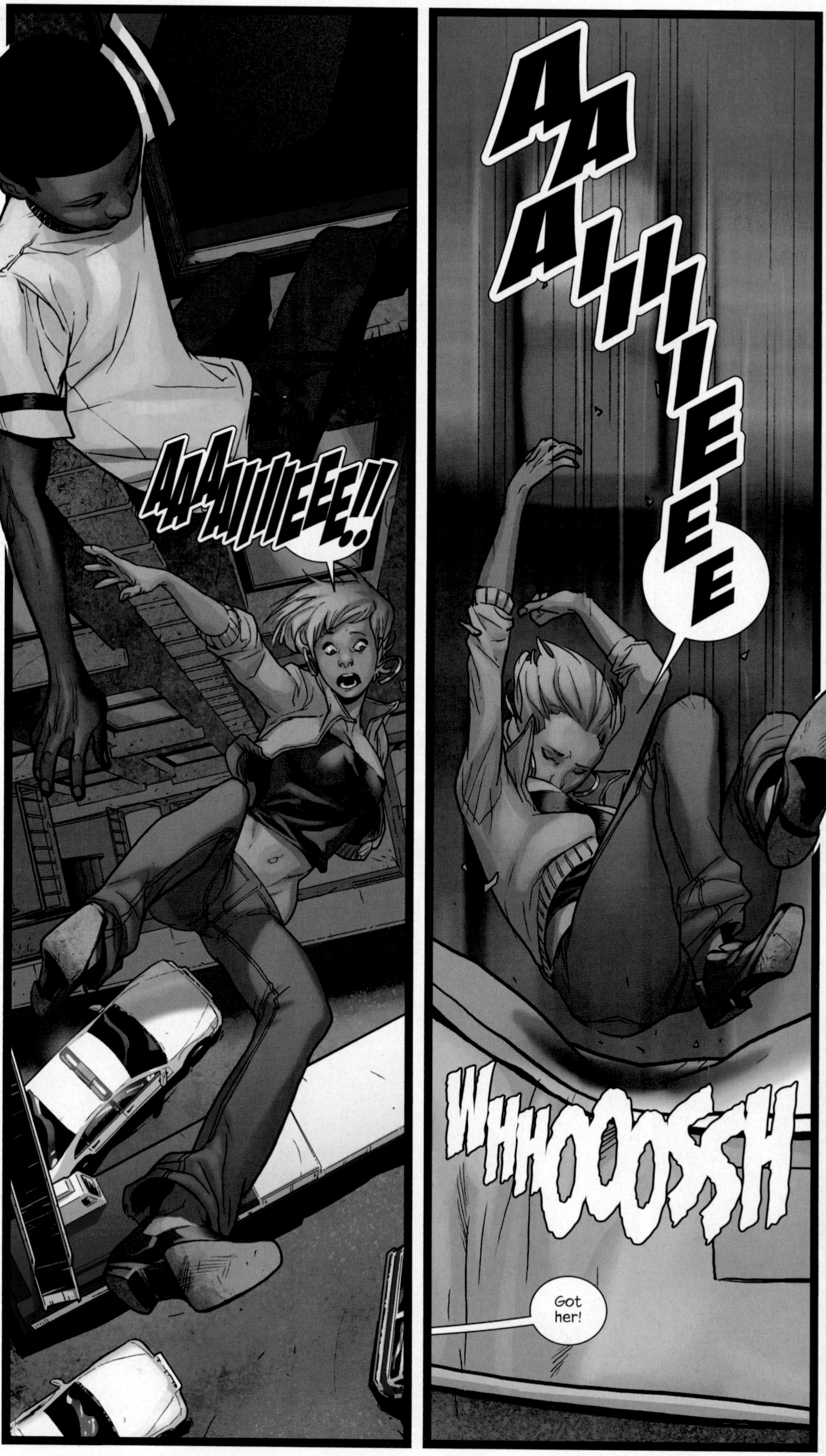
AAAAIIIIEEE!!
AAAIIIIIEEEE
WHHOOOSH
Got her!

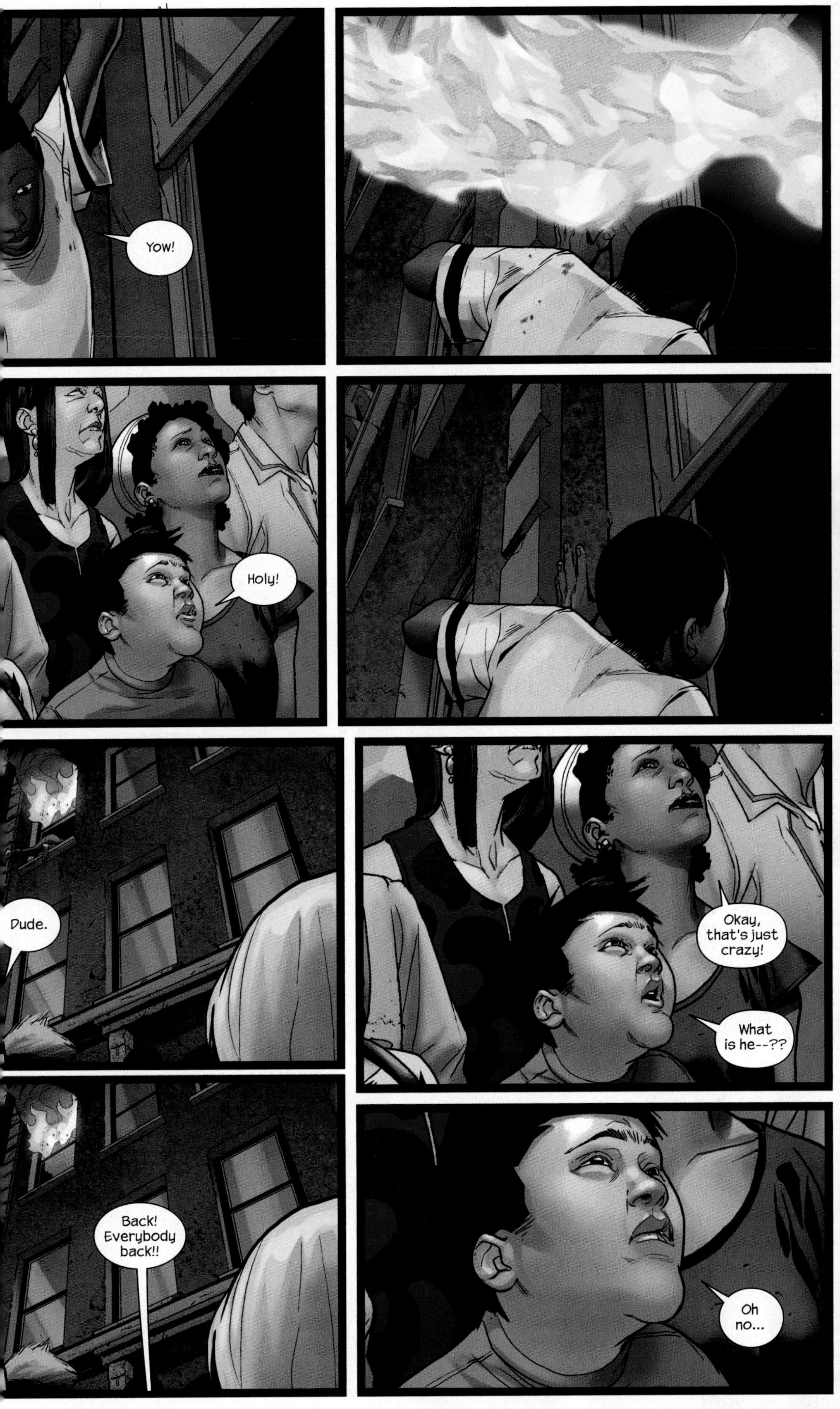

YOW!
Holy!
Dude.
Okay, that's just crazy!
What is he--??
Back! Everybody back!!
Oh no...

Woof!

Ruff!

FUMP

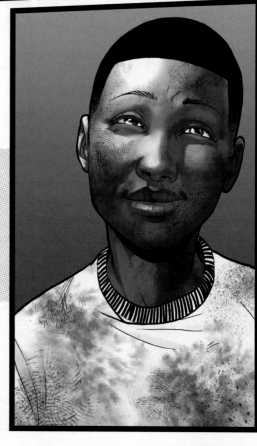

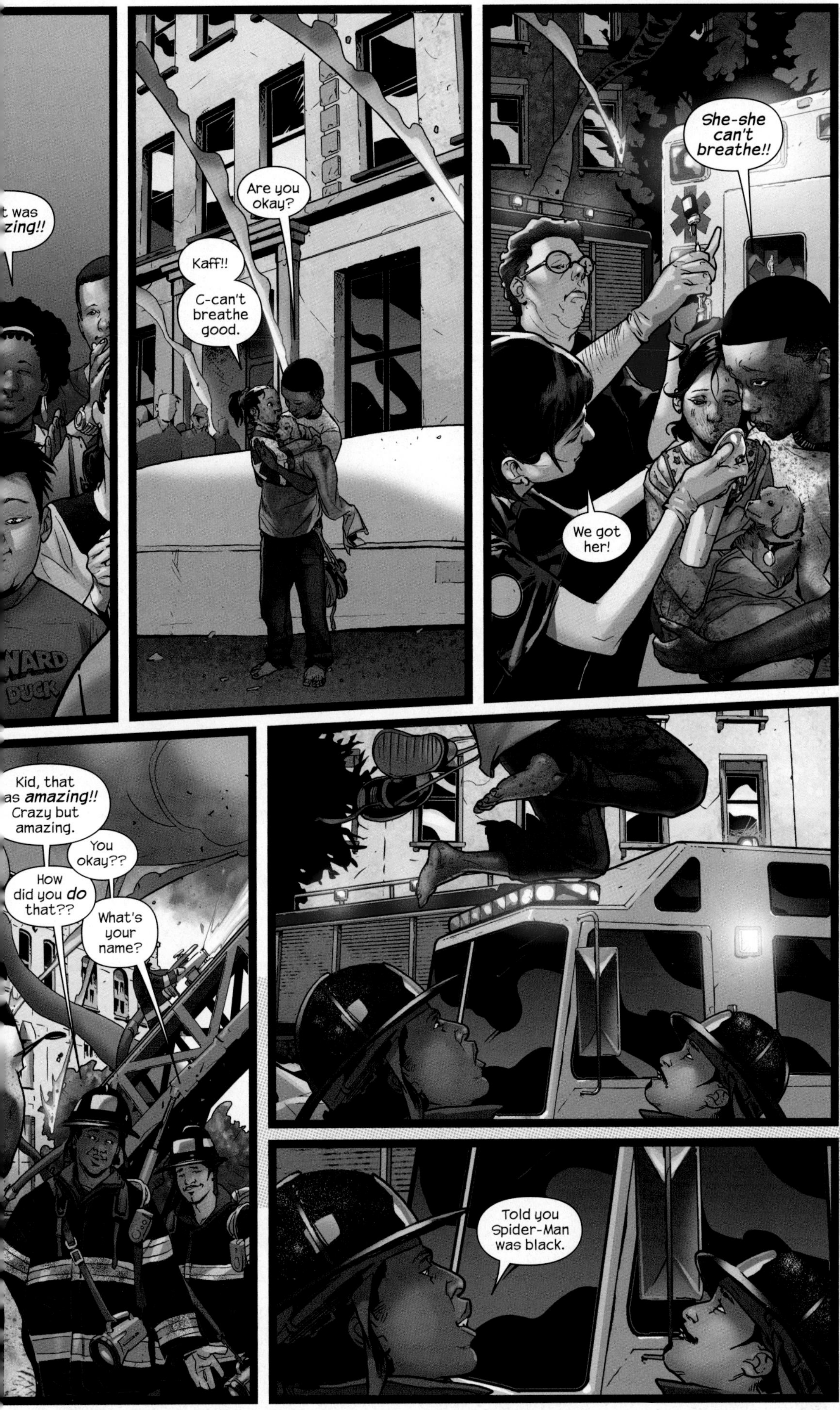

t was
zing!!
Are you okay?
Kaff!!
C-can't breathe good.
She-she can't breathe!!
We got her!
Kid, that as amazing!! Crazy but amazing.
You okay??
How did you do that??
What's your name?
Told you Spider-Man was black.

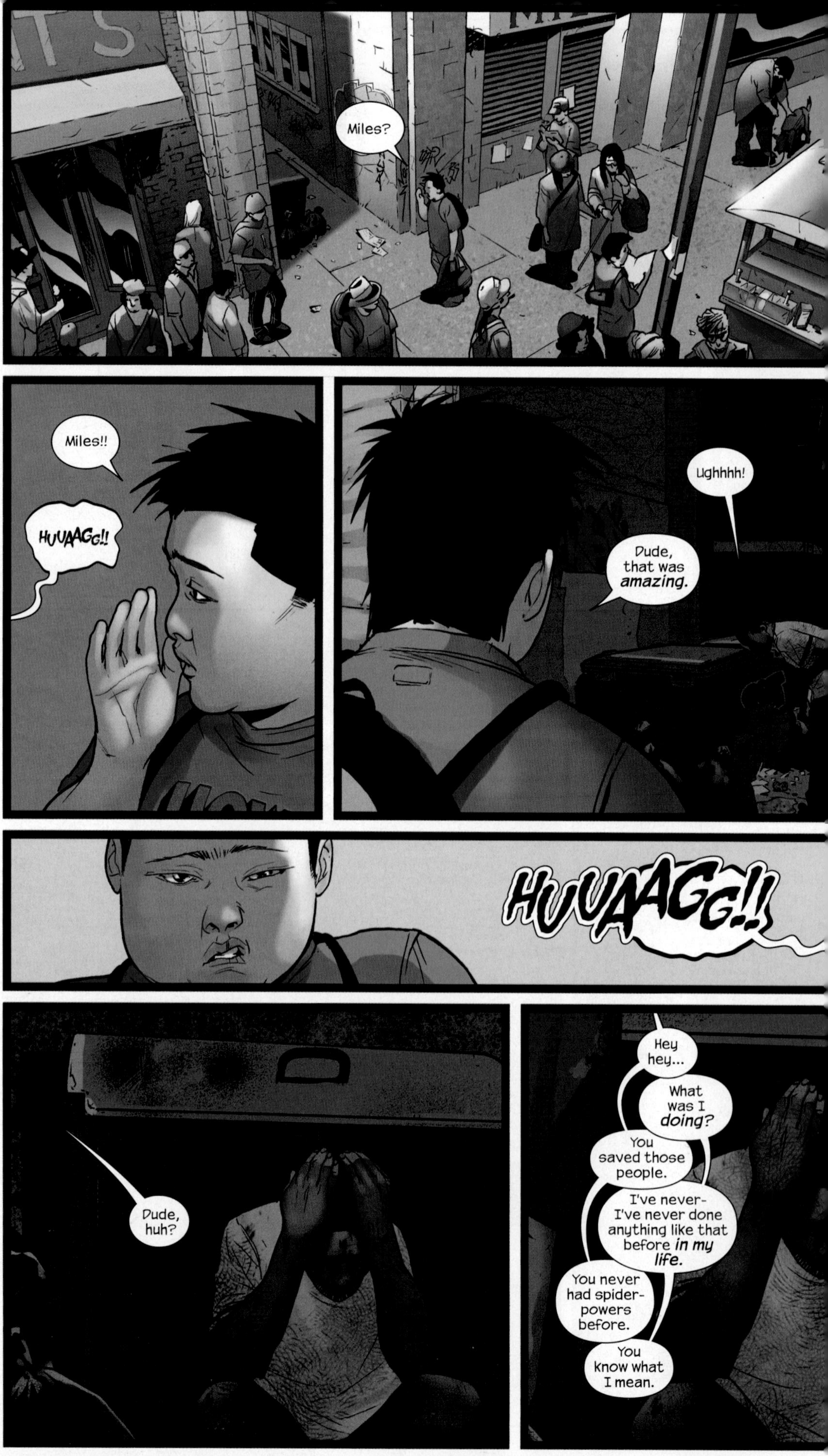
Miles?
Miles!!
HUUAAGG!!
Ughhhh!
Dude, that was *amazing.*
HUUAAGG!!
Dude, huh?
Hey hey...
What was I *doing?*
You saved those people.
I've never- I've never done anything like that before *in my life.*
You never had spider-powers before.
You know what I mean.

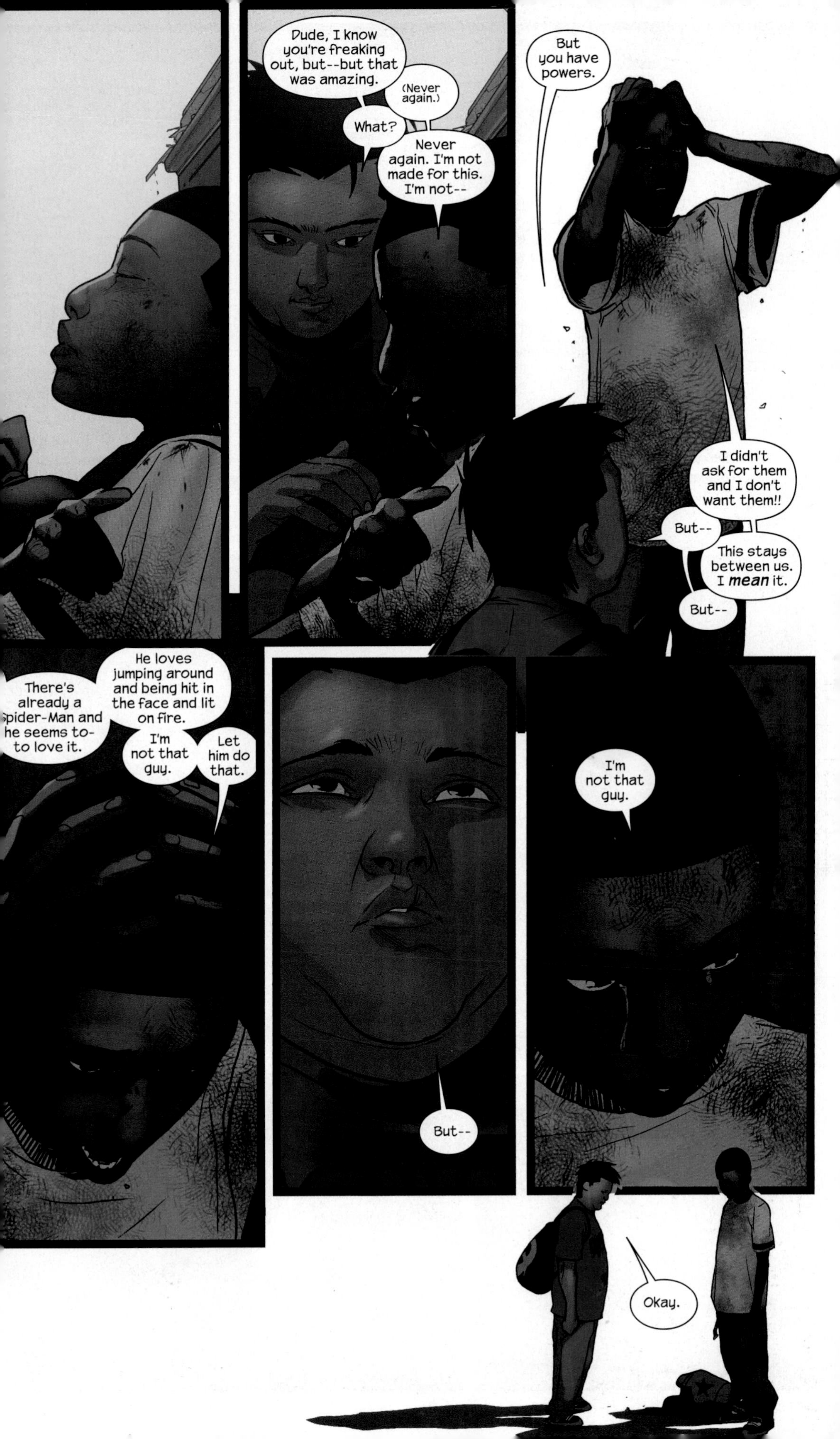

Dude, I know you're freaking out, but--but that was amazing.
(Never again.)
What?
Never again. I'm not made for this. I'm not--
But you have powers.
I didn't ask for them and I don't want them!!
But--
This stays between us. I *mean* it.
But--
There's already a Spider-Man and he seems to-to love it.
He loves jumping around and being hit in the face and lit on fire.
I'm not that guy.
Let him do that.
But--
I'm not that guy.
Okay.

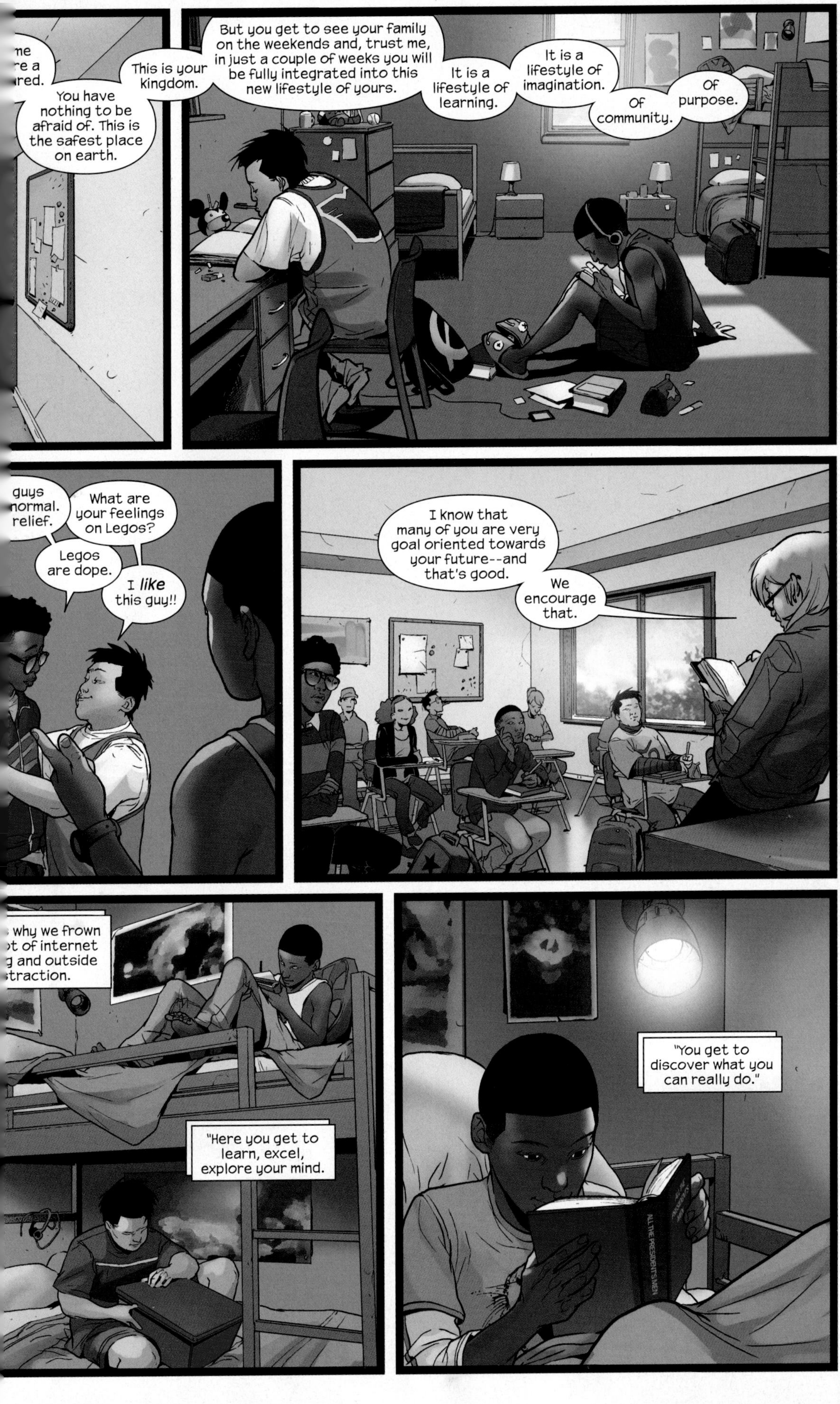

me
re a
red.
You have nothing to be afraid of. This is the safest place on earth.
This is your kingdom.
But you get to see your family on the weekends and, trust me, in just a couple of weeks you will be fully integrated into this new lifestyle of yours.
It is a lifestyle of learning.
It is a lifestyle of imagination.
Of community.
Of purpose.
guys
normal.
relief.
What are your feelings on Legos?
Legos are dope.
I *like* this guy!!
I know that many of you are very goal oriented towards your future--and that's good.
We encourage that.
why we frown
ot of internet
g and outside
straction.
"Here you get to learn, excel, explore your mind.
"You get to discover what you can really do."
ALL THE PRESIDENT'S MEN

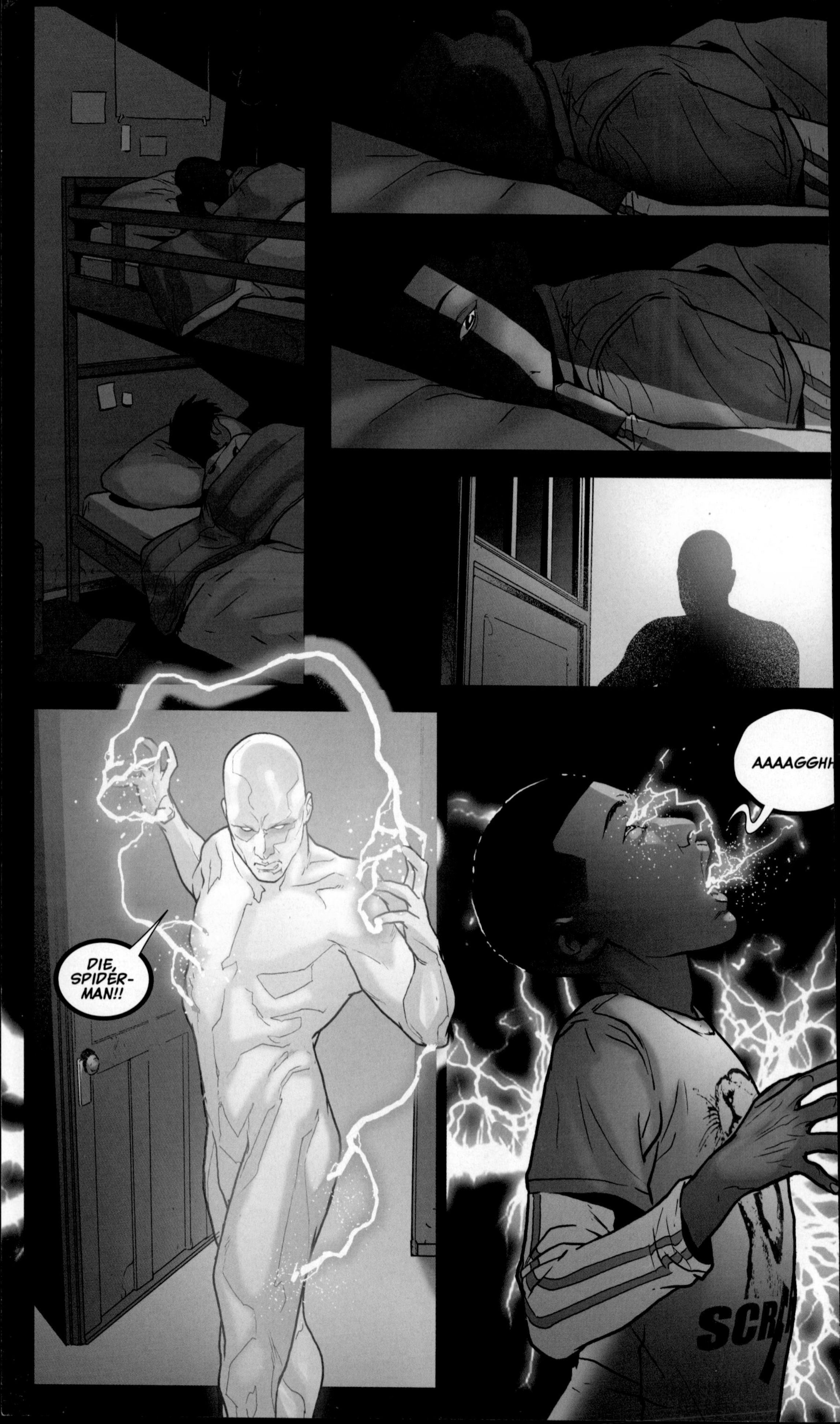
DIE, SPIDER-MAN!!
AAAAGGHH
SCR

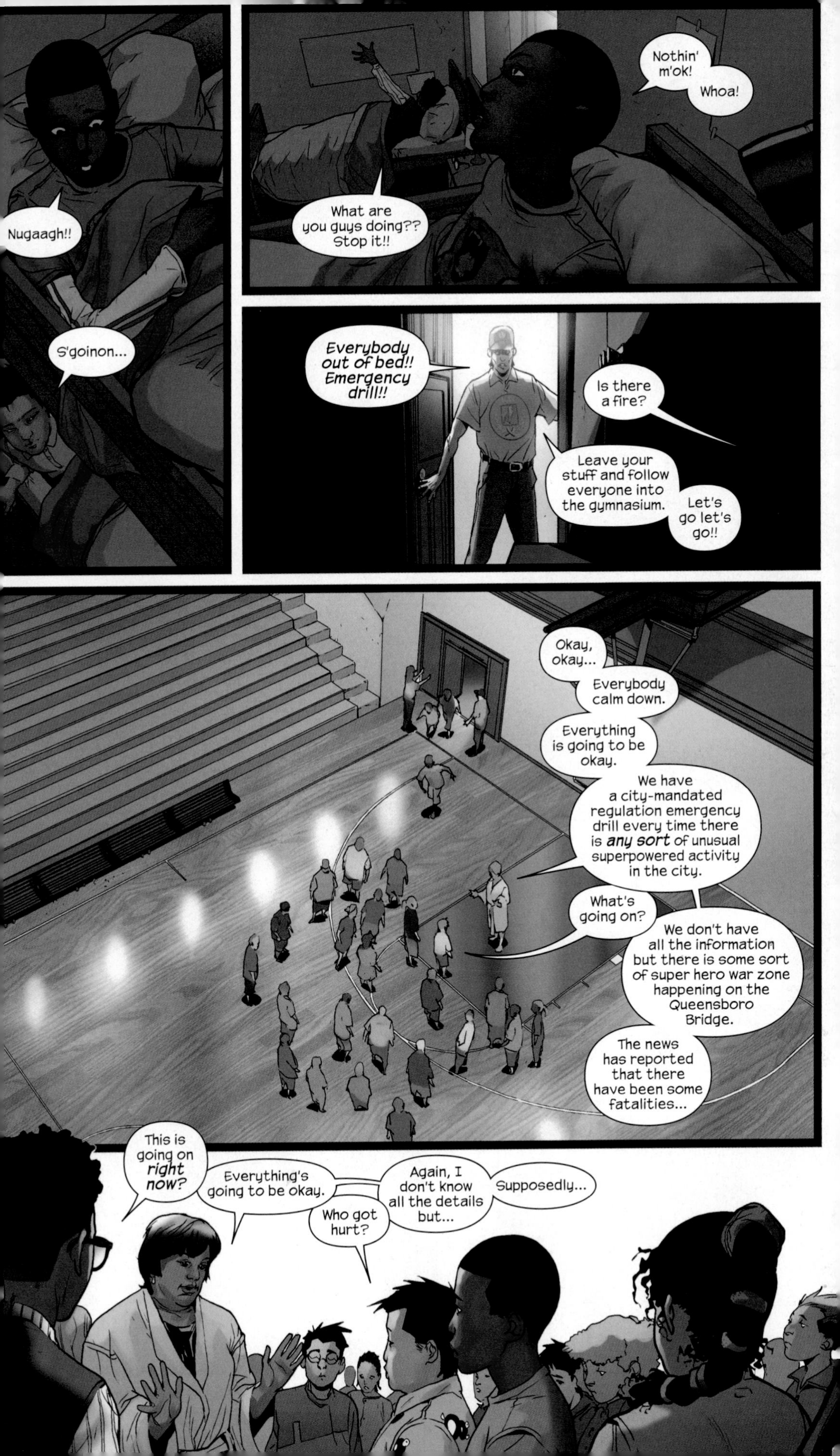
Nugaagh!!
S'goinon...
What are you guys doing?? Stop it!!
Nothin' m'ok!
Whoa!
Everybody out of bed!! Emergency drill!!
Is there a fire?
Leave your stuff and follow everyone into the gymnasium.
Let's go let's go!!
Okay, okay...
Everybody calm down.
Everything is going to be okay.
We have a city-mandated regulation emergency drill every time there is any sort of unusual superpowered activity in the city.
What's going on?
We don't have all the information but there is some sort of super hero war zone happening on the Queensboro Bridge.
The news has reported that there have been some fatalities...
This is going on right now?
Everything's going to be okay.
Who got hurt?
Again, I don't know all the details but...
Supposedly...

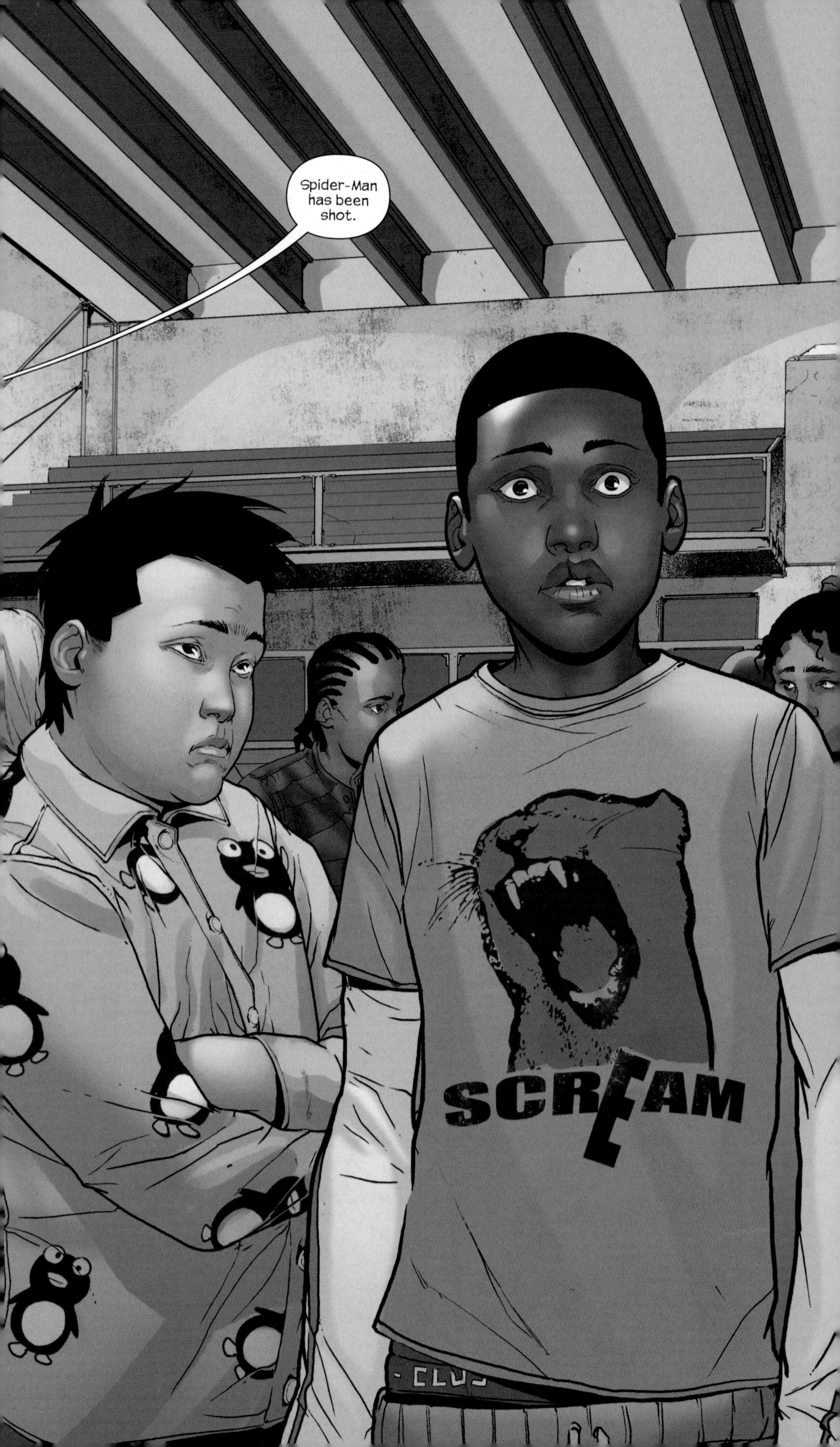
Spider-Man has been shot.
SCREAM

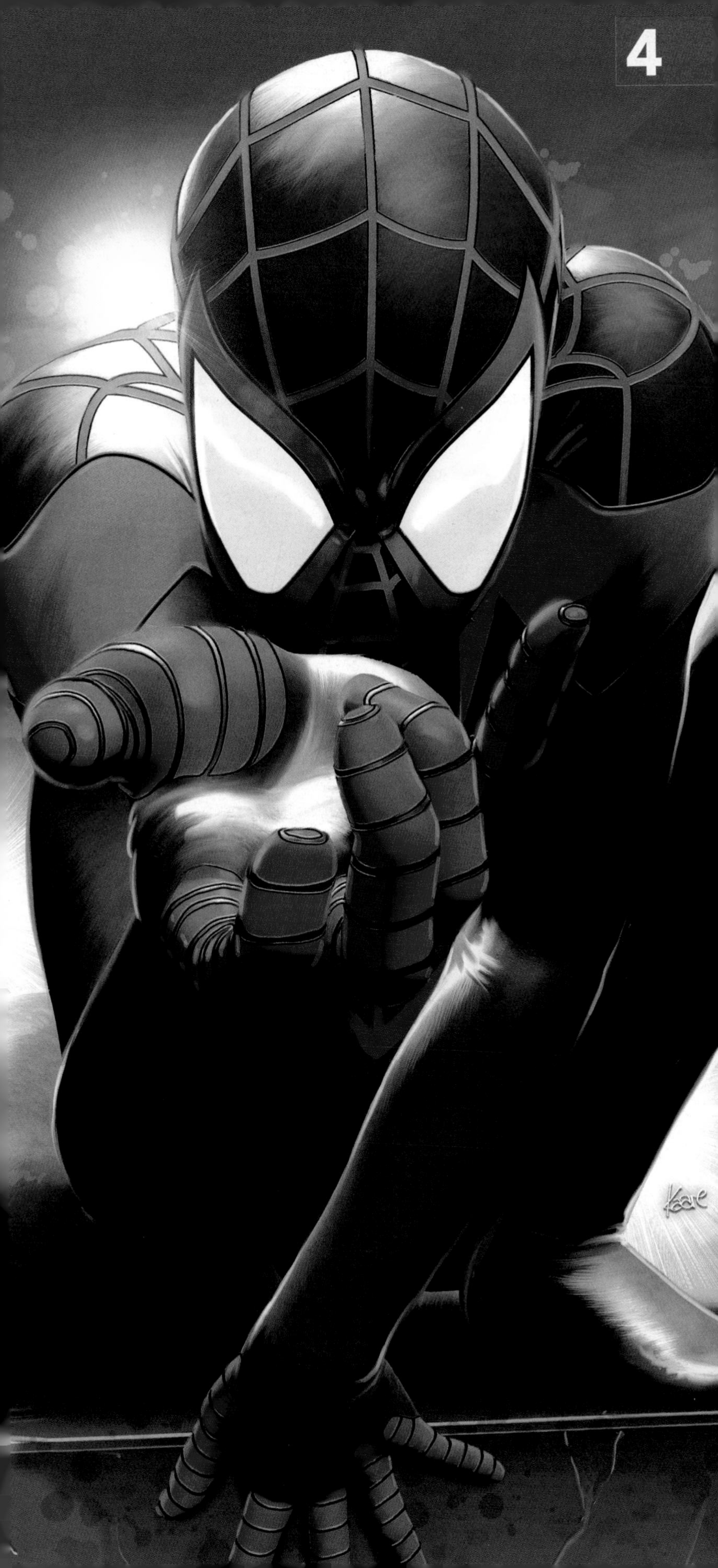
4

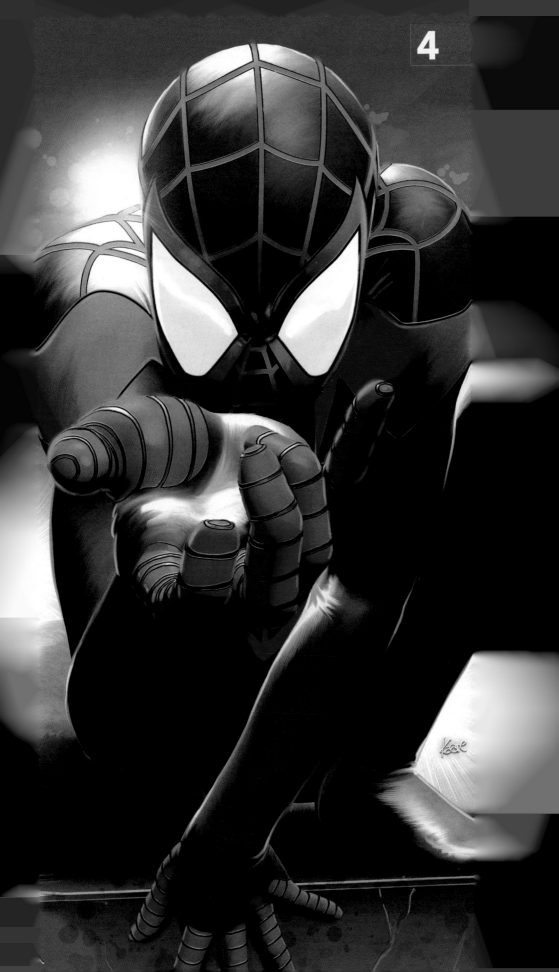

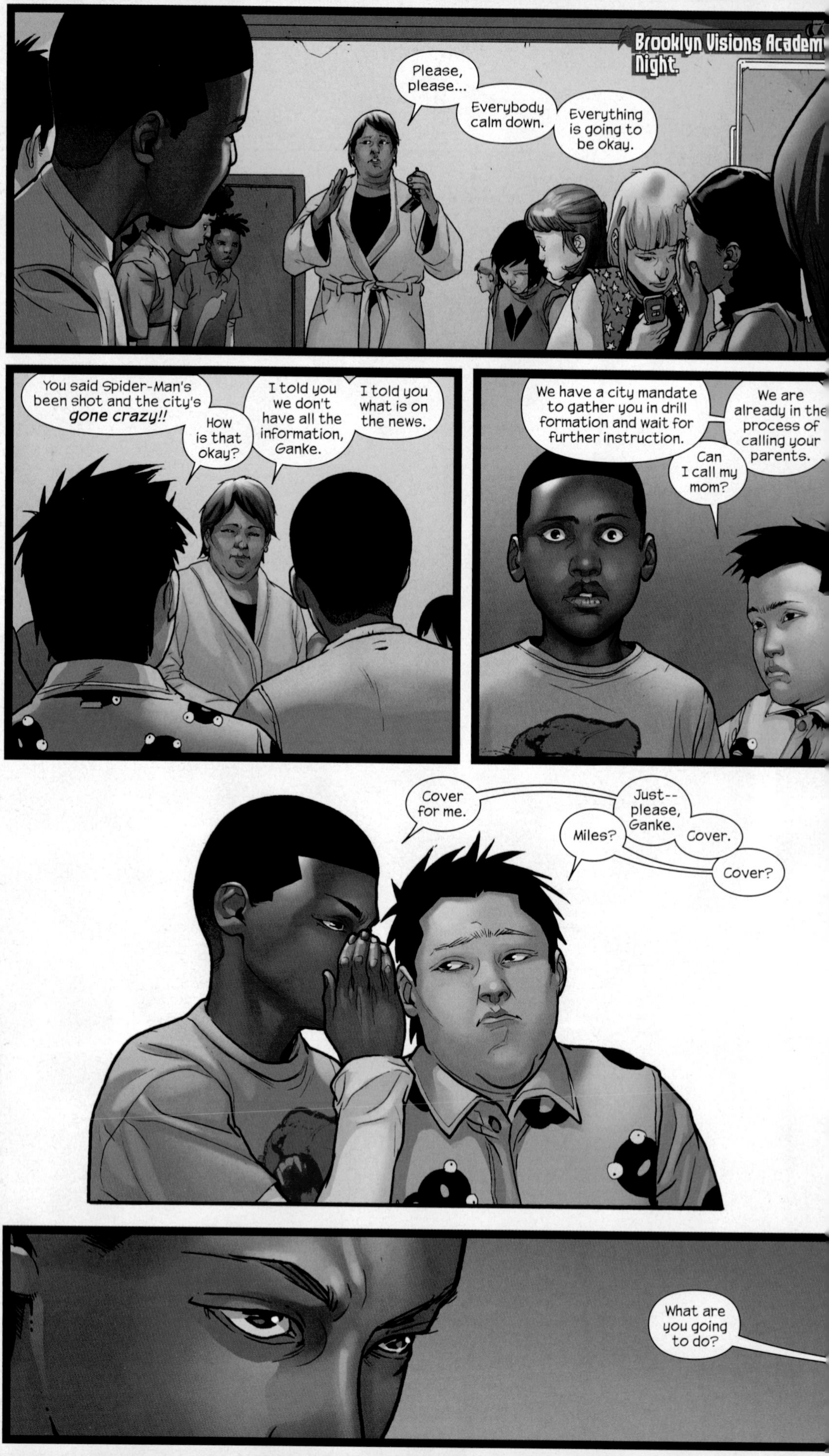
Brooklyn Visions Academ
Night.
Please, please...
Everybody calm down.
Everything is going to be okay.
You said Spider-Man's been shot and the city's gone crazy!!
How is that okay?
I told you we don't have all the information, Ganke.
I told you what is on the news.
We have a city mandate to gather you in drill formation and wait for further instruction.
We are already in the process of calling your parents.
Can I call my mom?
Cover for me.
Just-- please, Ganke.
Miles?
Cover.
Cover?
What are you going to do?

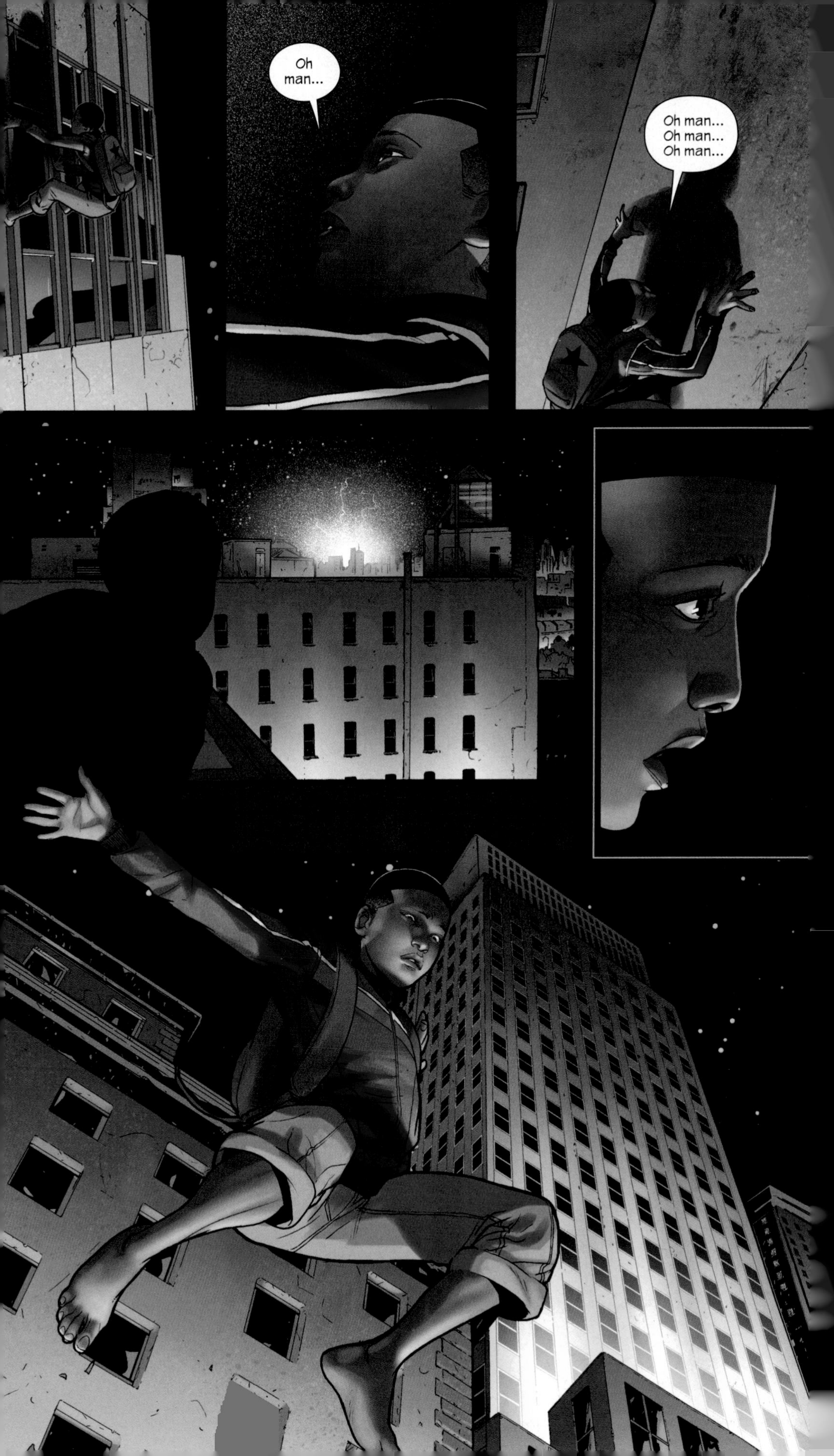
Oh man...
Oh man...
Oh man...
Oh man...

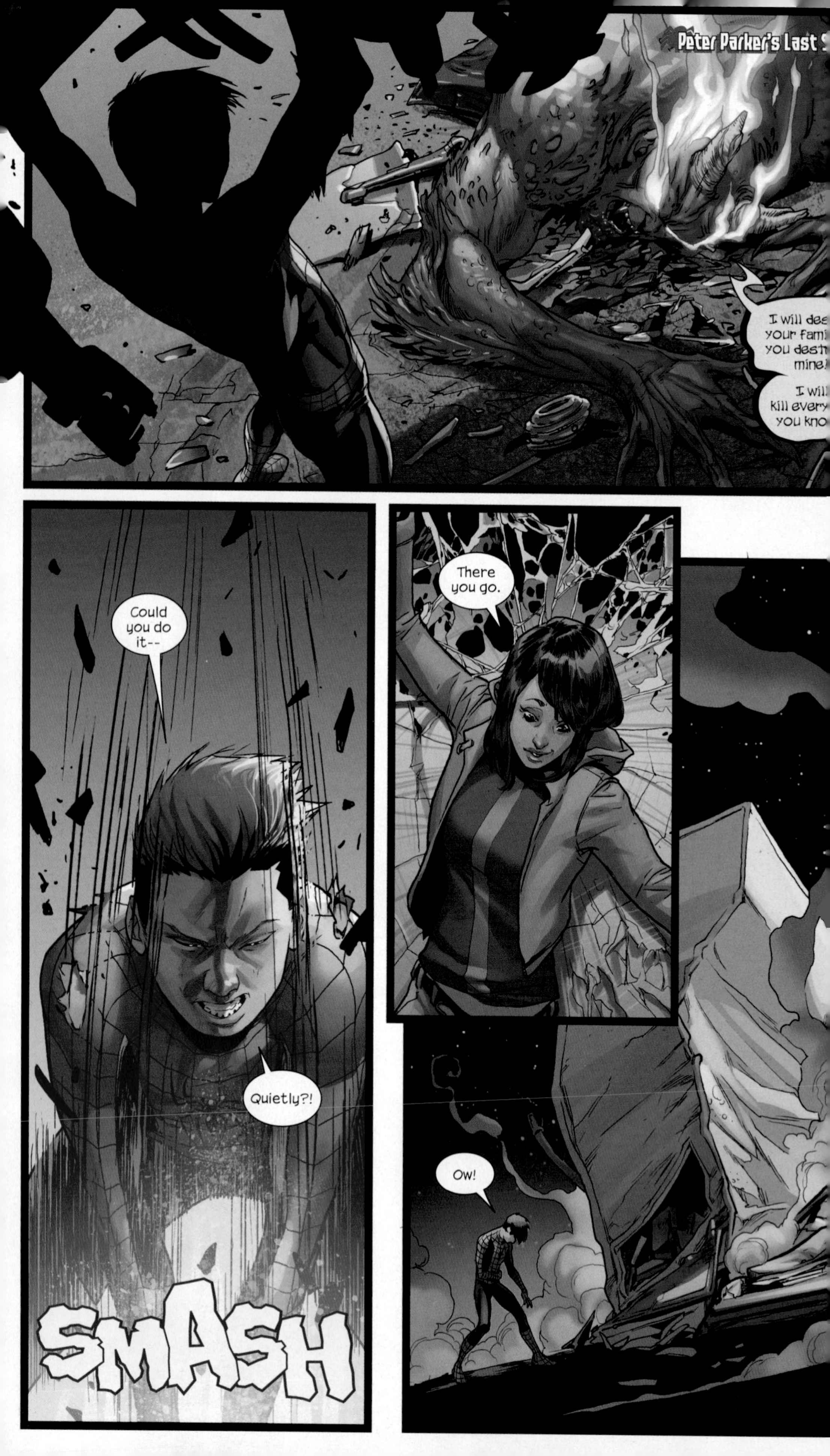
I will de
your fami
you destr
mine!
I will
kill every
you kno
Could you do it--
Quietly?!
There you go.
SMASH
Ow!

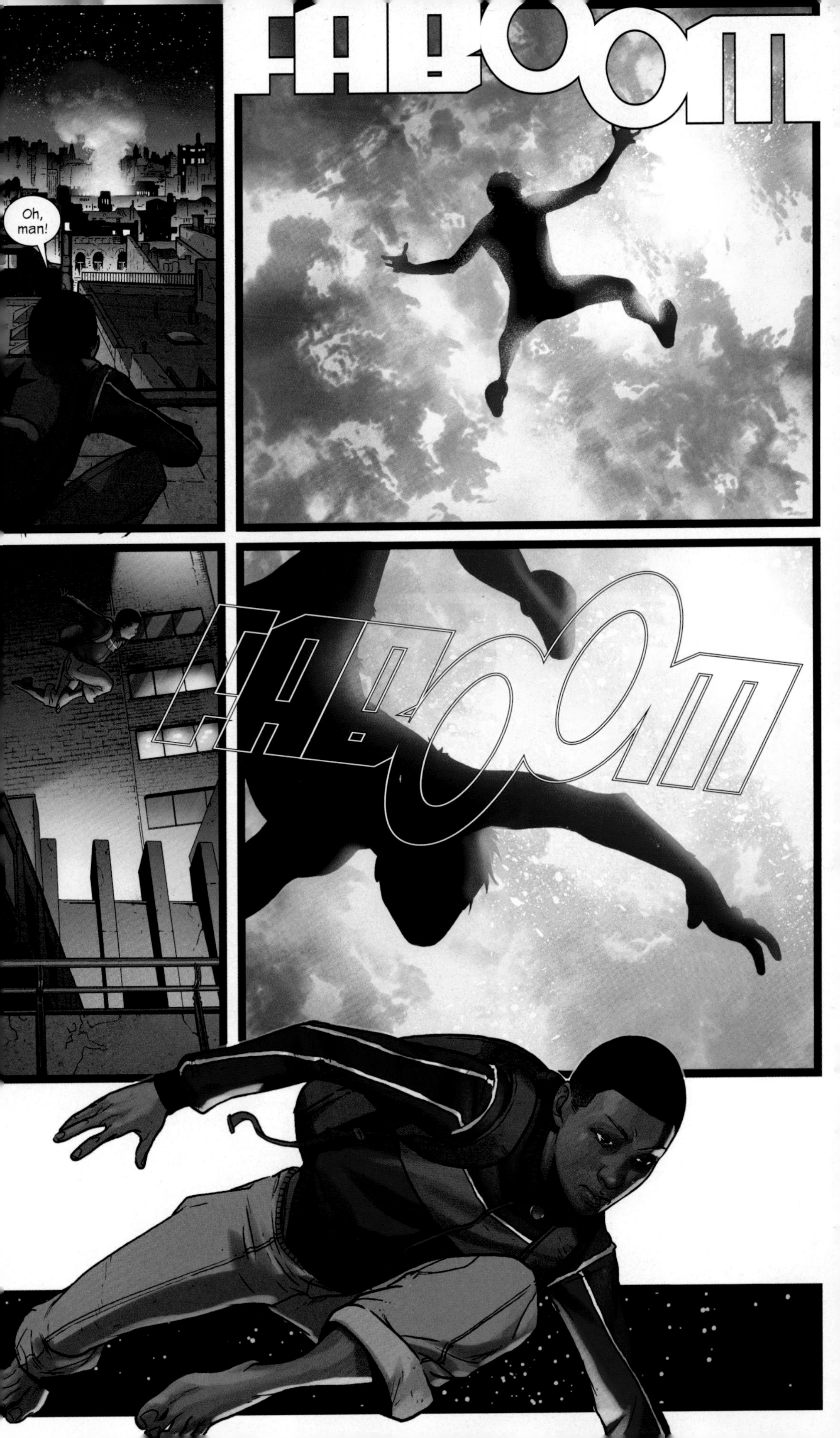
KABOOM
Oh, man!
KABOOM

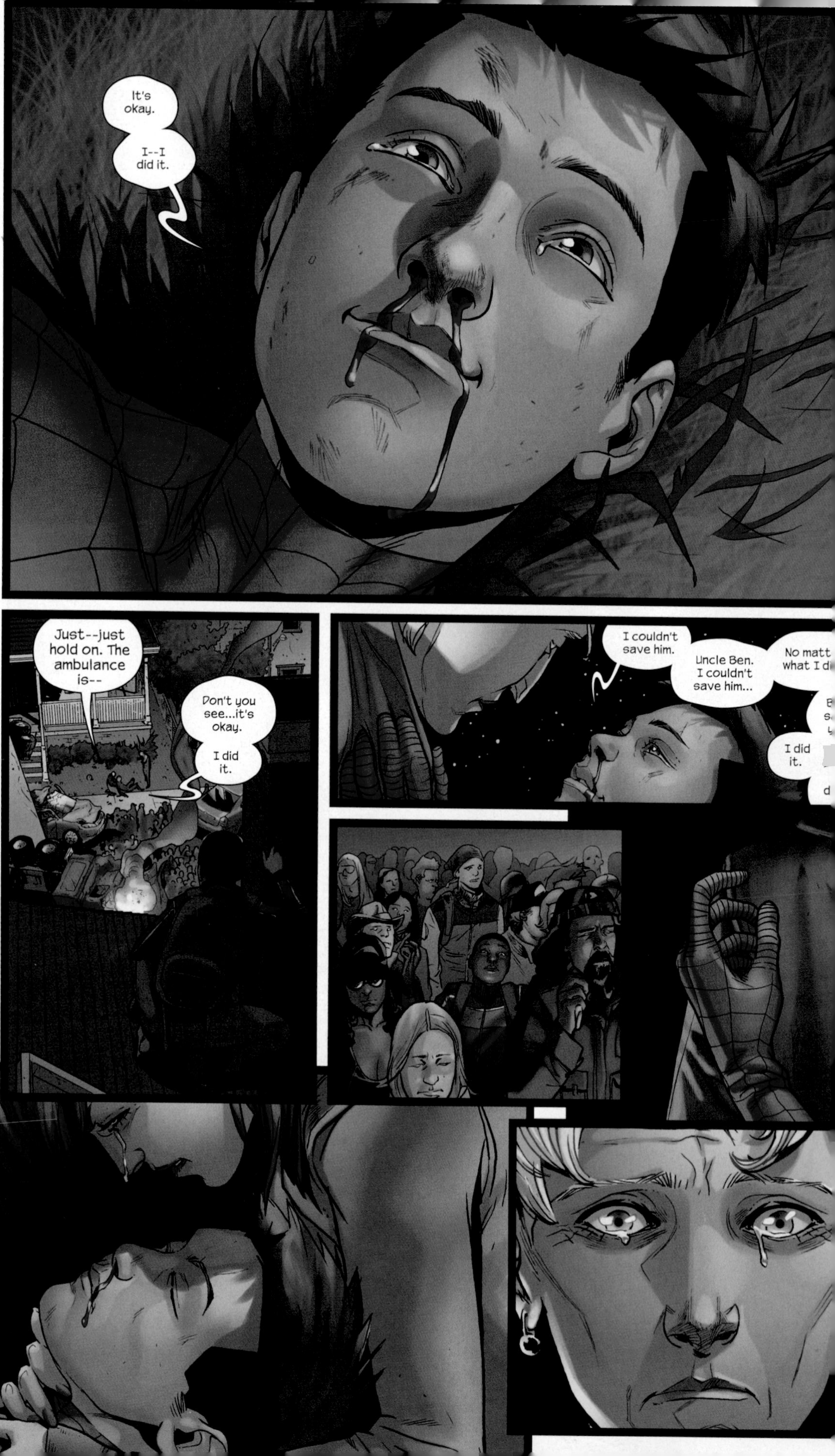
It's okay.
I--I did it.
Just--just hold on. The ambulance is--
Don't you see...it's okay.
I did it.
I couldn't save him.
Uncle Ben. I couldn't save him...
No matt what I di
I did it.

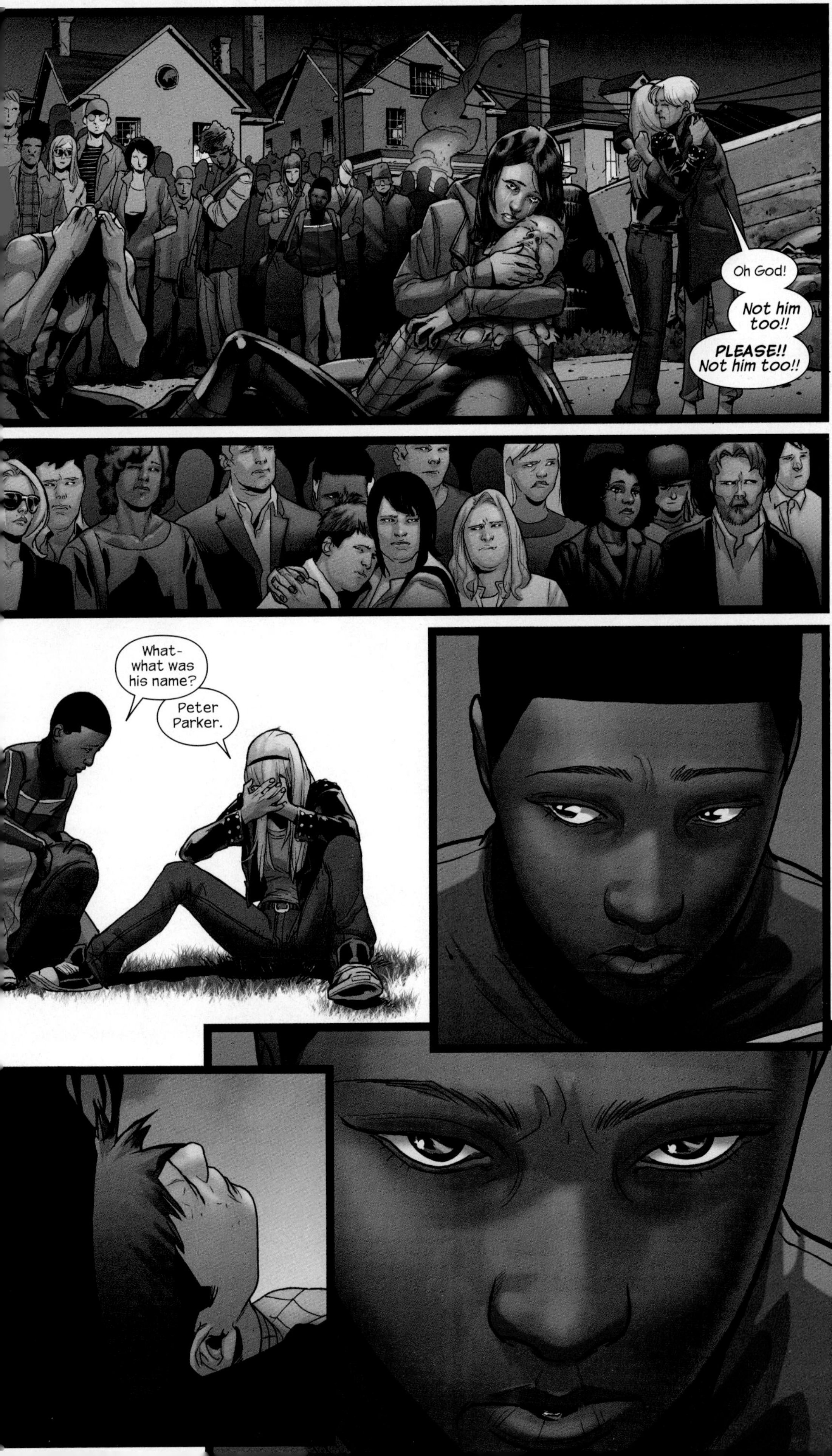
Oh God!
Not him too!!
PLEASE!! Not him too!!
What- what was his name?
Peter Parker.

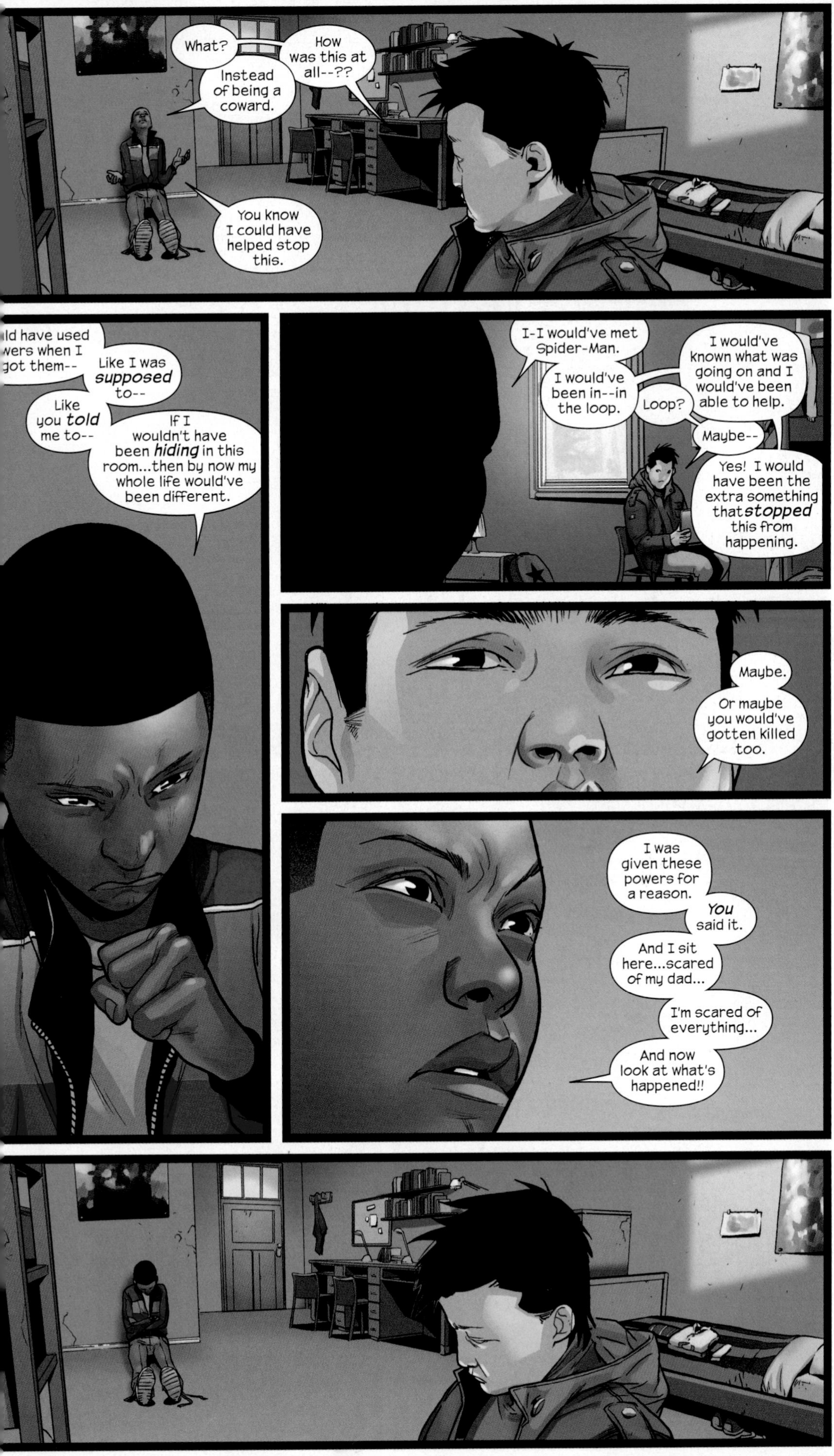
What?
How was this at all--??
Instead of being a coward.
You know I could have helped stop this.
ld have used wers when I got them--
Like I was *supposed* to--
Like you *told* me to--
If I wouldn't have been *hiding* in this room...then by now my whole life would've been different.
I-I would've met Spider-Man.
I would've been in--in the loop.
Loop?
I would've known what was going on and I would've been able to help.
Maybe--
Yes! I would have been the extra something that *stopped* this from happening.
Maybe.
Or maybe you would've gotten killed too.
I was given these powers for a reason.
*You* said it.
And I sit here...scared of my dad...
I'm scared of everything...
And now look at what's happened!!

Or Maybe-- Maybe *this* is what you were given the powers for. Maybe you're supposed to be Spider-Man now that we don't have one anymore.

Maybe you're the Spider-Man in the on-deck circle...and now it's your turn.

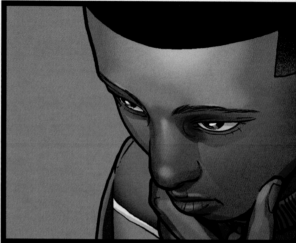

This is crazy.

All the bridges are closed.

You think we'll get the day off school?

What?

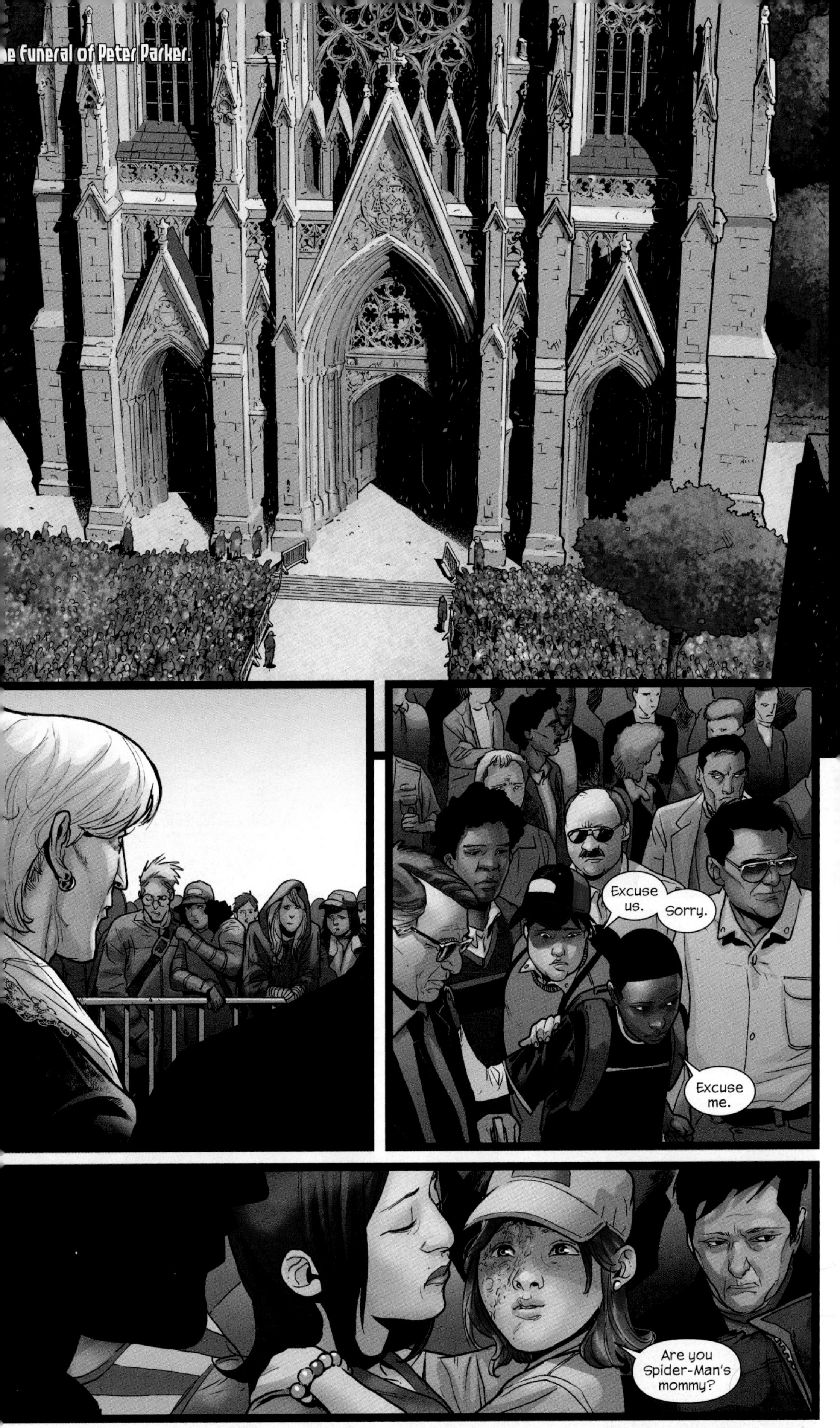
e Funeral of Peter Parker.
Excuse us.
Sorry.
Excuse me.
Are you Spider-Man's mommy?

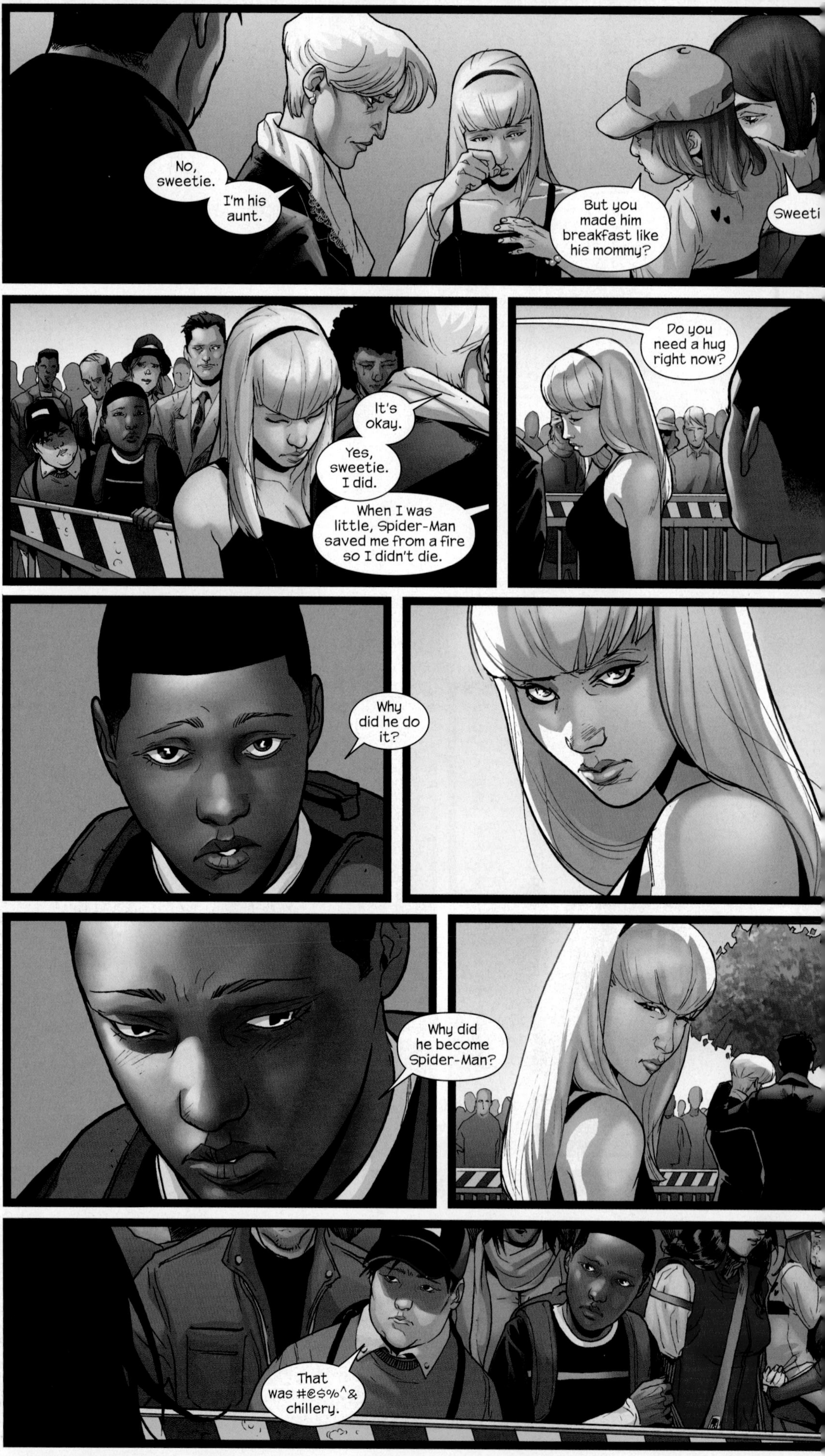
No, sweetie.
I'm his aunt.
But you made him breakfast like his mommy?
Sweeti
It's okay.
Yes, sweetie. I did.
When I was little, Spider-Man saved me from a fire so I didn't die.
Do you need a hug right now?
Why did he do it?
Why did he become Spider-Man?
That was #@$%^& chillery.

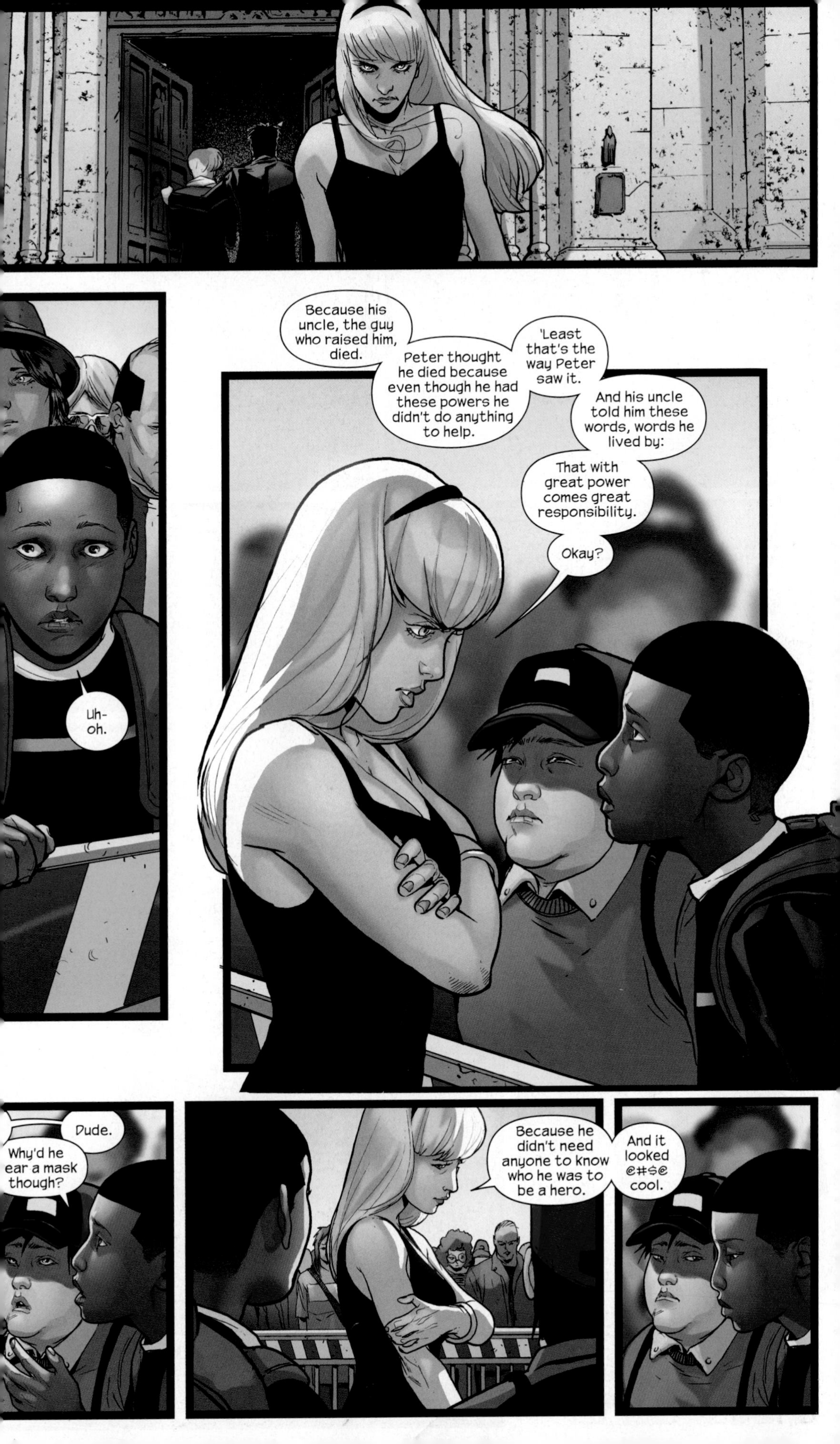

Because his uncle, the guy who raised him, died.
Peter thought he died because even though he had these powers he didn't do anything to help.
'Least that's the way Peter saw it.
And his uncle told him these words, words he lived by:
That with great power comes great responsibility.
Okay?
Uh-oh.
Dude.
Why'd he ear a mask though?
Because he didn't need anyone to know who he was to be a hero.
And it looked @#$@ cool.

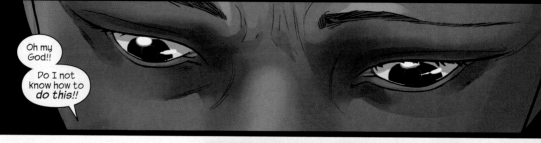

Oh my God!!

Do I not know how to *do this*!!

Say thank you.

What did you do?

No.

You say thank you because I just made your life insanely easy.

SPIDER-MAN
costume & mask

*Halloween exclusive*

You've got to be kidding me.

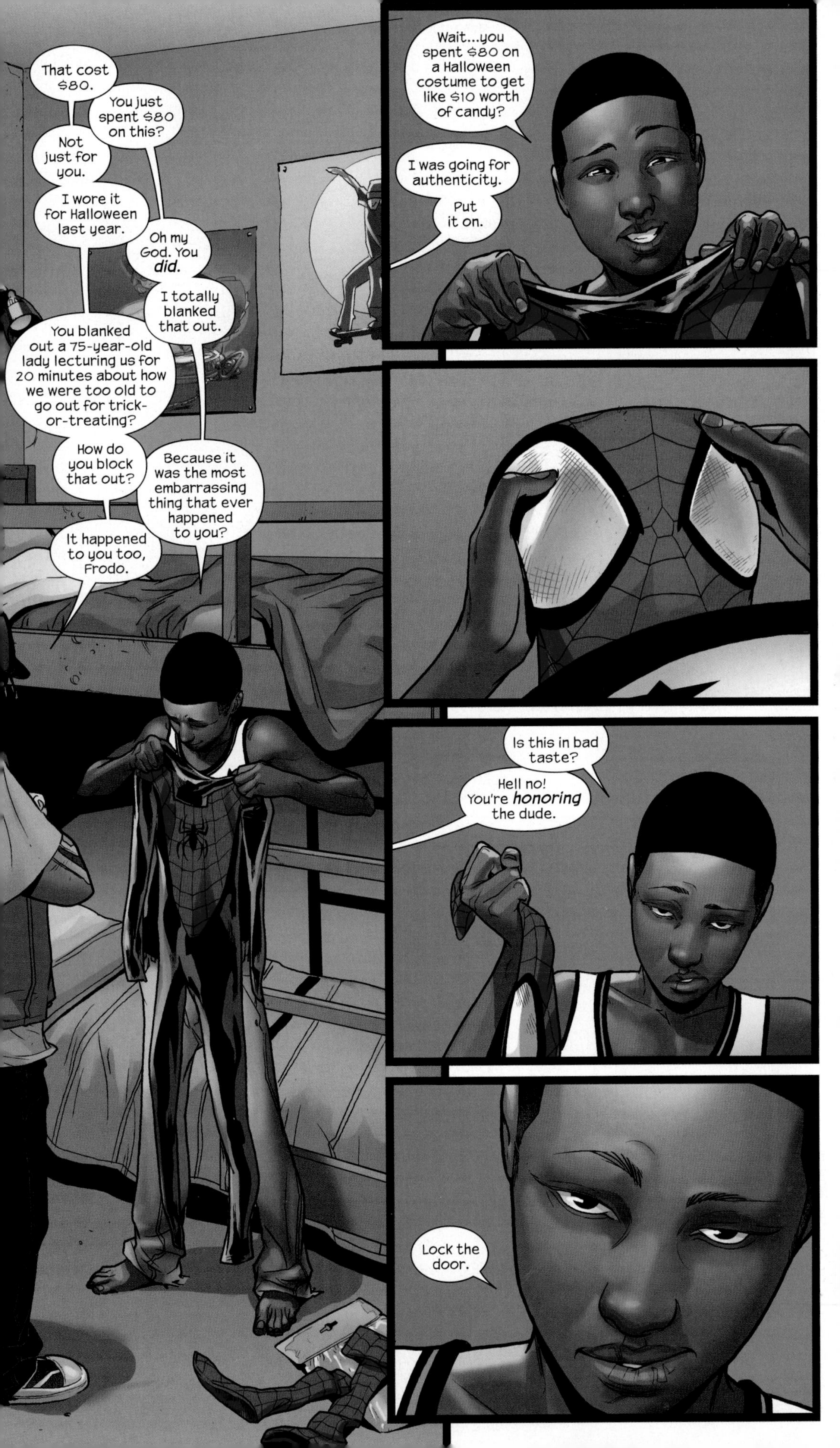

That cost $80.
You just spent $80 on this?
Not just for you.
I wore it for Halloween last year.
Oh my God. You *did.*
I totally blanked that out.
You blanked out a 75-year-old lady lecturing us for 20 minutes about how we were too old to go out for trick-or-treating?
How do you block that out?
Because it was the most embarrassing thing that ever happened to you?
It happened to you too, Frodo.
Wait...you spent $80 on a Halloween costume to get like $10 worth of candy?
I was going for authenticity.
Put it on.
Is this in bad taste?
Hell no! You're ***honoring*** the dude.
Lock the door.

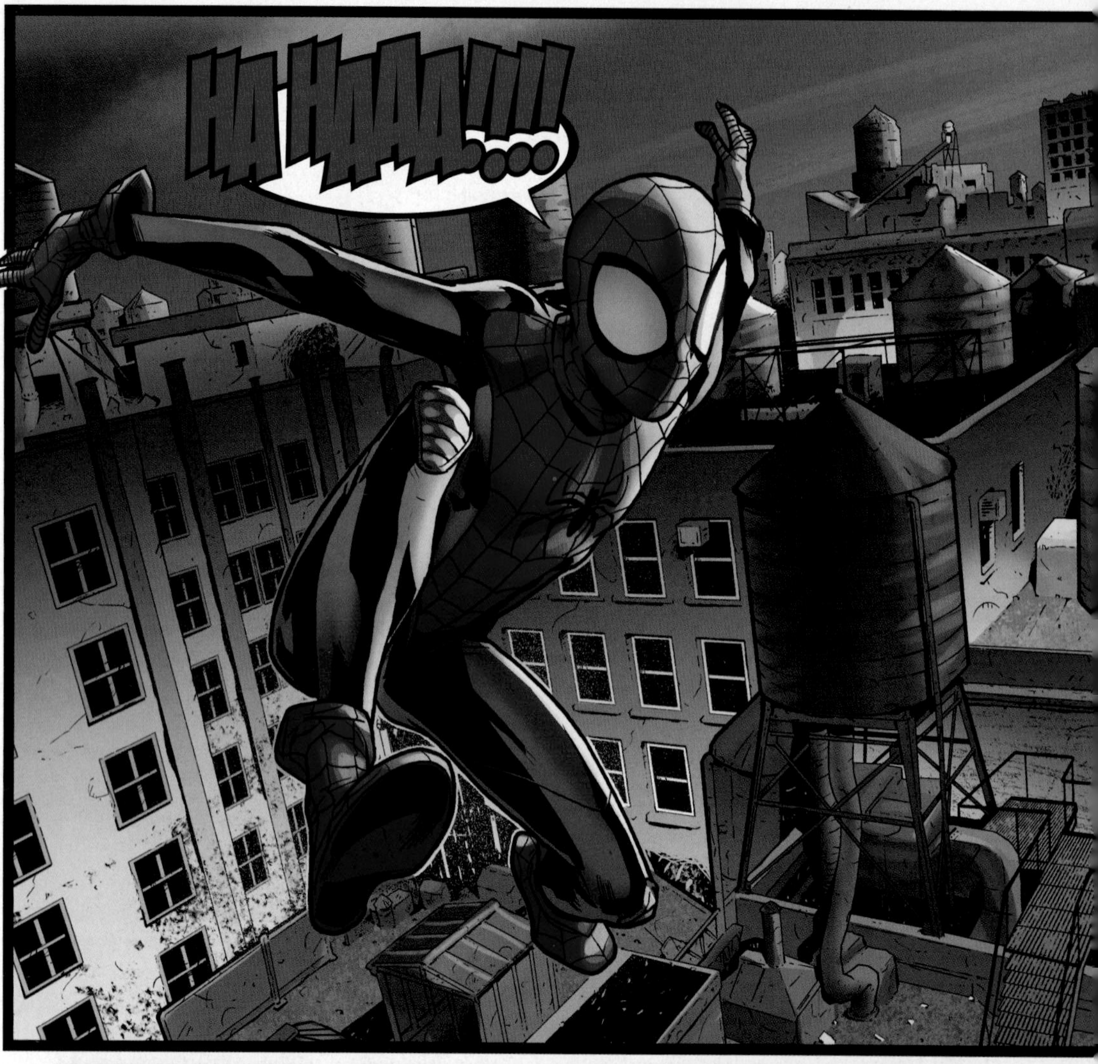
HA HAAA!!!!...

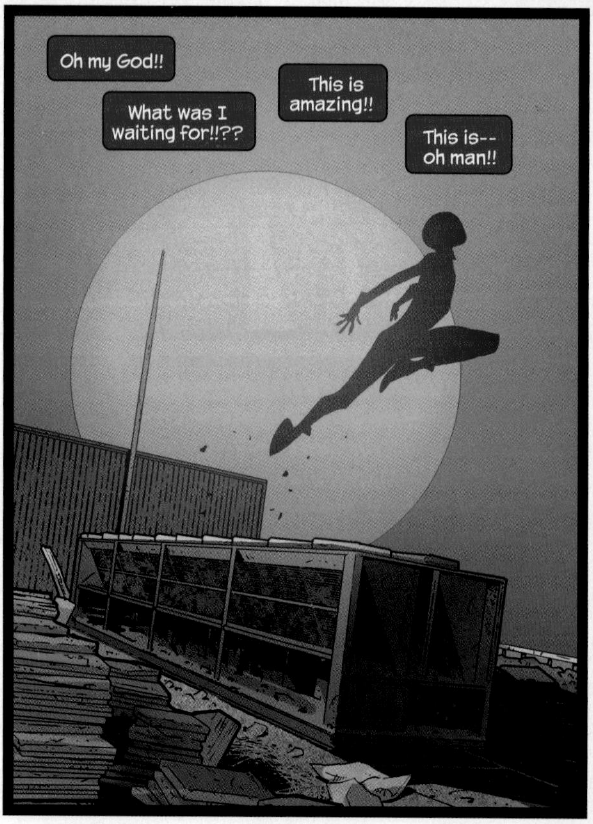
Oh my God!!
What was I waiting for!!??
This is amazing!!
This is-- oh man!!

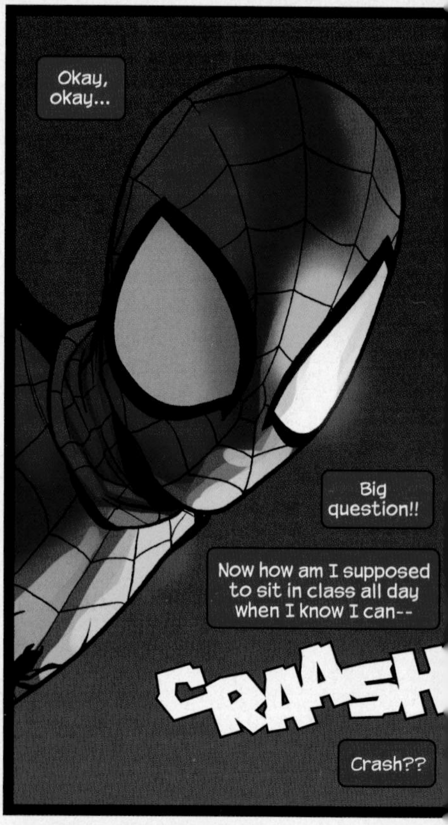
Okay, okay...
Big question!!
Now how am I supposed to sit in class all day when I know I can--
CRAASH
Crash??

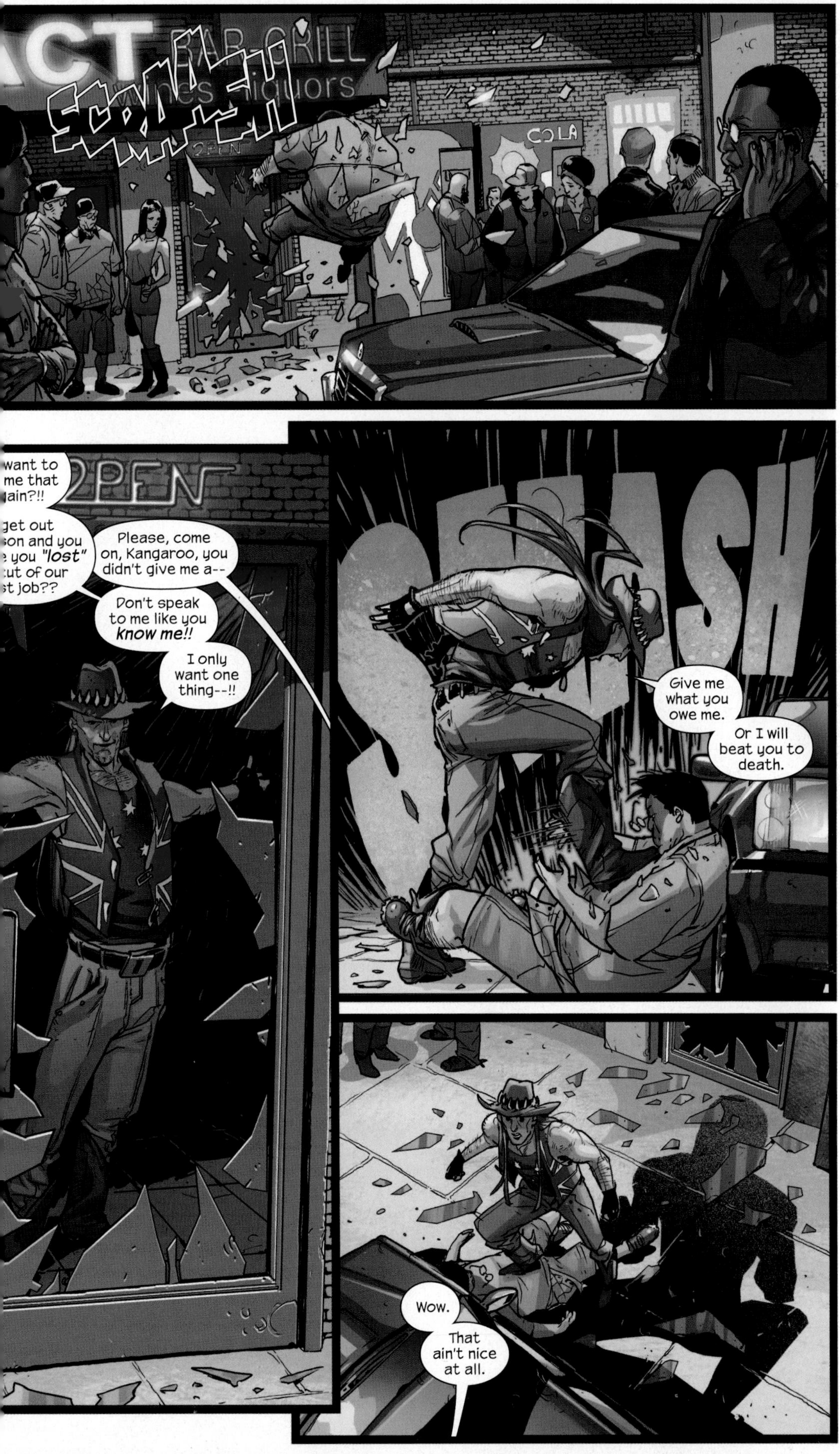
BAR-GRILL
COLA
Please, come on, Kangaroo, you didn't give me a--
Don't speak to me like you *know me!!*
I only want one thing--!!
Give me what you owe me.
Or I will beat you to death.
Wow.
That ain't nice at all.

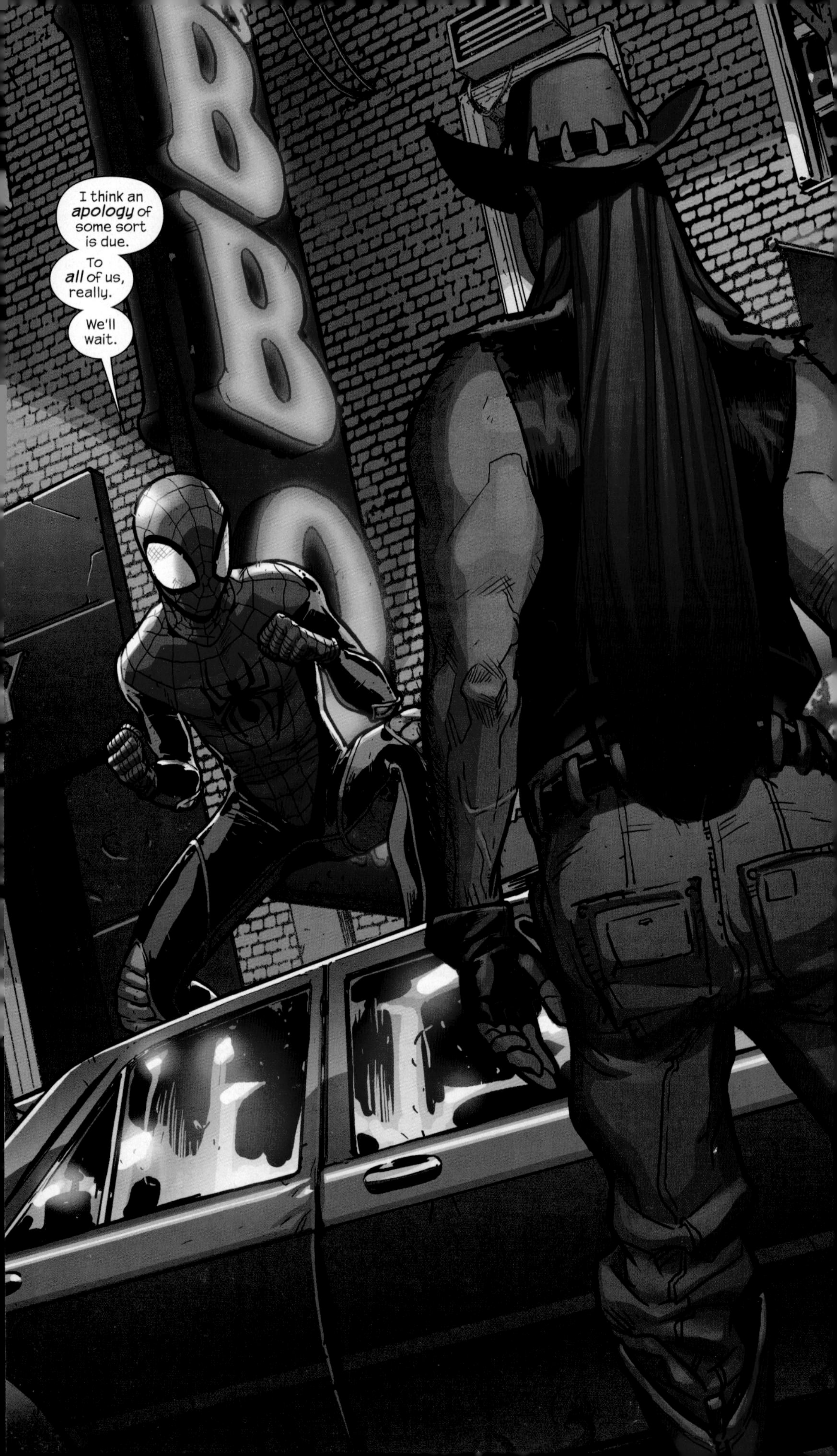
I think an apology of some sort is due.
To all of us, really.
We'll wait.

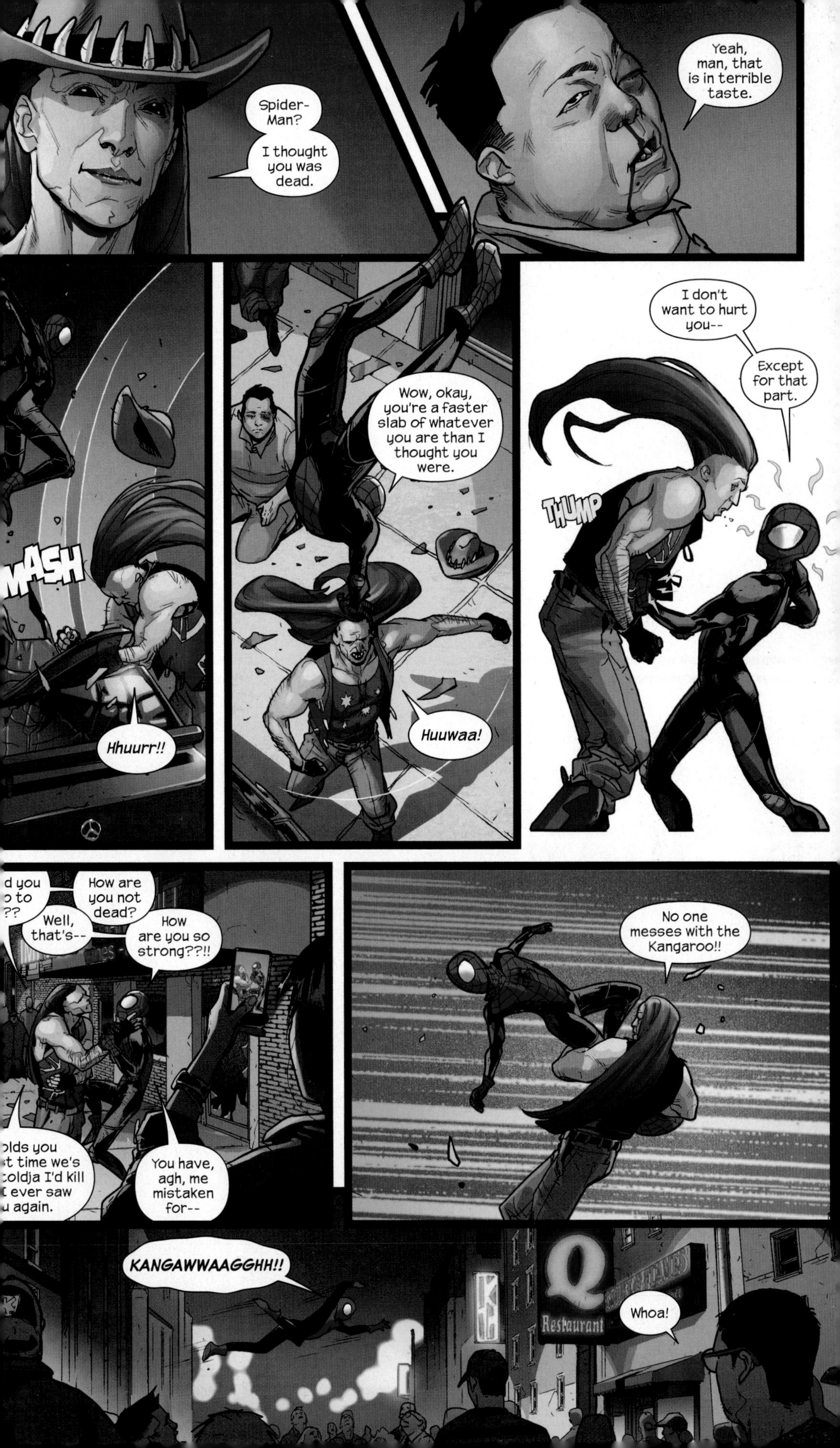
Spider-Man?
I thought you was dead.
Yeah, man, that is in terrible taste.
MASH
Hhuurr!!
Wow, okay, you're a faster slab of whatever you are than I thought you were.
Huuwaa!
I don't want to hurt you--
Except for that part.
THUMP
How are you not dead?
Well, that's--
How are you so strong??!!
You have, agh, me mistaken for--
No one messes with the Kangaroo!!
KANGAWWAAGGHH!!
Whoa!
Restaurant

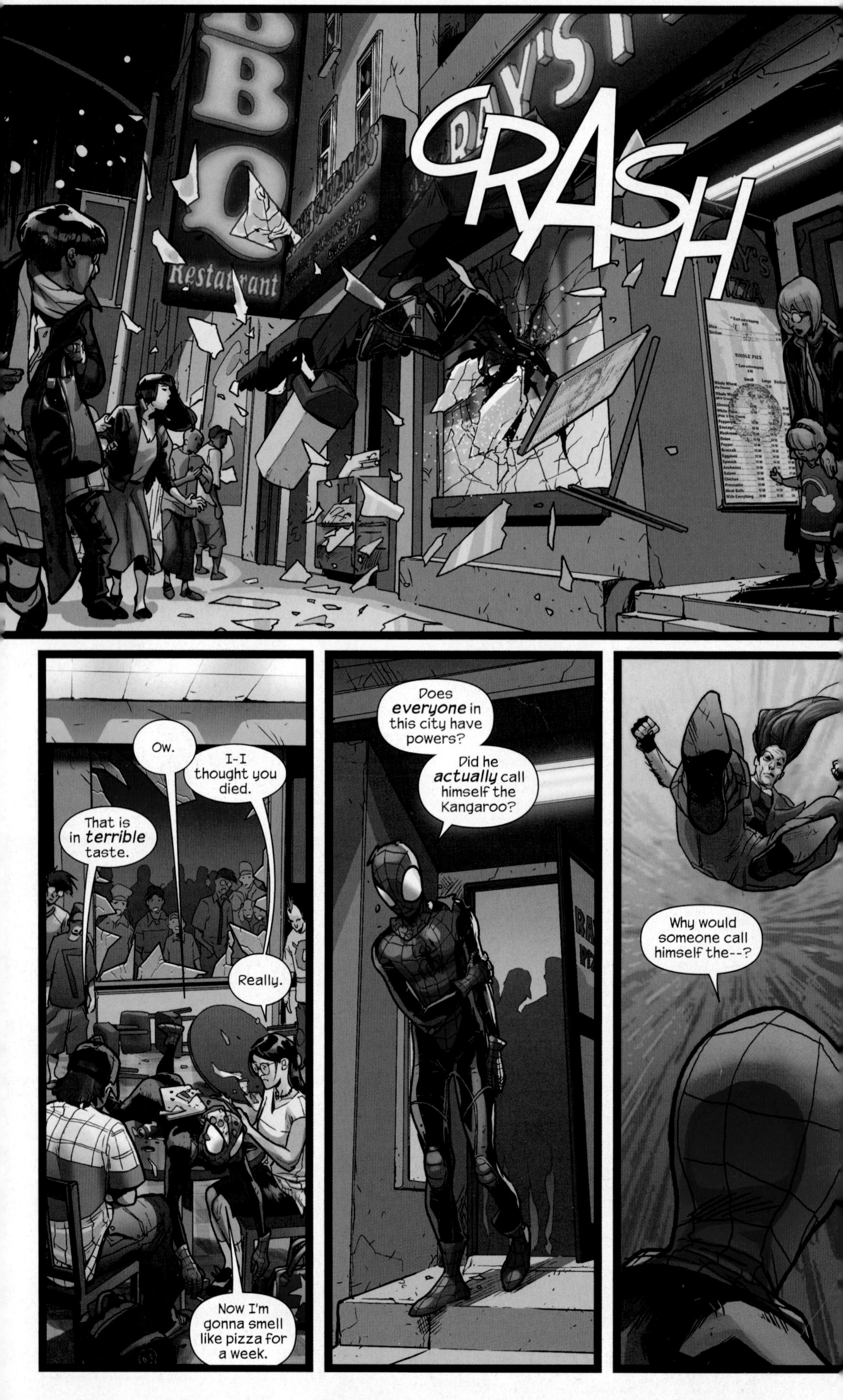

BBQ
Restaurant
CRASH
Ray's Pizza
WHOLE PIES
Ow.
I-I thought you died.
That is in *terrible* taste.
Really.
Now I'm gonna smell like pizza for a week.
Does *everyone* in this city have powers?
Did he *actually* call himself the Kangaroo?
Why would someone call himself the--?

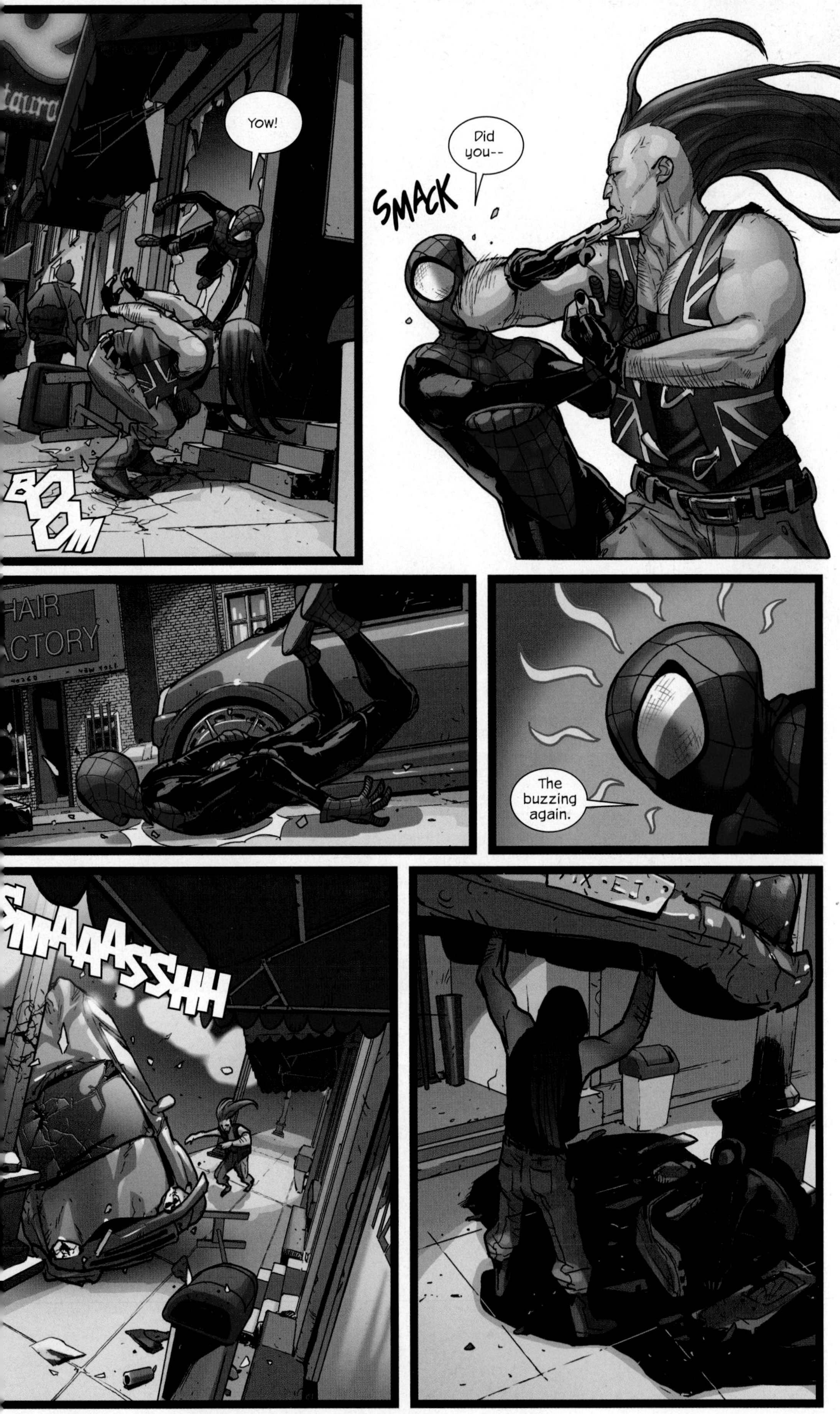
YOW!
BOOM
Did you--
SMACK
HAIR
ACTORY
The buzzing again.
SMAAASSHH

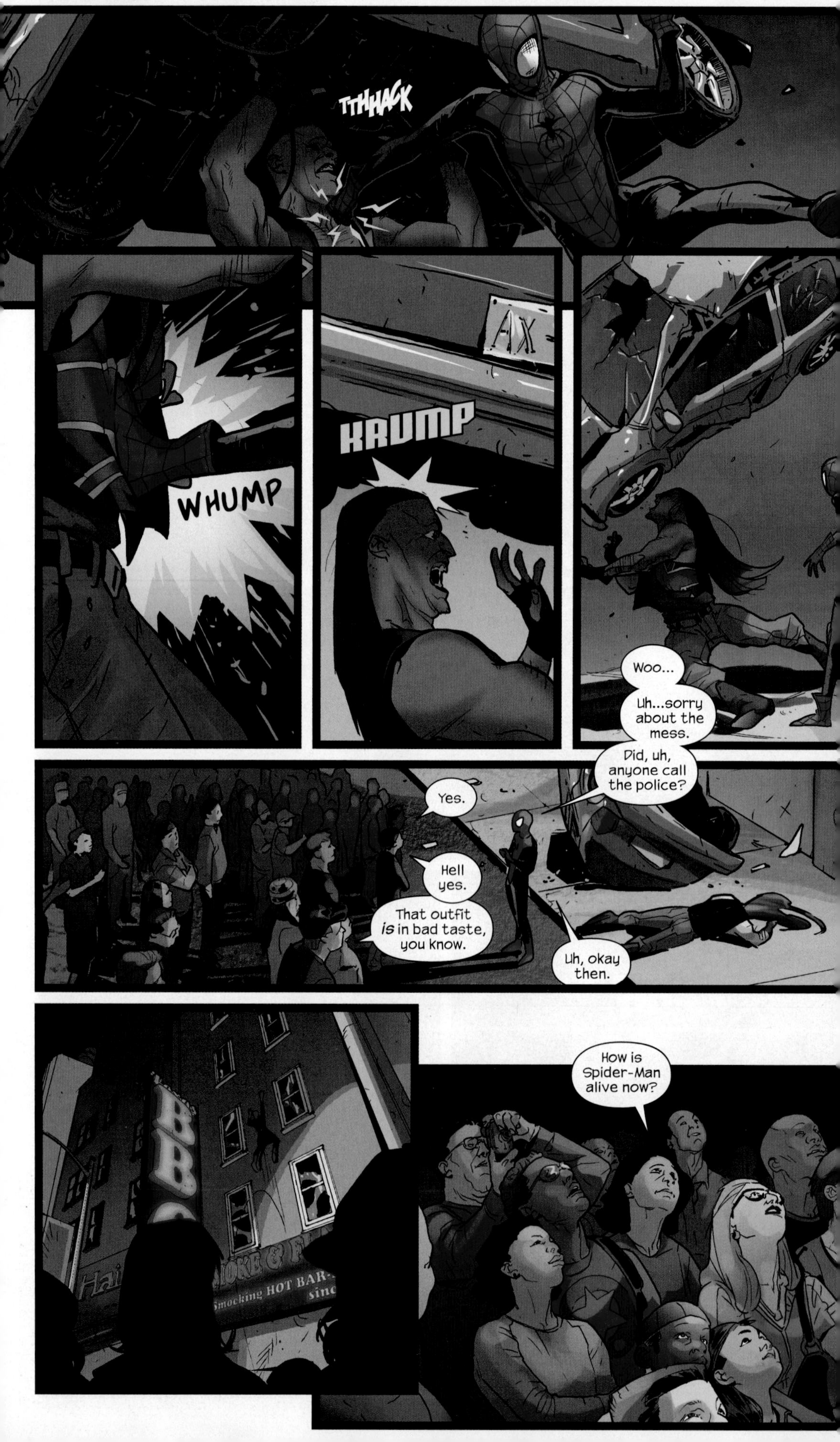
TTHHACK
WHUMP
KRUMP
Woo...
Uh...sorry about the mess.
Did, uh, anyone call the police?
Yes.
Hell yes.
That outfit *is* in bad taste, you know.
Uh, okay then.
How is Spider-Man alive now?
BBQ
Smoking HOT BAR-

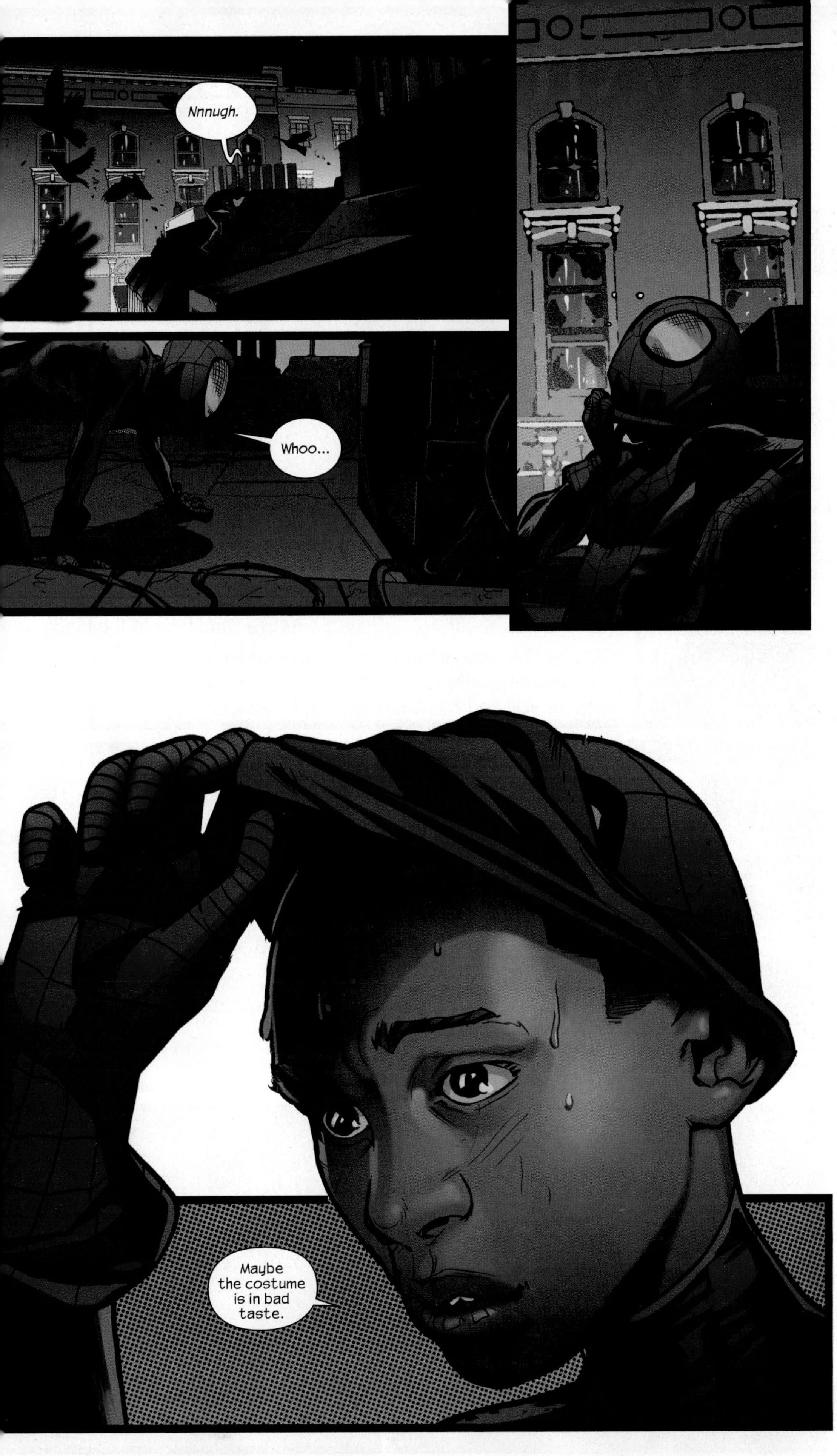
Nnnugh.
Whoo...
Maybe the costume is in bad taste.

# DAILY ❖ BUGLE

**News**
games - scores - lotteries

**Gossip**
video - photos - blogs

**Sports**
subscribe

Li
NYC Loca

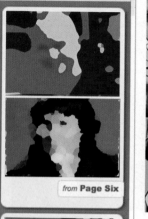

from **Page Six**

## SPIDER-MAN NO MORE... PLEASE!!

### COPYCAT HERO RIPS UP CITY

By Frederick Foswell-reporter

"It really was in bad taste."
Was the opinion of one of the dozens of New Yorkers who were witness to the calamitous debut of a young man who took it upon himself to dress as Spider-Man and take to the night.

Though he was victorious in a powered street fight with a career criminal who calls himself the Kangaroo, witnesses say that his lack of skill and naivete made the battle a clumsy dance of

Maybe it *was* in bad taste.

Ya think?

Wow, the Bugle is really dumping on you.

*Really?*

Uh, really.

I thought they *loved* Spider-Man.

I reme they to dun him t

I just thought I'd get a chance to--

THUMP THUMP

Uh-oh.

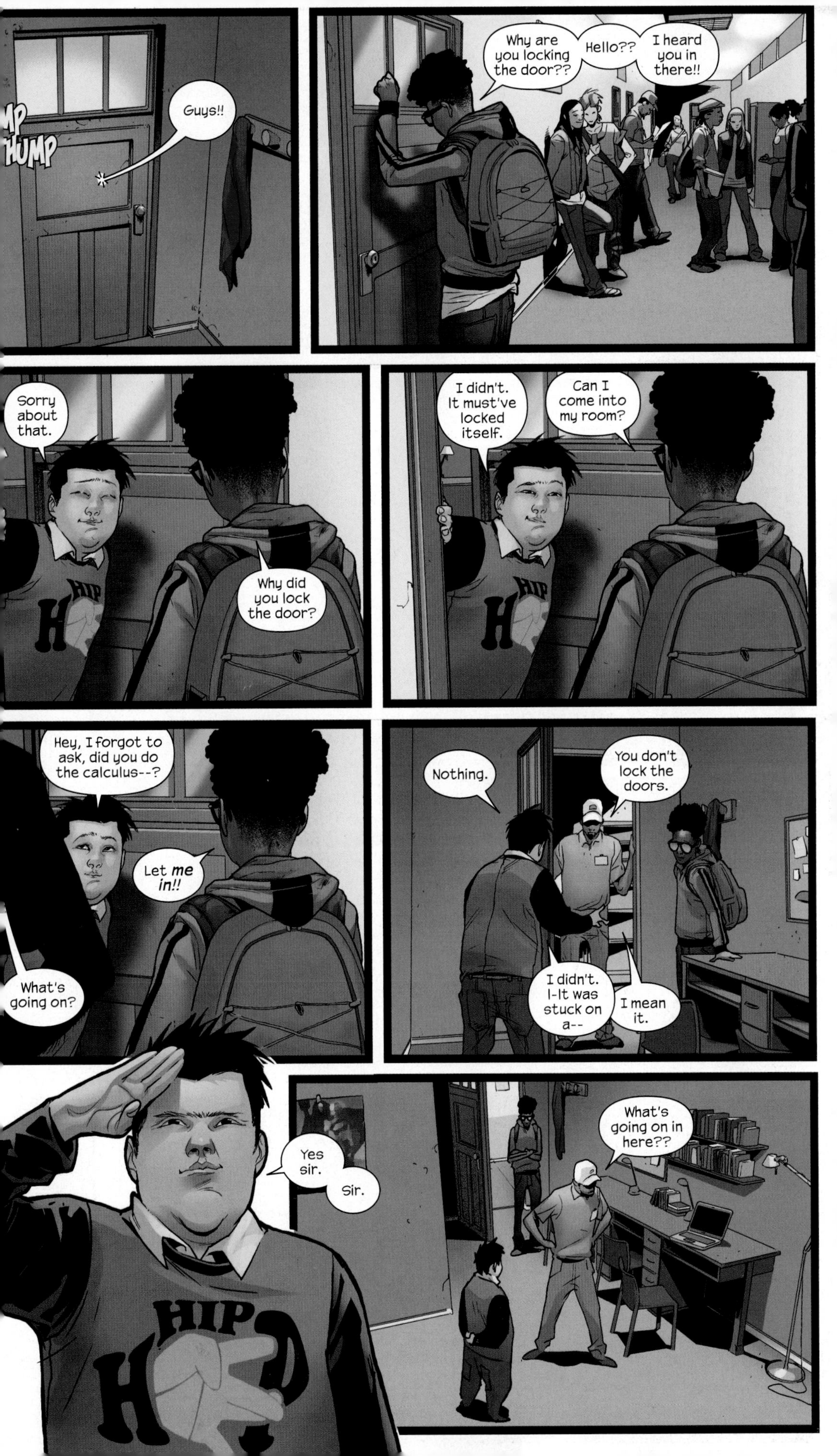
MP
HUMP
Guys!!
Why are you locking the door??
Hello??
I heard you in there!!
Sorry about that.
Why did you lock the door?
I didn't. It must've locked itself.
Can I come into my room?
Hey, I forgot to ask, did you do the calculus--?
Let me in!!
What's going on?
Nothing.
You don't lock the doors.
I didn't. I-It was stuck on a--
I mean it.
Yes sir.
Sir.
What's going on in here??

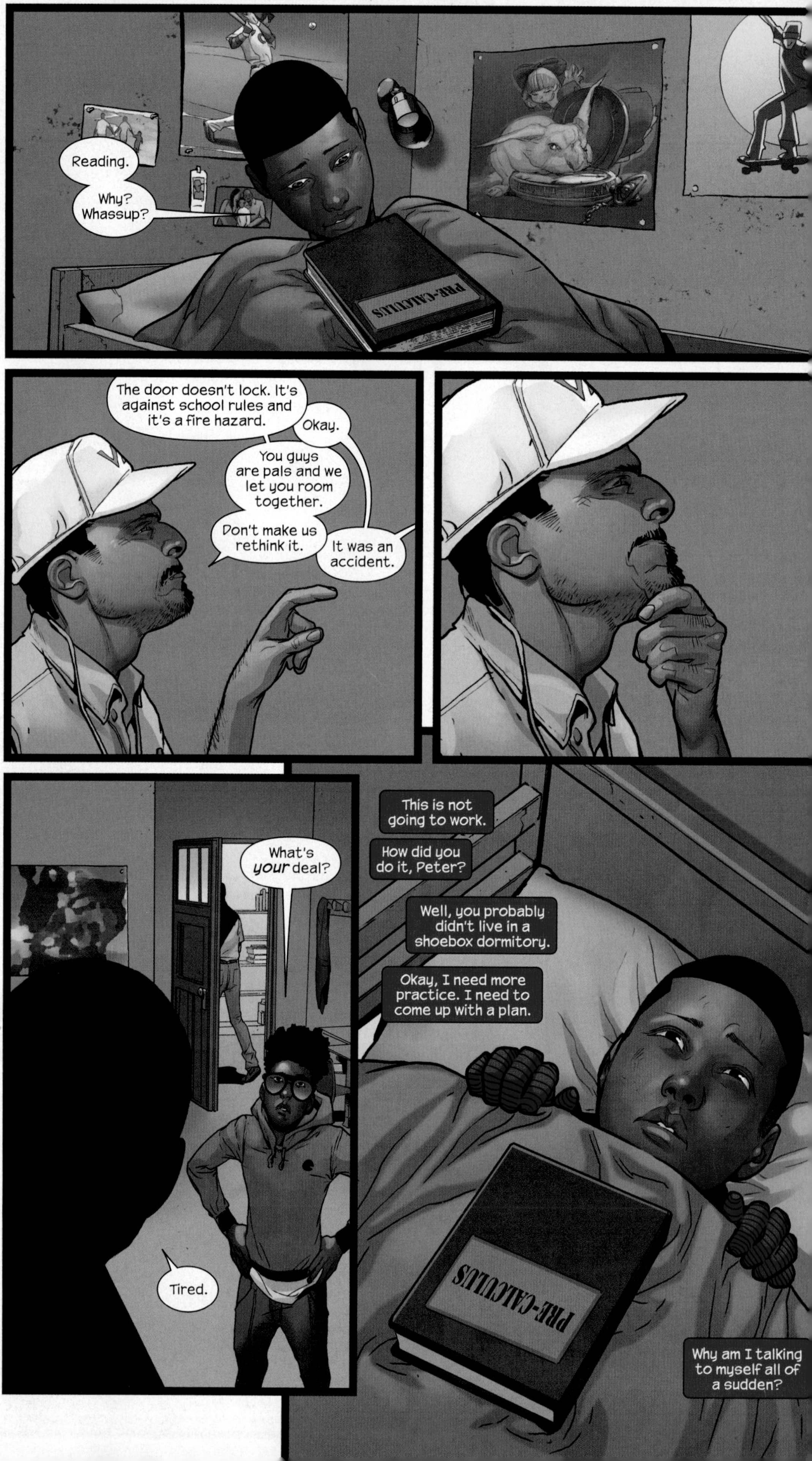

Reading.
Why? Whassup?
The door doesn't lock. It's against school rules and it's a fire hazard.
Okay.
You guys are pals and we let you room together.
Don't make us rethink it.
It was an accident.
PRE-CALCULUS
What's *your* deal?
Tired.
This is not going to work.
How did you do it, Peter?
Well, you probably didn't live in a shoebox dormitory.
Okay, I need more practice. I need to come up with a plan.
PRE-CALCULUS
Why am I talking to myself all of a sudden?

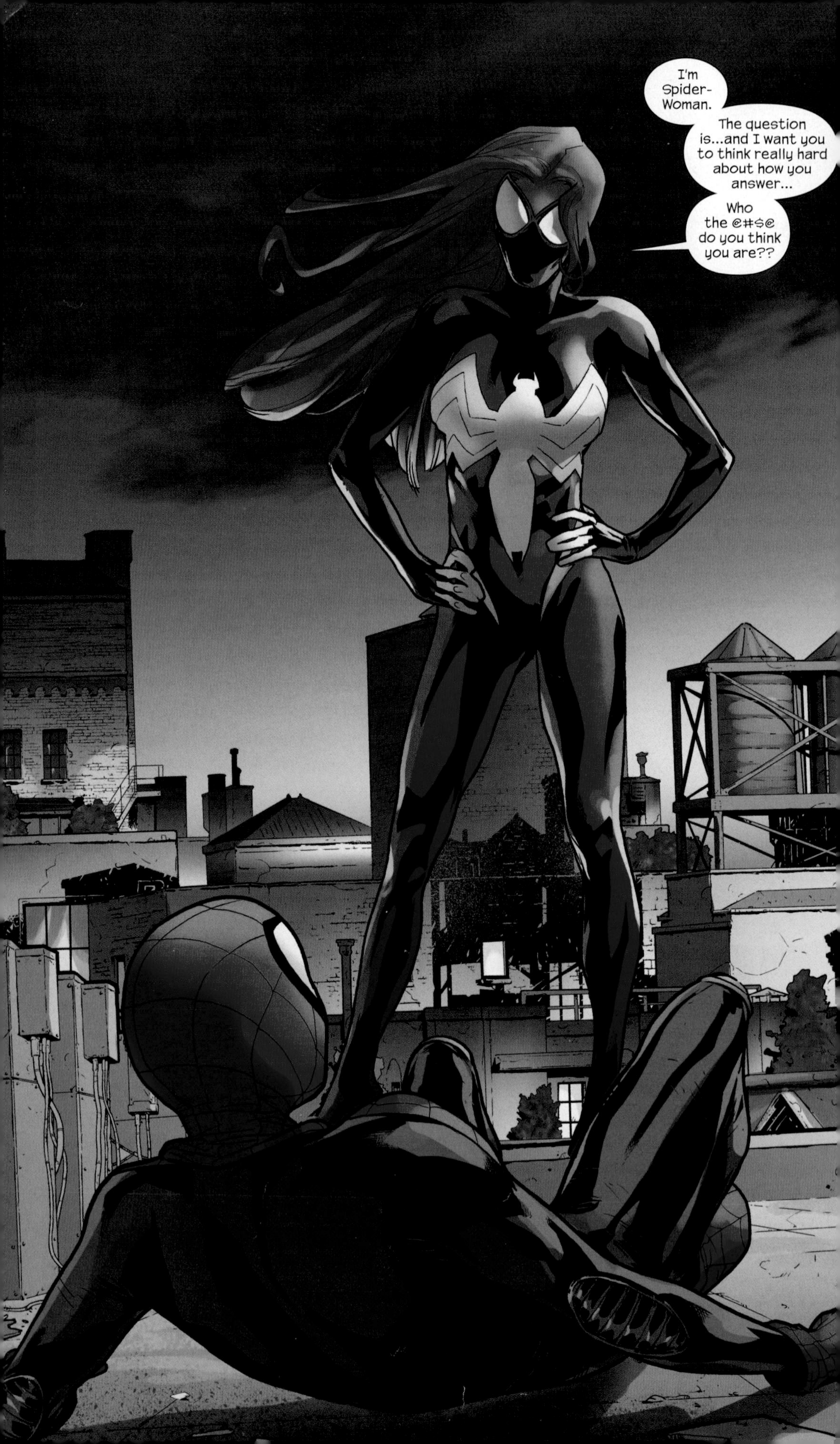
I'm Spider-Woman.
The question is...and I want you to think really hard about how you answer...
Who the @#$@ do you think you are??

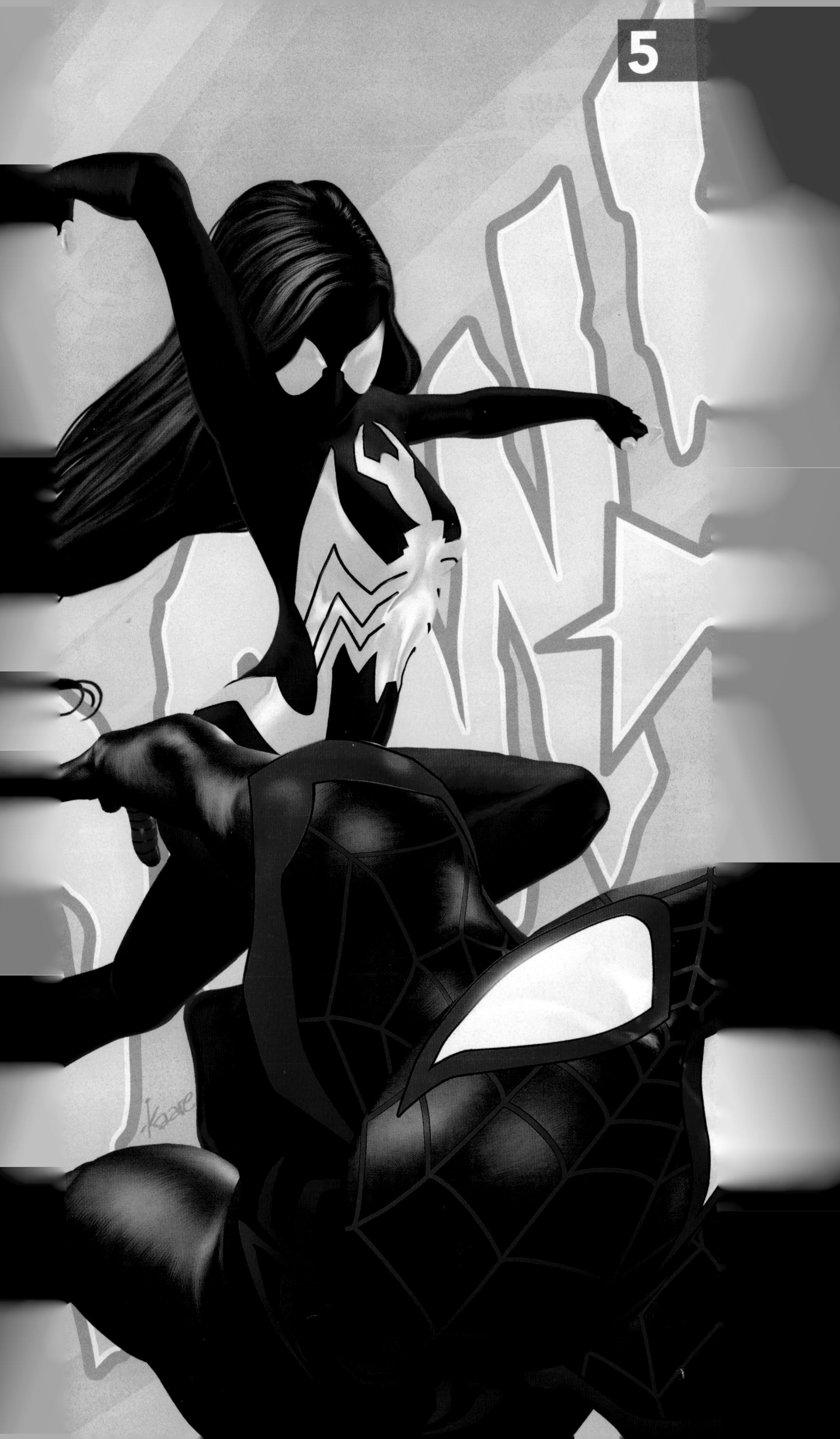
5
Kaare

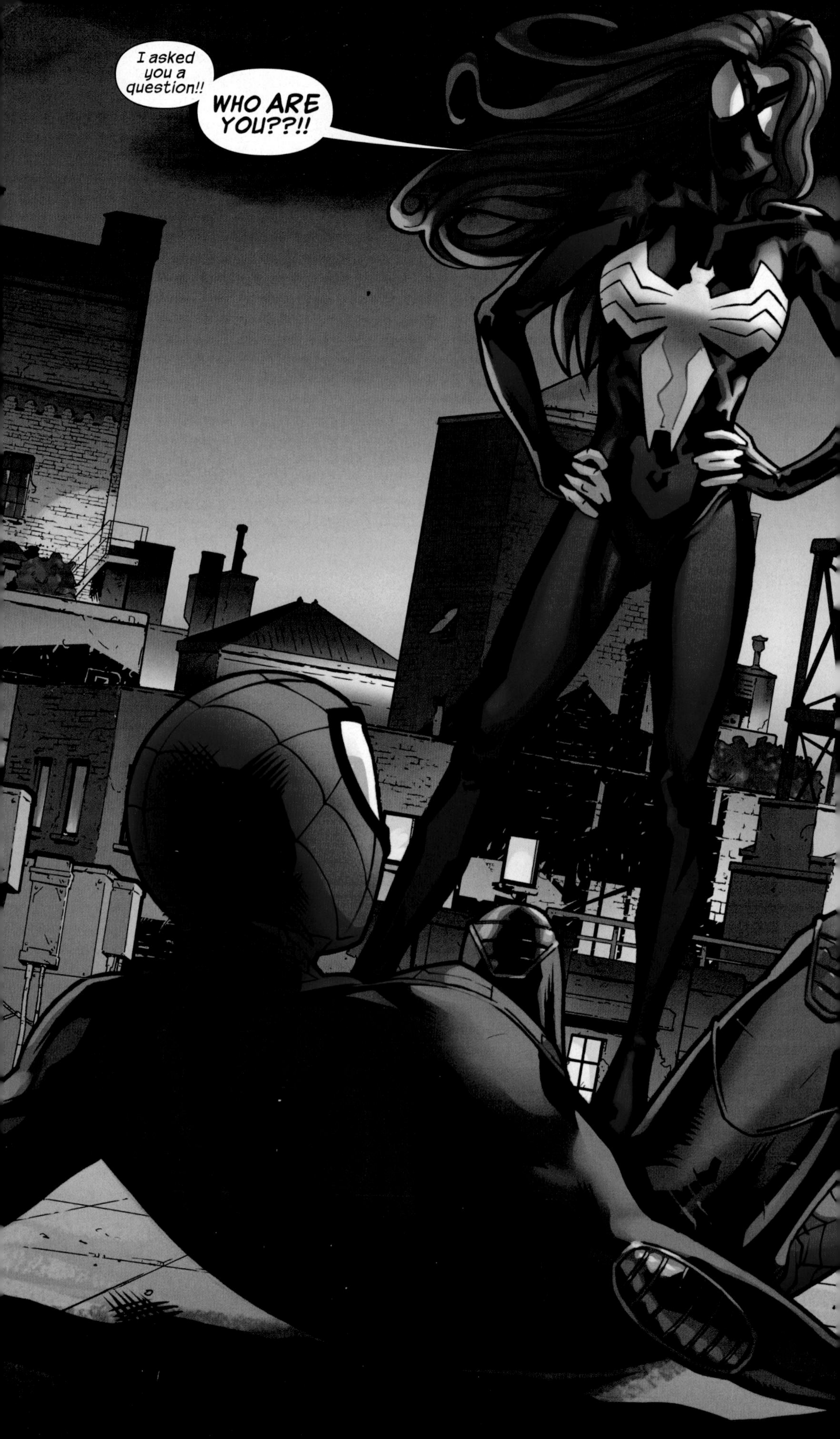
I asked you a question!!
WHO ARE YOU??!!

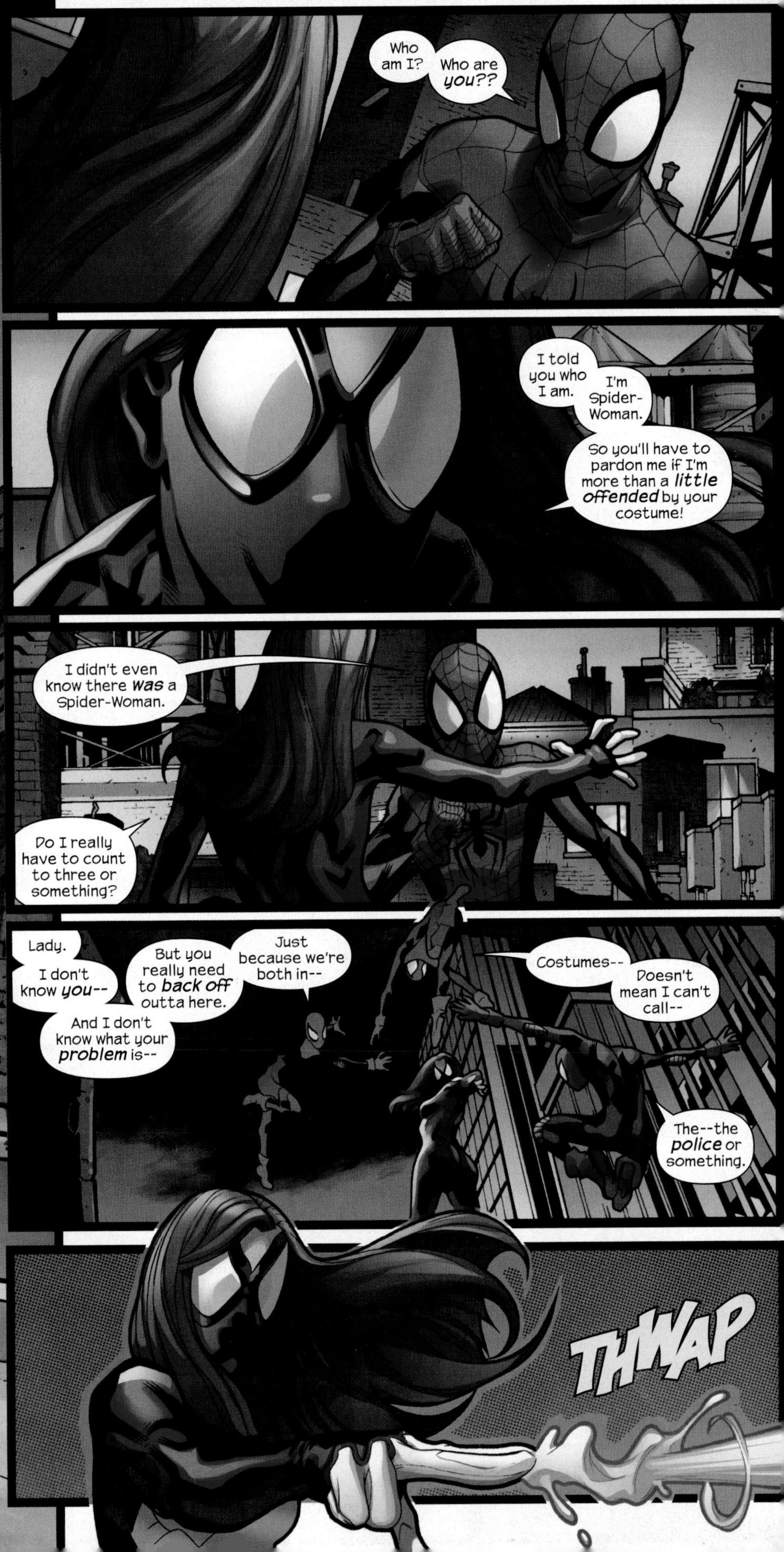

Who am I?
Who are *you??*
I told you who I am.
I'm Spider-Woman.
So you'll have to pardon me if I'm more than a ***little offended*** by your costume!
I didn't even know there ***was*** a Spider-Woman.
Do I really have to count to three or something?
Lady.
I don't know ***you***--
And I don't know what your ***problem*** is--
But you really need to ***back off*** outta here.
Just because we're both in--
Costumes--
Doesn't mean I can't call--
The--the ***police*** or something.
THWAP

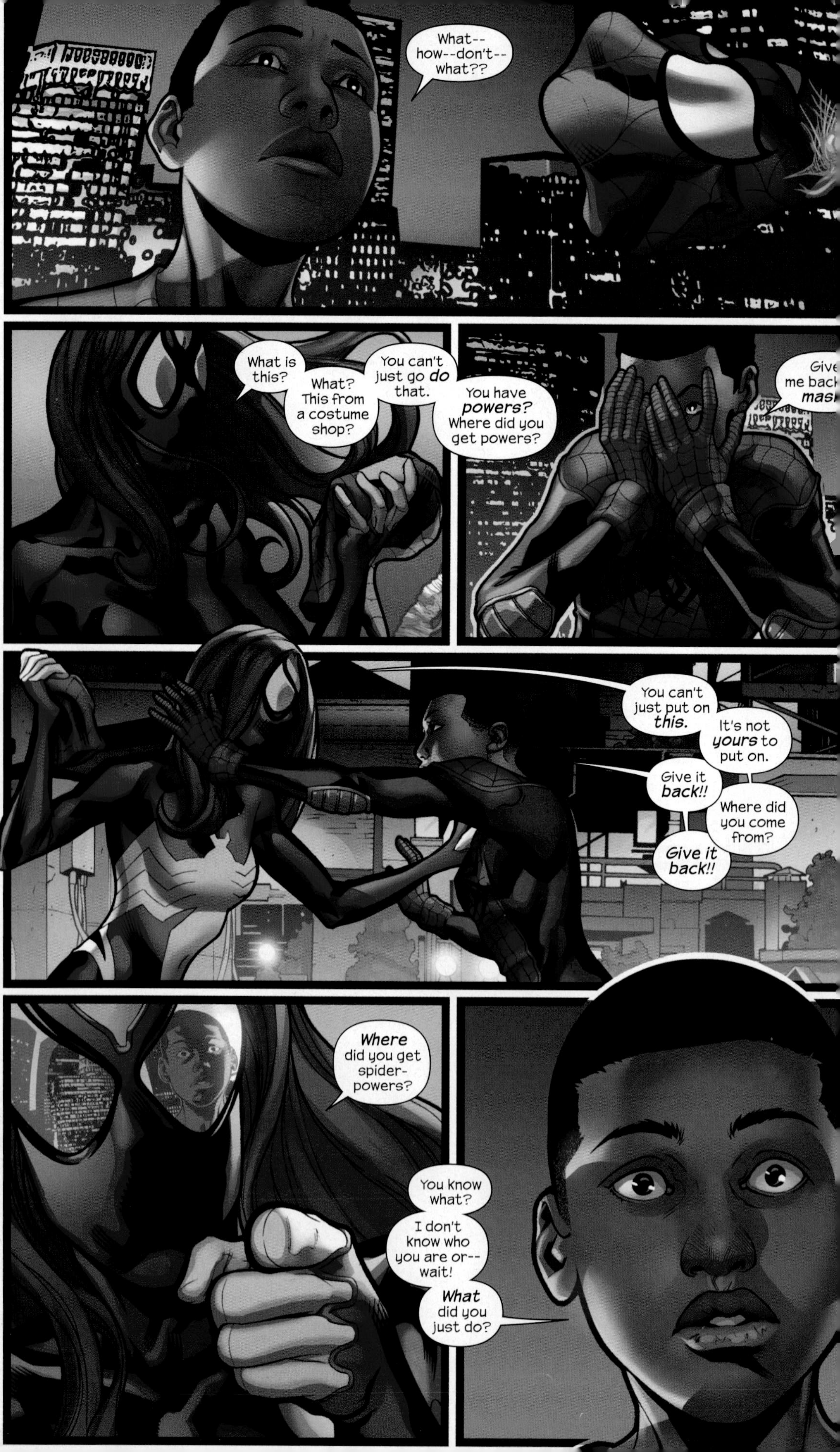
What--how--don't--what??
What is this?
What? This from a costume shop?
You can't just go *do* that.
You have *powers?* Where did you get powers?
Give me back mas
You can't just put on *this.*
It's not *yours* to put on.
Give it *back!!*
Where did you come from?
*Give it back!!*
*Where* did you get spider-powers?
You know what?
I don't know who you are or-- wait!
*What* did you just do?

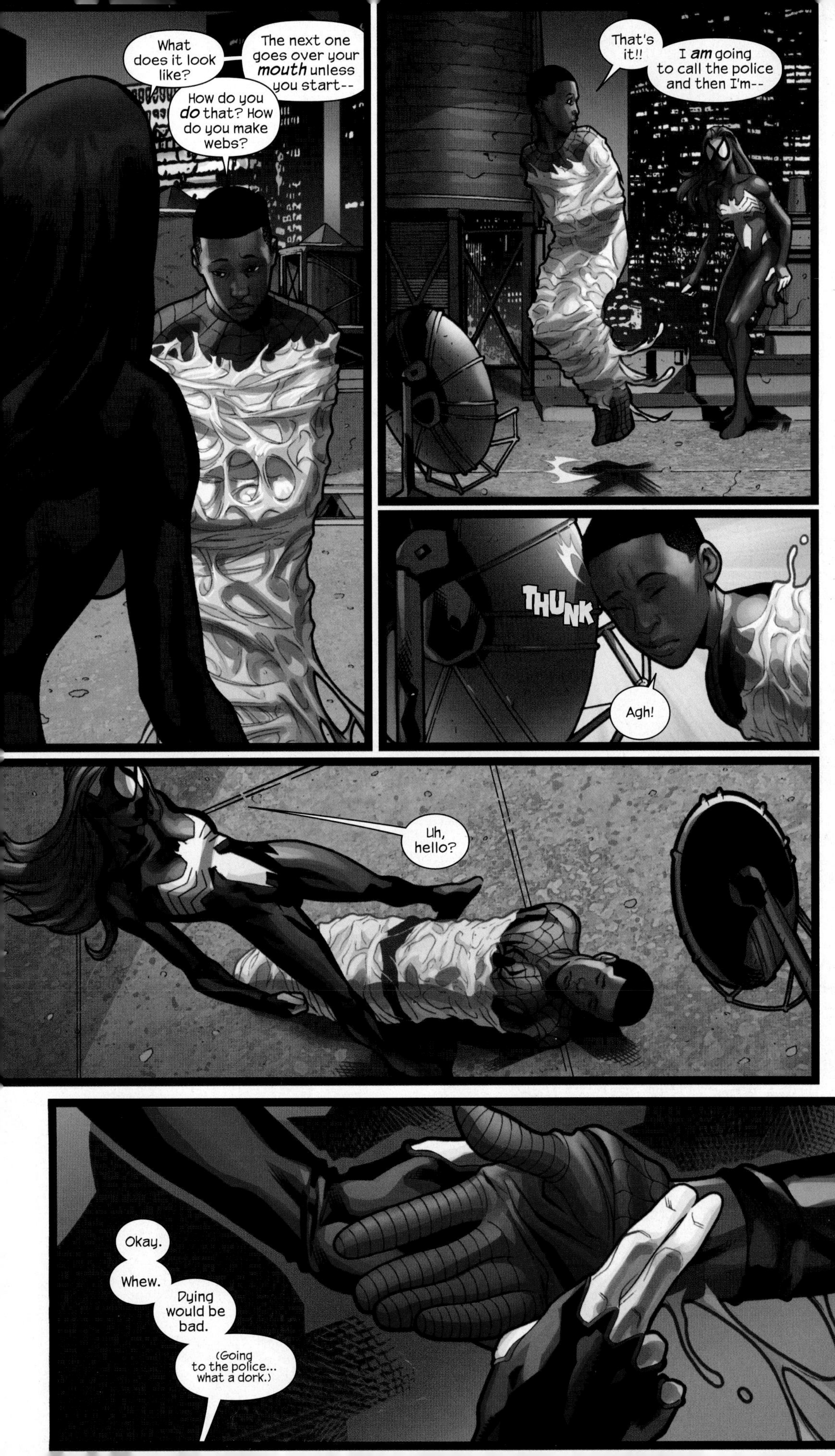
What does it look like?
The next one goes over your *mouth* unless you start--
How do you *do* that? How do you make webs?
That's it!!
I *am* going to call the police and then I'm--
THUNK
Agh!
Uh, hello?
Okay.
Whew.
Dying would be bad.
(Going to the police... what a dork.)

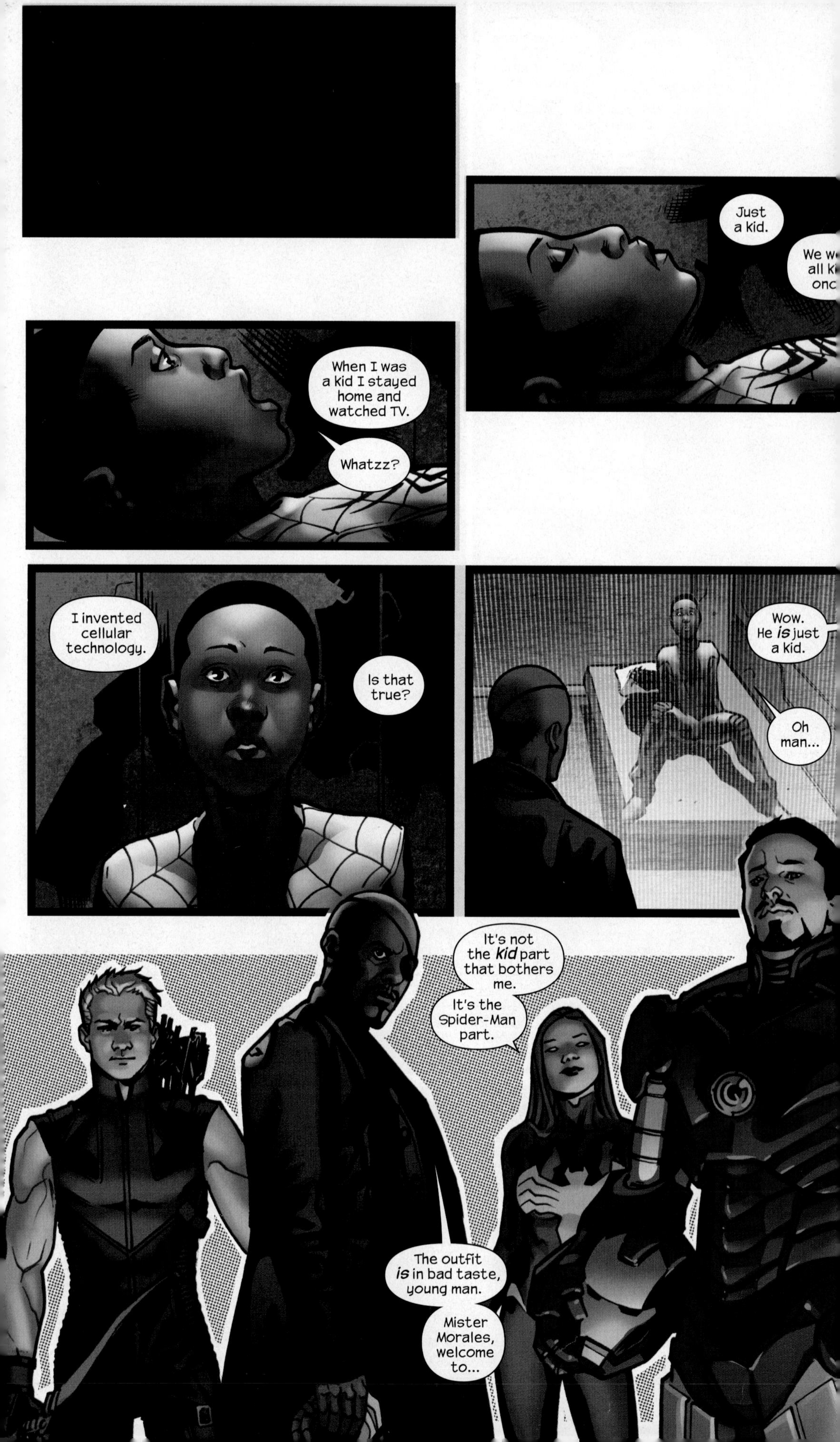
Just a kid.
When I was a kid I stayed home and watched TV.
Whatzz?
I invented cellular technology.
Is that true?
Wow. He *is* just a kid.
Oh man...
It's not the *kid* part that bothers me.
It's the Spider-Man part.
The outfit *is* in bad taste, young man.
Mister Morales, welcome to...

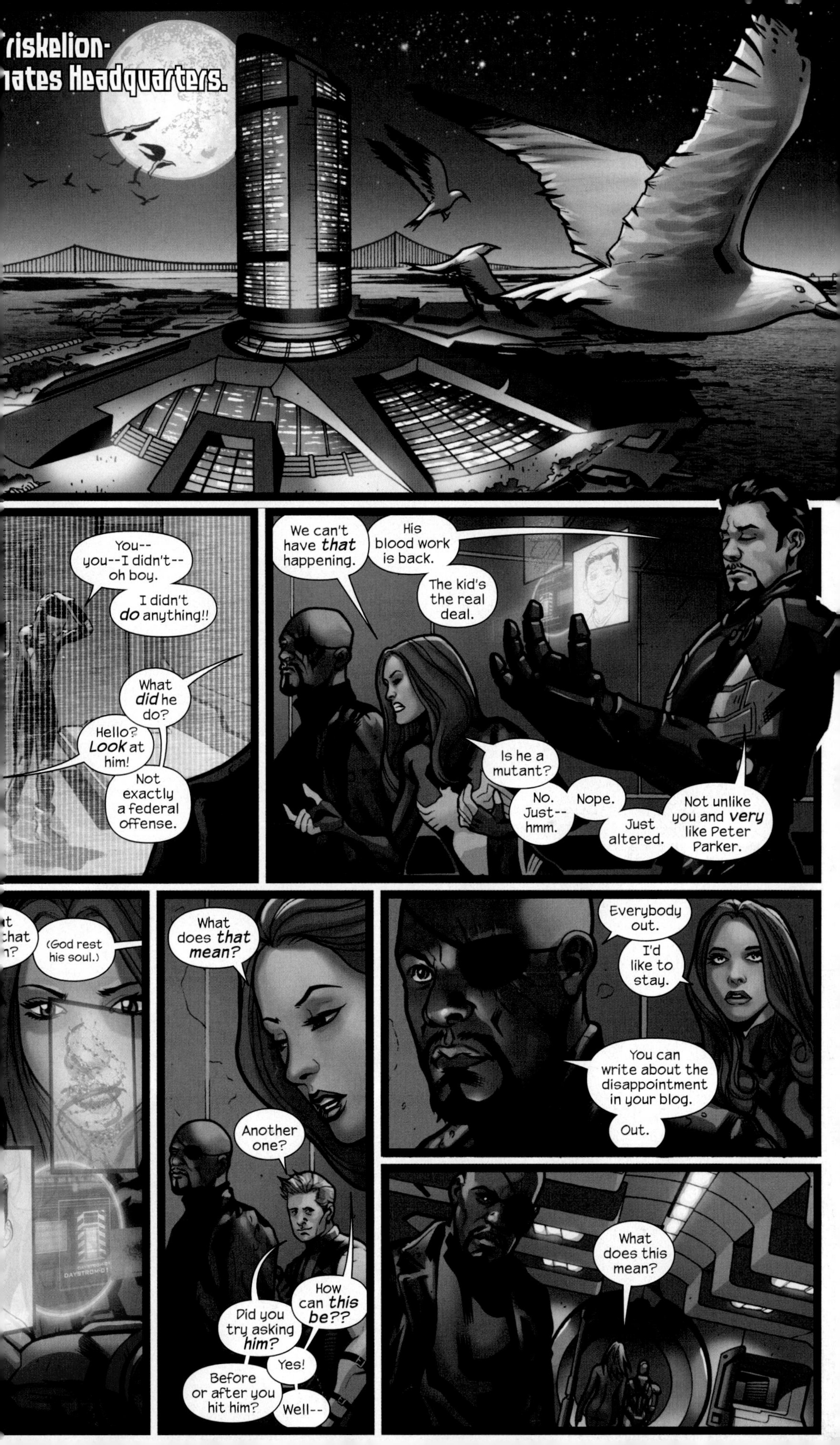
riskelion-
ates Headquarters.
You-- you--I didn't-- oh boy.
I didn't *do* anything!!
What *did* he do?
Hello? *Look* at him!
Not exactly a federal offense.
We can't have *that* happening.
His blood work is back.
The kid's the real deal.
Is he a mutant?
No. Just-- hmm.
Nope.
Just altered.
Not unlike you and *very* like Peter Parker.
(God rest his soul.)
What does *that* mean?
Another one?
How can *this* be??
Did you try asking *him*?
Yes!
Before or after you hit him?
Well--
Everybody out.
I'd like to stay.
You can write about the disappointment in your blog.
Out.
What does this mean?

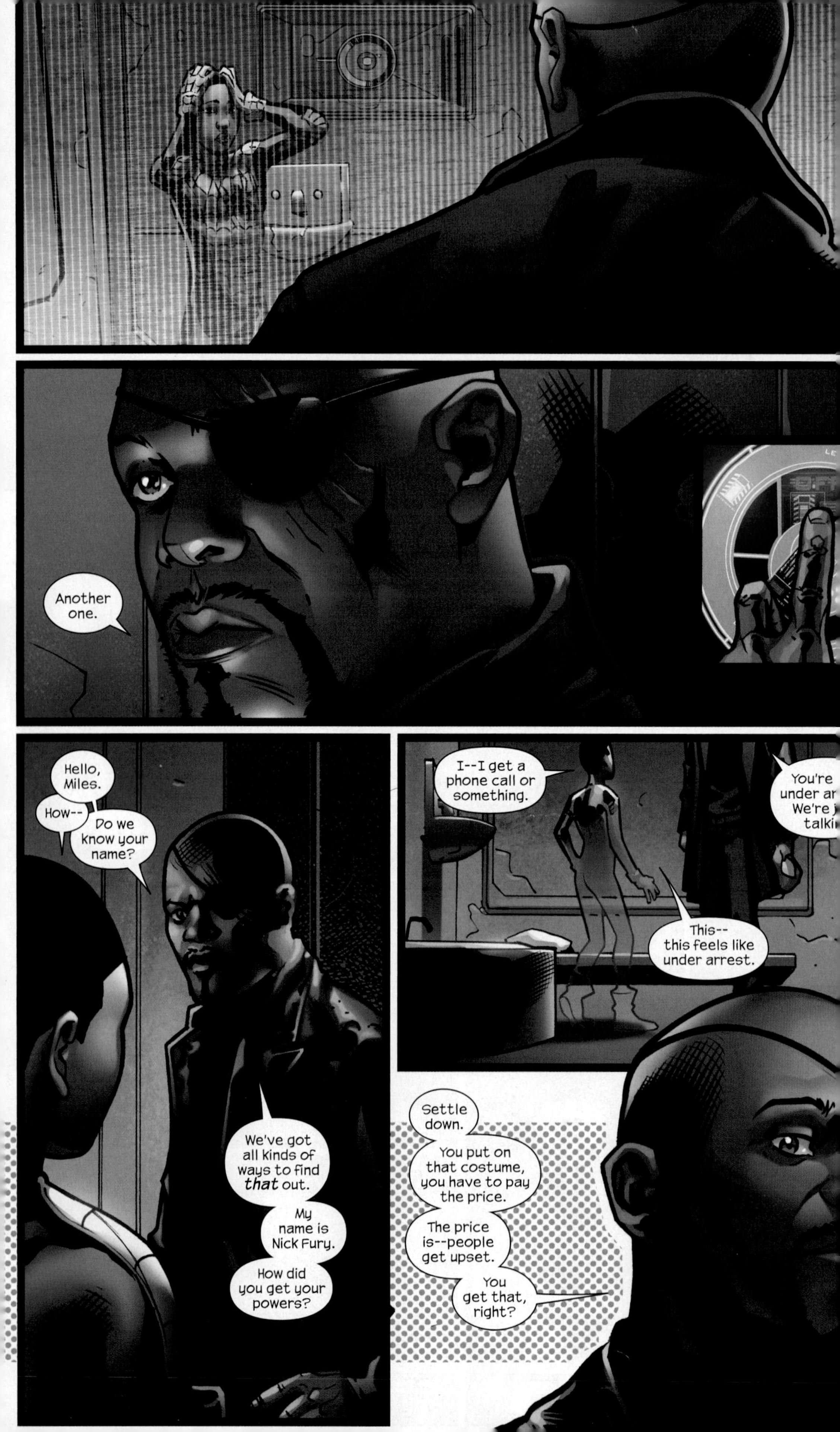
Another one.
Hello, Miles.
How--
Do we know your name?
We've got all kinds of ways to find *that* out.
My name is Nick Fury.
How did you get your powers?
I--I get a phone call or something.
You're
This-- this feels like under arrest.
Settle down.
You put on that costume, you have to pay the price.
The price is--people get upset.
You get that, right?

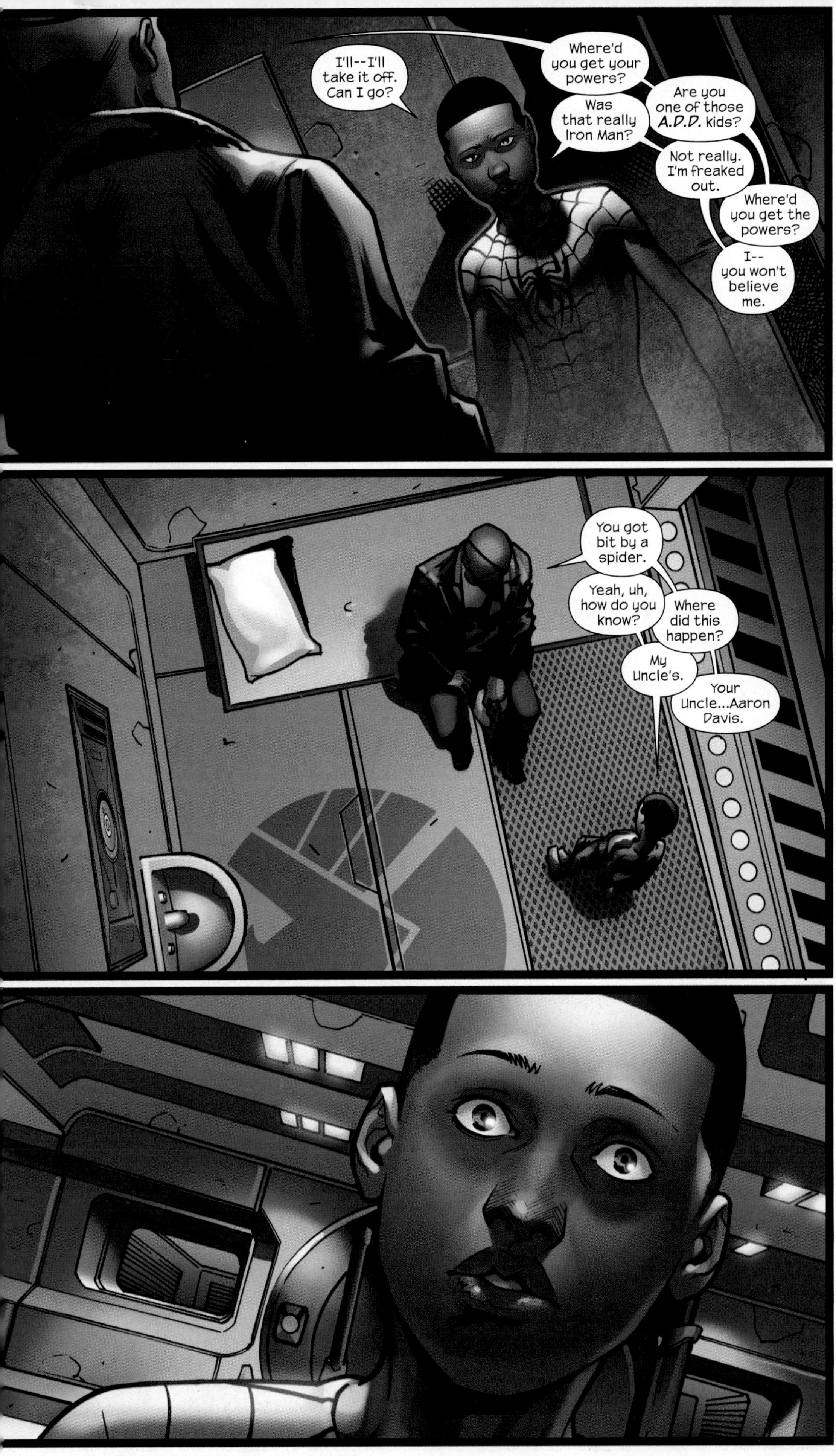
Where'd you get your powers?
I'll--I'll take it off. Can I go?
Was that really Iron Man?
Are you one of those *A.D.D.* kids?
Not really. I'm freaked out.
Where'd you get the powers?
I--you won't believe me.
You got bit by a spider.
Yeah, uh, how do you know?
Where did this happen?
My Uncle's.
Your Uncle...Aaron Davis.

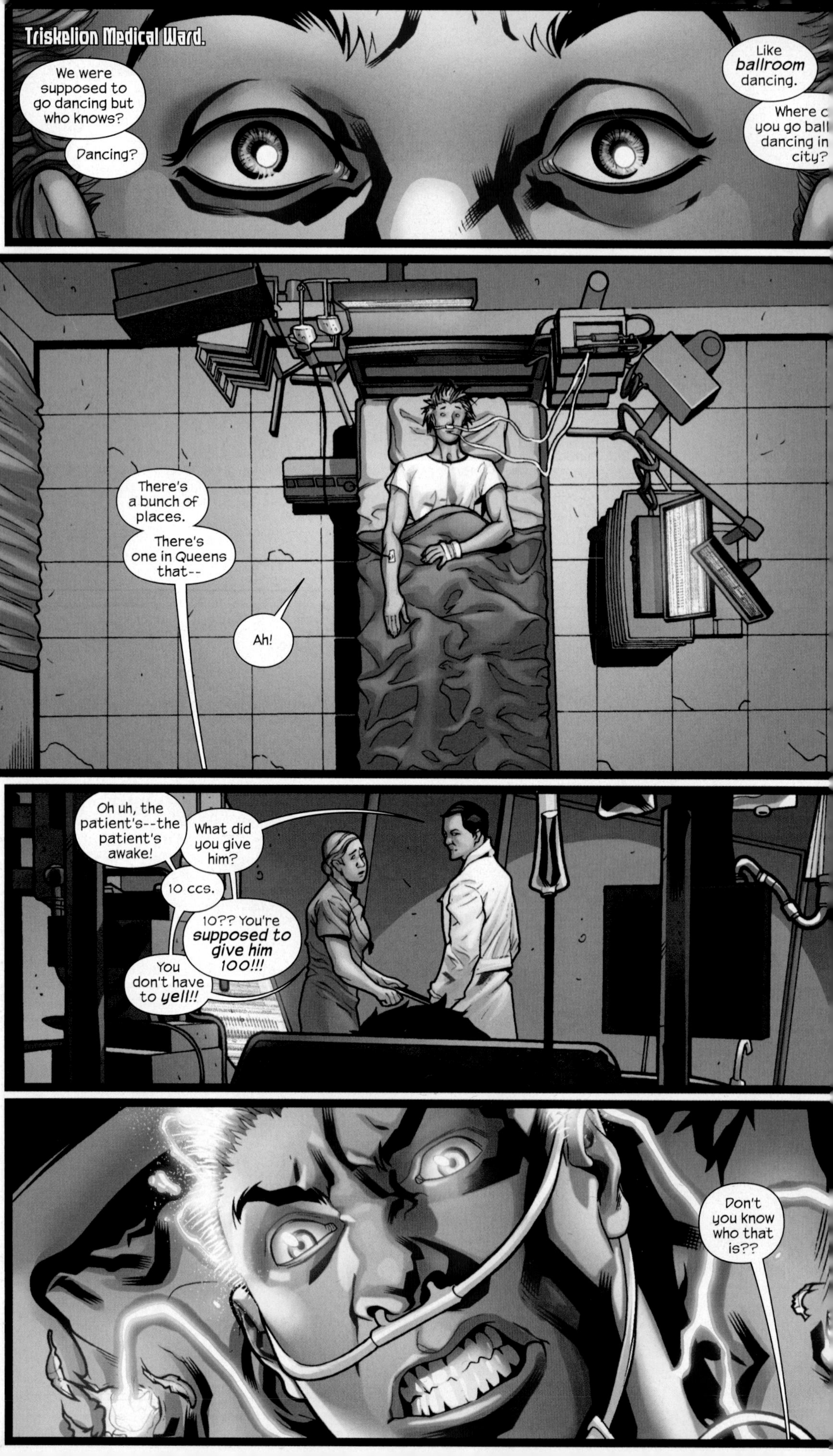

Triskelion Medical Ward.
We were supposed to go dancing but who knows?
Dancing?
Like ballroom dancing.
Where c you go ball dancing in city?
There's a bunch of places.
There's one in Queens that--
Ah!
Oh uh, the patient's--the patient's awake!
What did you give him?
10 ccs.
10?? You're supposed to give him 100!!!
You don't have to yell!!
Don't you know who that is??

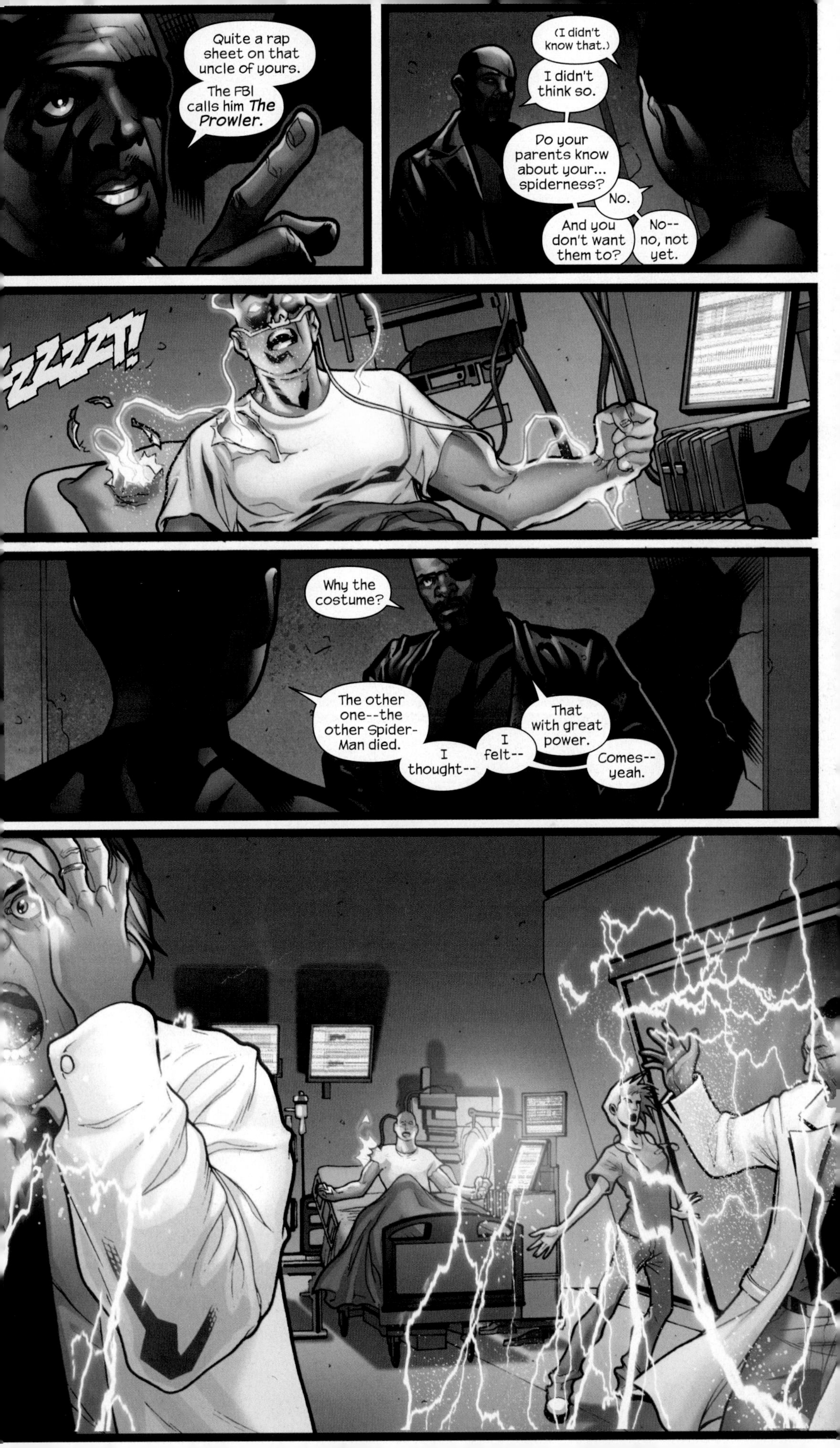
Quite a rap sheet on that uncle of yours.
The FBI calls him *The Prowler.*
(I didn't know that.)
I didn't think so.
Do your parents know about your... spiderness?
No.
And you don't want them to?
No-- no, not yet.
ZZZZZT!
Why the costume?
The other one--the other Spider-Man died.
I thought--
I felt--
That with great power.
Comes-- yeah.

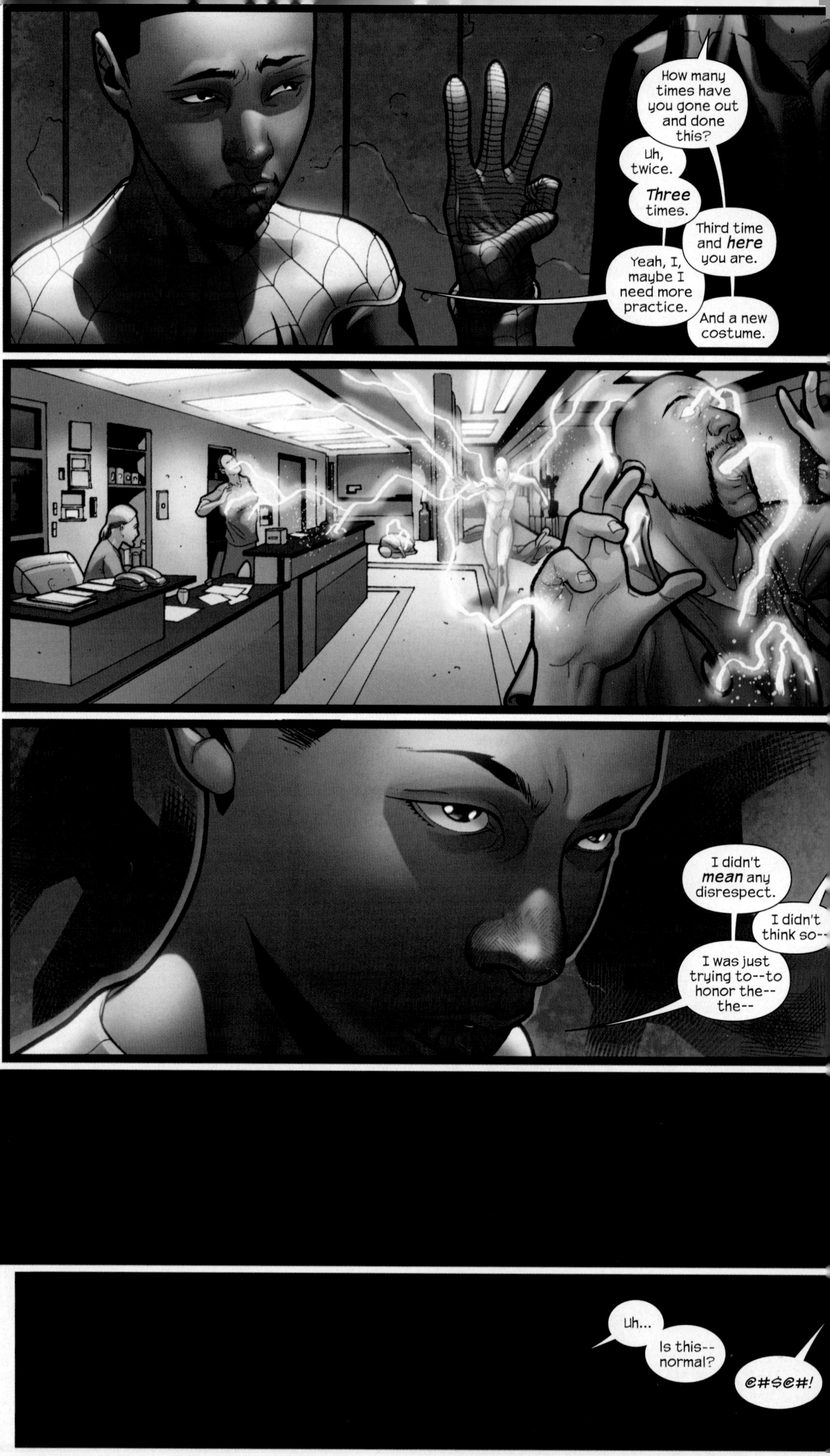
How many times have you gone out and done this?
Uh, twice.
*Three* times.
Third time and *here* you are.
Yeah, I, maybe I need more practice.
And a new costume.
I didn't *mean* any disrespect.
I didn't think so--
I was just trying to--to honor the-- the--
Uh...
Is this-- normal?
@#$@#!

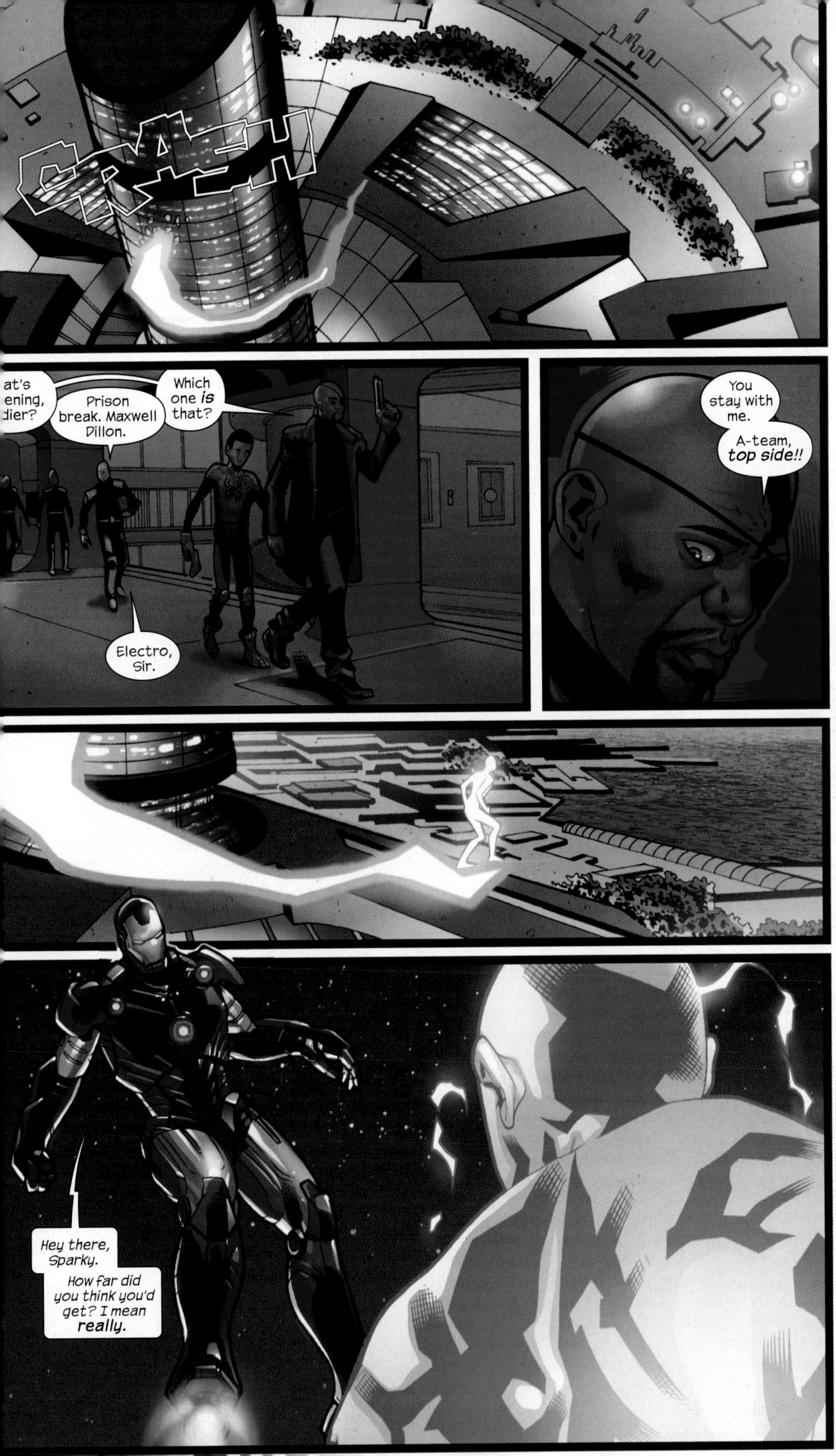
CRASH
at's
ening,
dier?
Prison break. Maxwell Dillon.
Which one *is* that?
Electro, Sir.
You stay with me.
A-team, ***top side!!***
Hey there, Sparky.
How far did you think you'd get? I mean **really.**

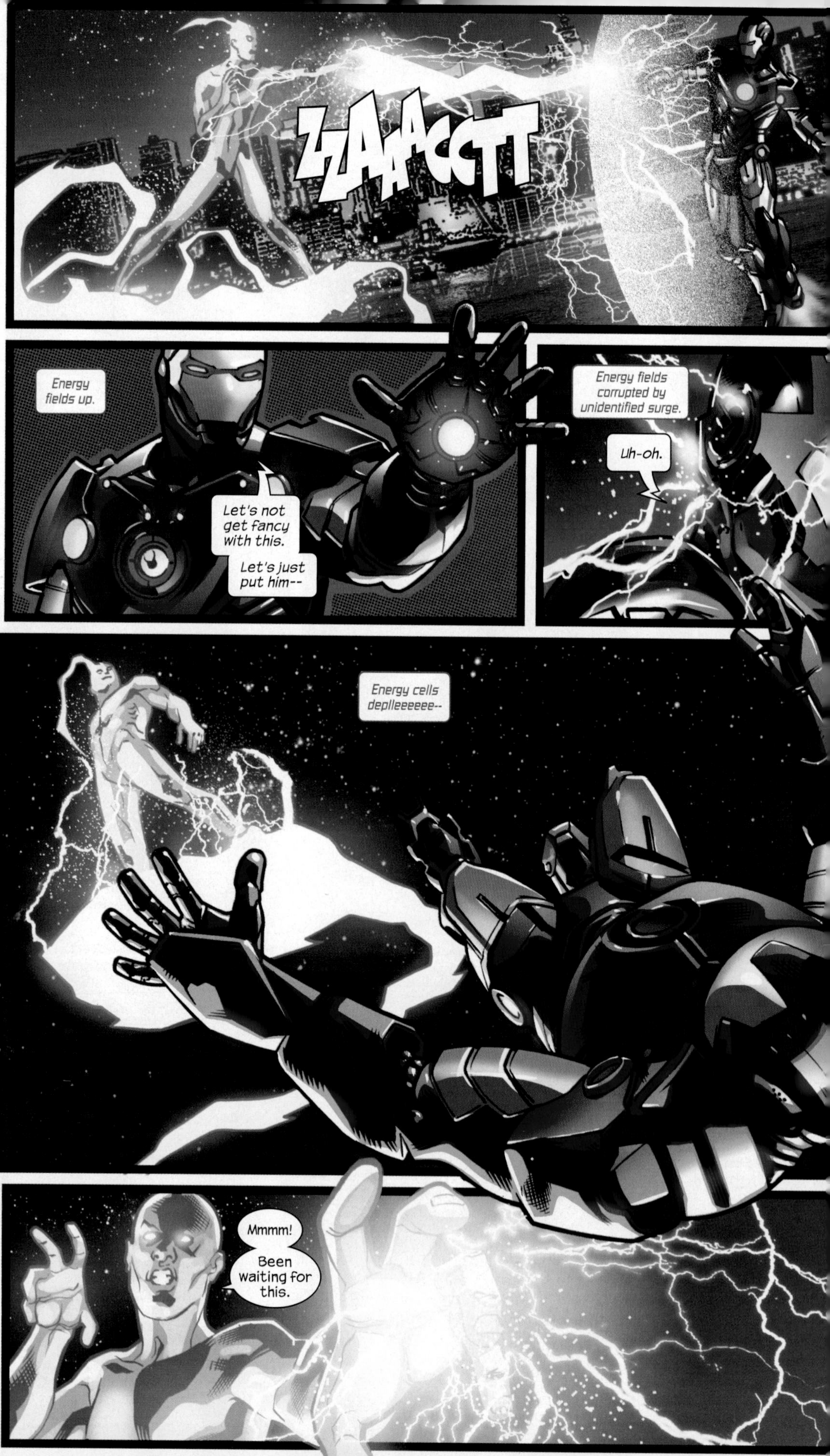
ZZZAAACCTT
Energy fields up.
Let's not get fancy with this.
Let's just put him--
Energy fields corrupted by unidentified surge.
Uh-oh.
Energy cells depleeeeee--
Mmmm!
Been waiting for this.

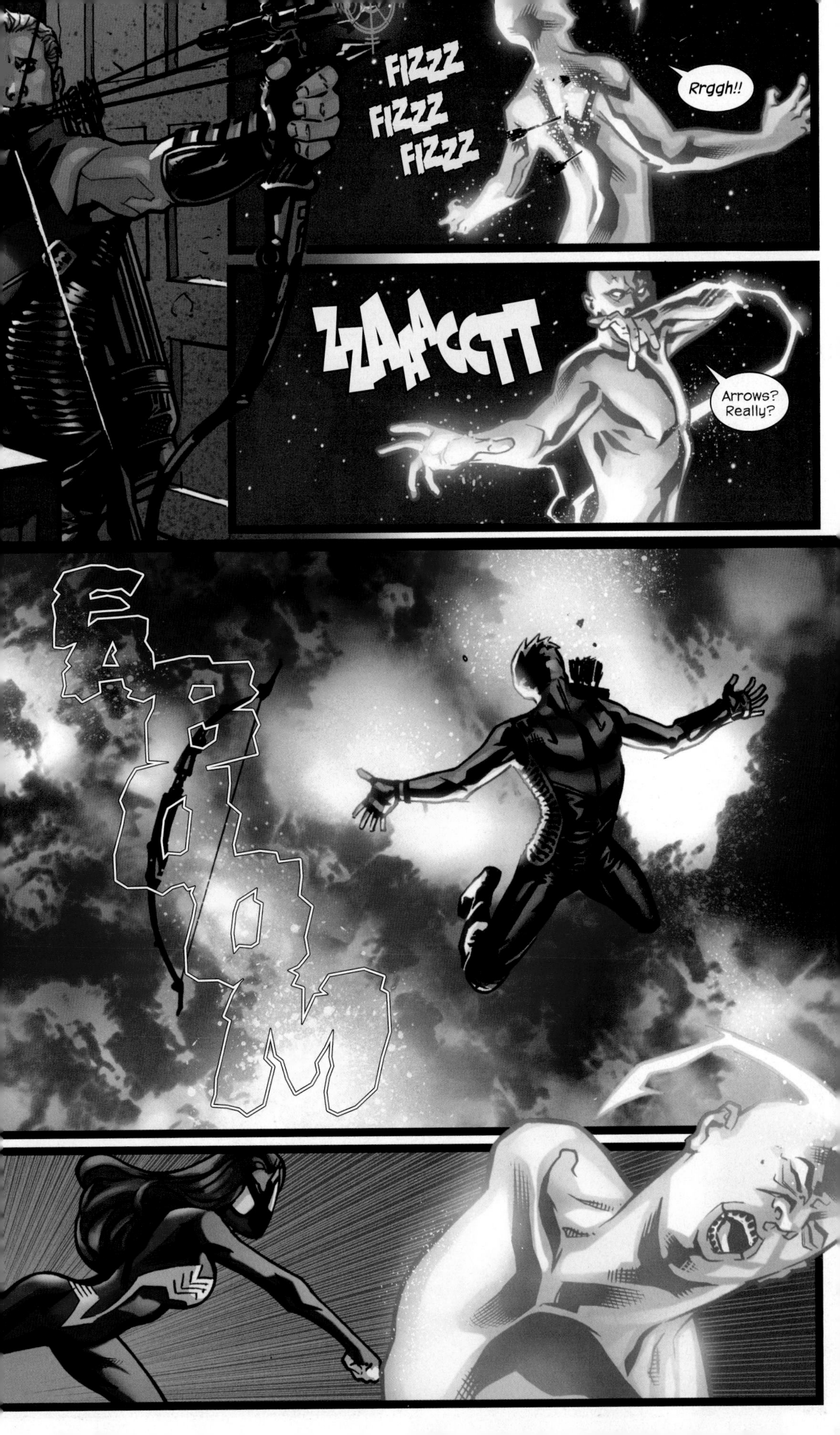
FIZZZ
FIZZZ
FIZZZ
Rrggh!!
ZZZAAACCTT
Arrows? Really?
KABLOOM

Don't even know *you* are.

Everybody take cover!!

SHUT THE PERIMETER!!

Take cover if you're not equipped!!

Heeeeey, eye patch!

EVERYONE OUT!!

Take cover!!

BAM BAM BAM

Yeah?

Tri
to ru
life,
hu

Gu
it's
tu

FSSHH
FSSHH
FSSHH

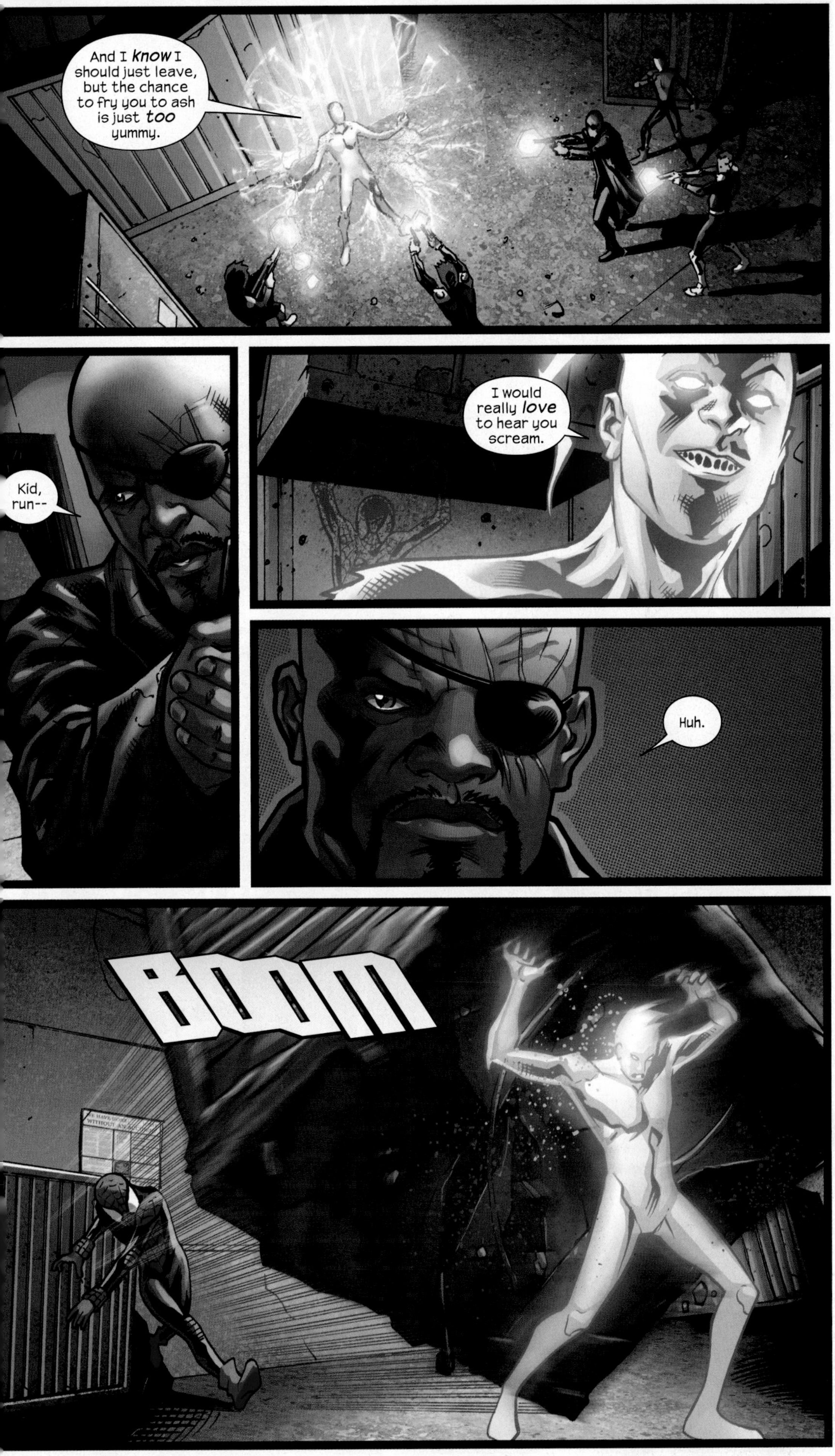

And I *know* I should just leave, but the chance to fry you to ash is just *too* yummy.
Kid, run--
I would really *love* to hear you scream.
Huh.
BOOM

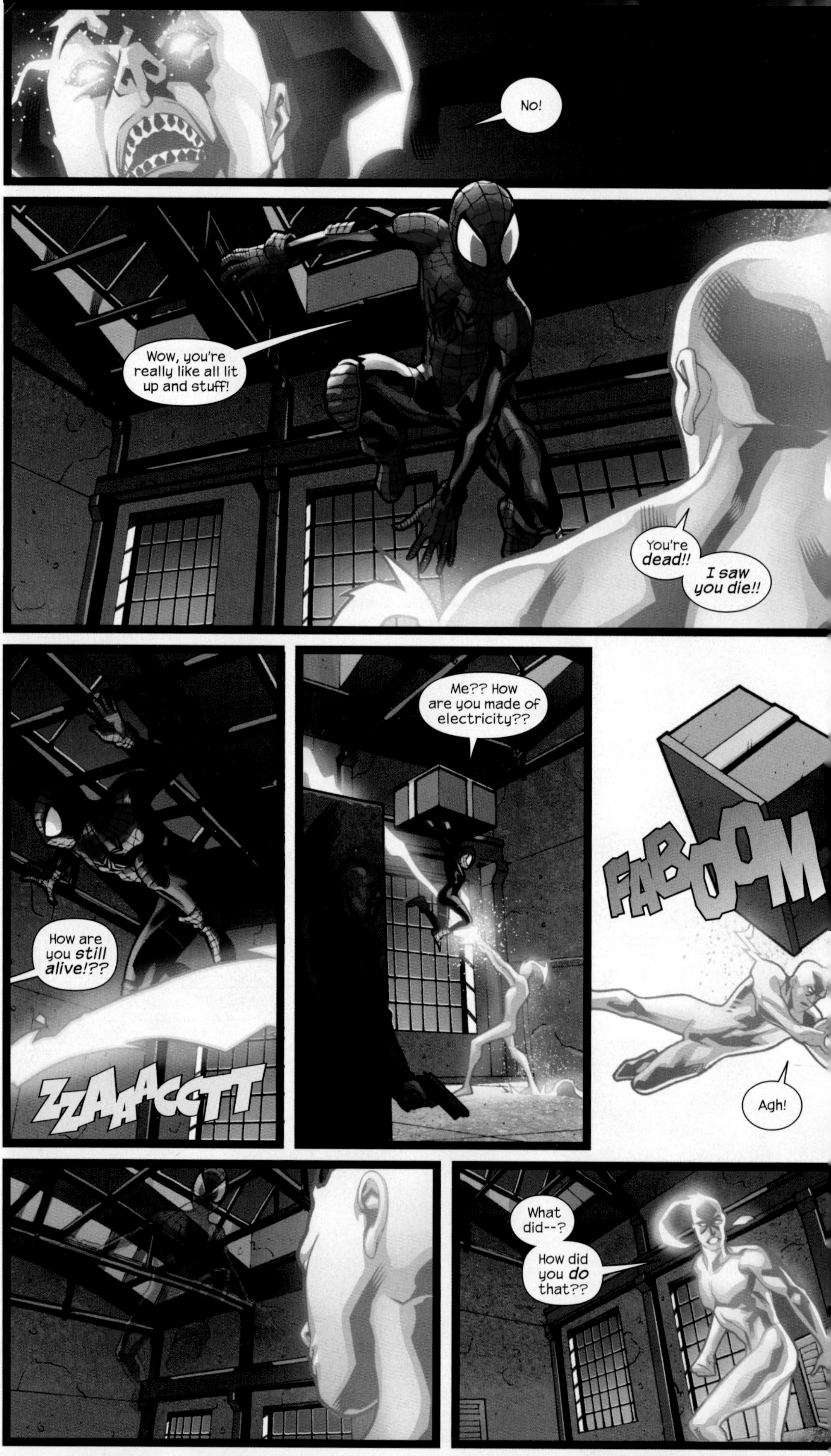
No!
Wow, you're really like all lit up and stuff!
You're dead!!
I saw you die!!
How are you still alive!??
ZZAAACCTT
Me?? How are you made of electricity??
FABOOM
Agh!
What did--?
How did you do that??

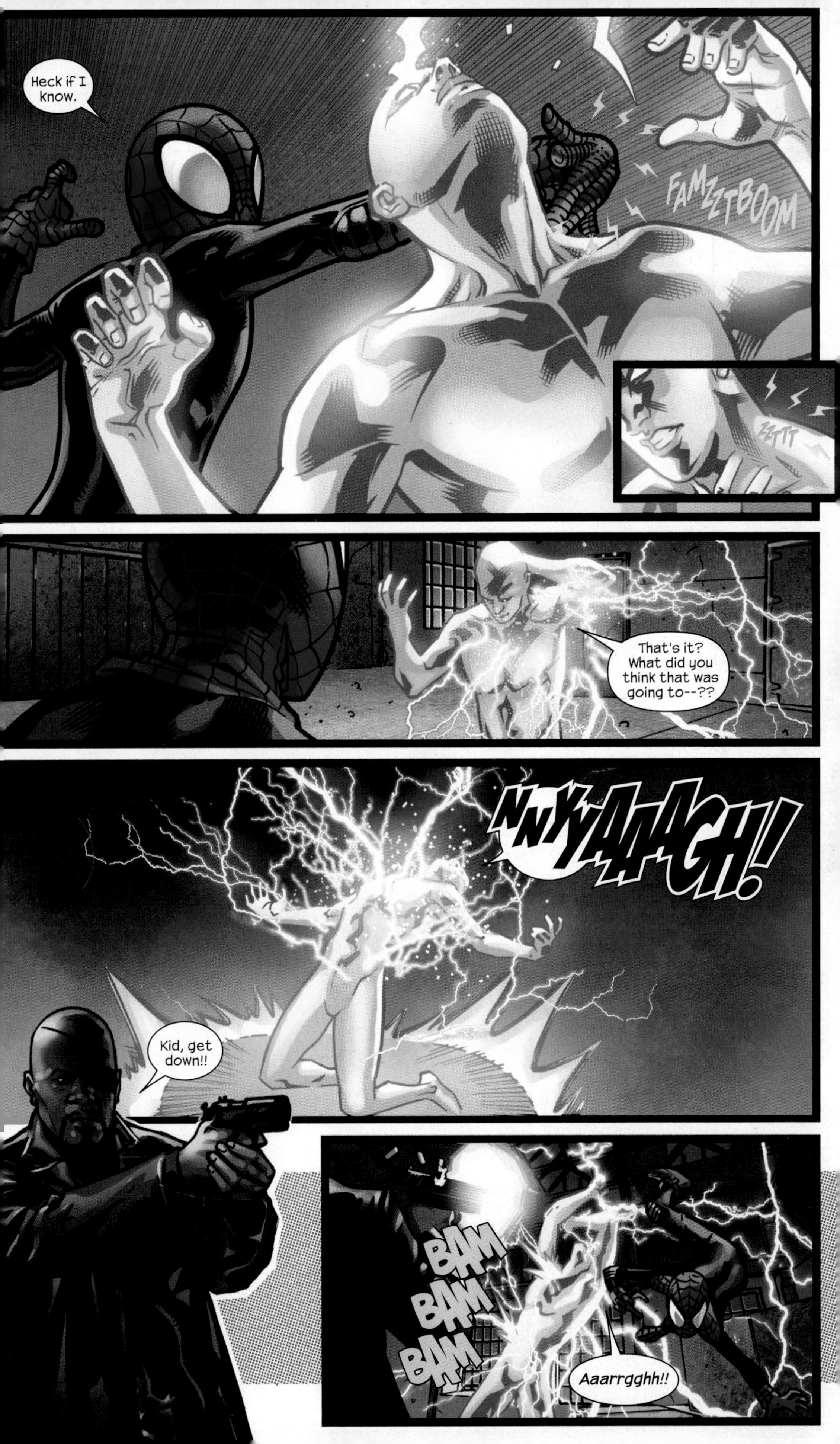
Heck if I know.
FAMZZTBOOM
ZZTTT
That's it? What did you think that was going to--??
NNYYAAAGH!
Kid, get down!!
BAM
BAM
BAM
Aaarrgghh!!

"That did **not** happen."

"It all did."

"You **beat** Electro."

"Is that his name?"

"How? What did you do?"

That thing-- when I punch someone--that little ZZT.

Whatever.

It disrupted his thingamabob.

I thought **maybe**--and I had to try something.

Your venom blast.

Did you know it would **do** that?

Dude.

**Dude, you're a super hero!!**

Oh my God!!

Sshh!!

Sorry.

Nick **Fury,** man!!

Shh!

Shh!!

And he just let you go home?

They had a big mess to clean up and I had to get back here.

What did he say?

He said he had to think about me.

What does that mean?

Dude, I'm still freaked out about the girl with the--

M

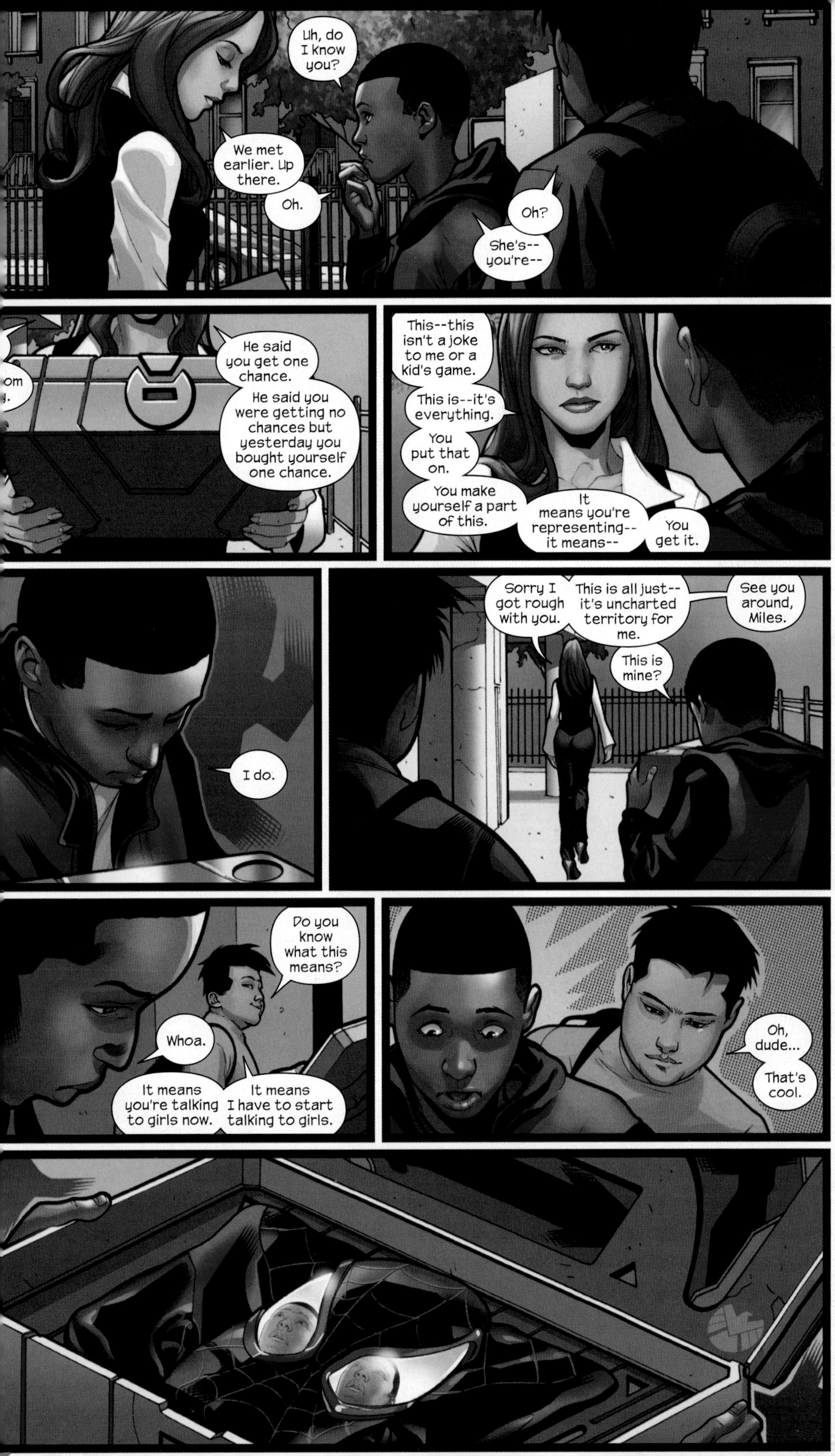

Uh, do I know you?
We met earlier. Up there.
Oh.
Oh?
She's-- you're--
He said you get one chance.
He said you were getting no chances but yesterday you bought yourself one chance.
This--this isn't a joke to me or a kid's game.
This is--it's everything.
You put that on.
You make yourself a part of this.
It means you're representing-- it means--
You get it.
I do.
Sorry I got rough with you.
This is all just-- it's uncharted territory for me.
See you around, Miles.
This is mine?
Do you know what this means?
Whoa.
It means you're talking to girls now.
It means I have to start talking to girls.
Oh, dude...
That's cool.

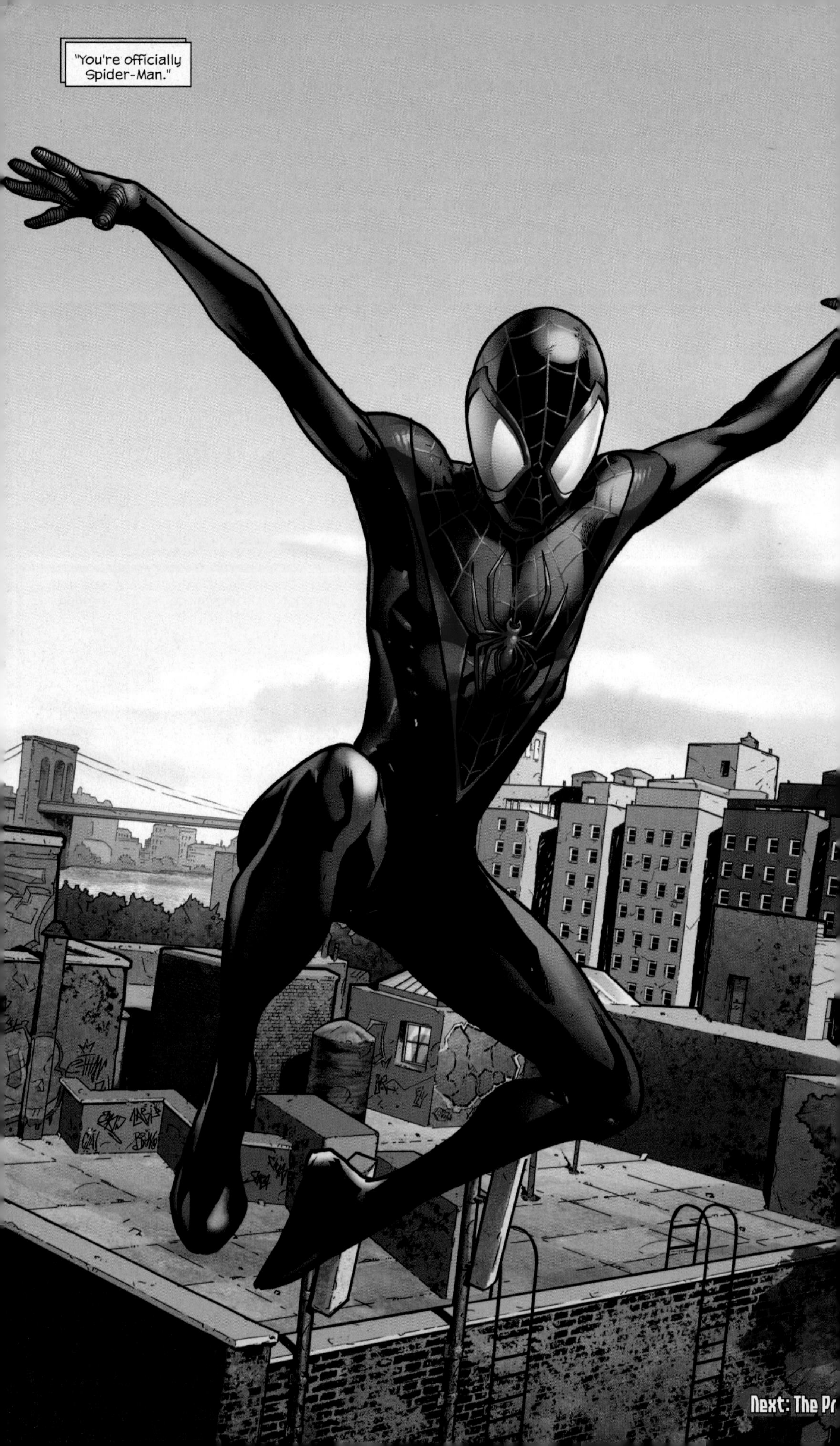
"You're officially Spider-Man."
Next: The Pr

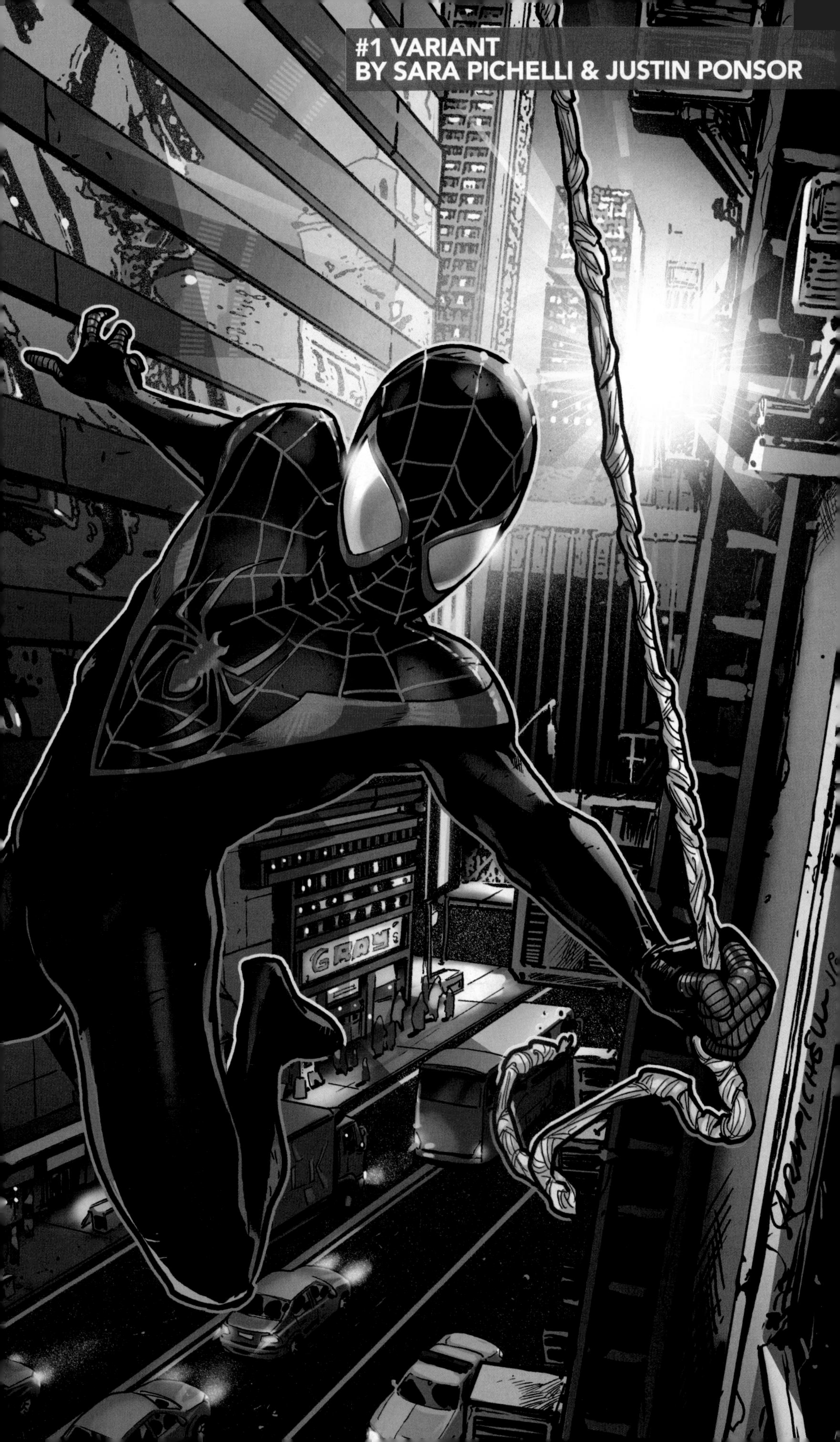
GRAY'S
#1 VARIANT
BY SARA PICHELLI & JUSTIN PONSOR

**#1 SKETCH VARIANT**
**BY SARA PICHELLI**

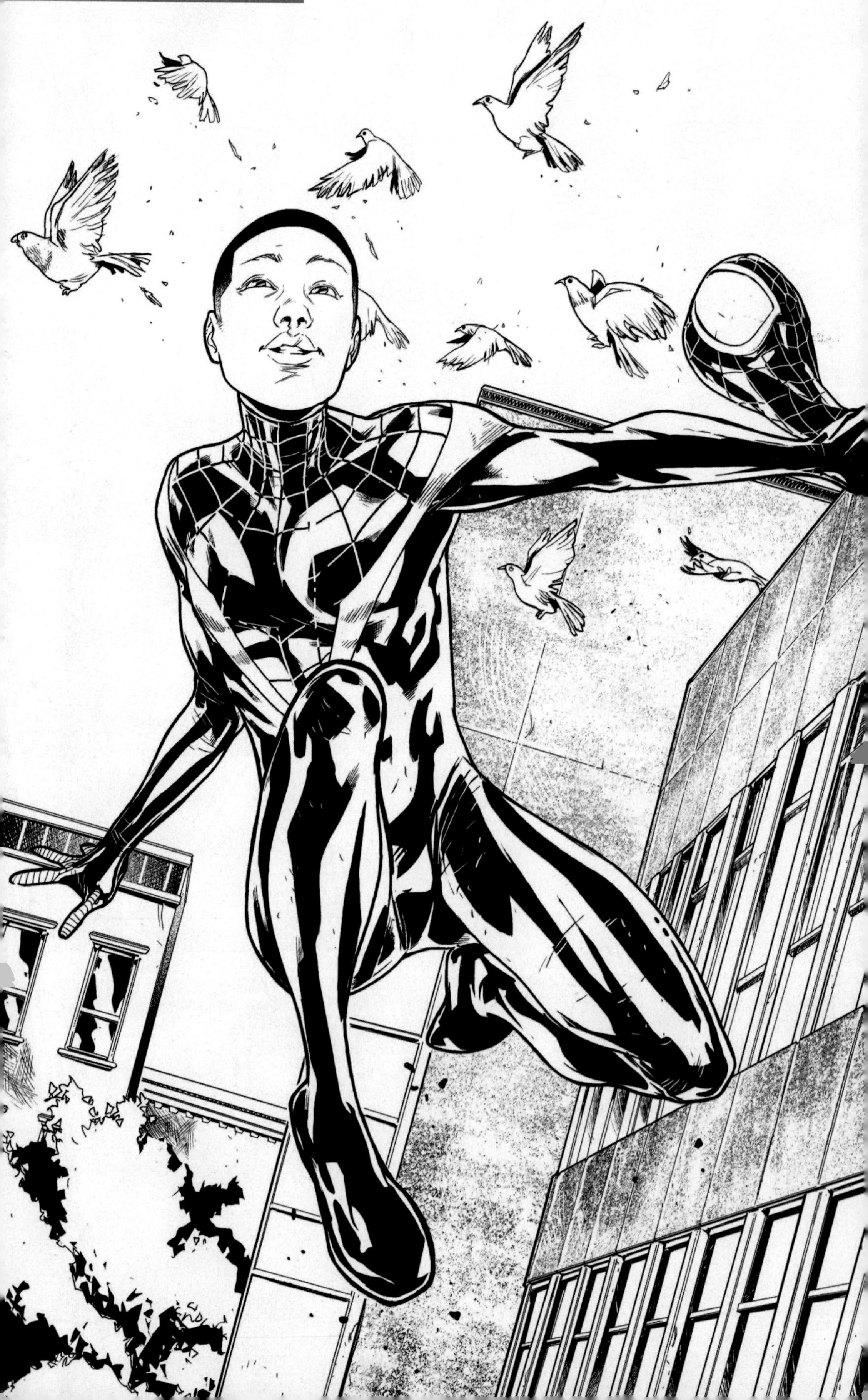

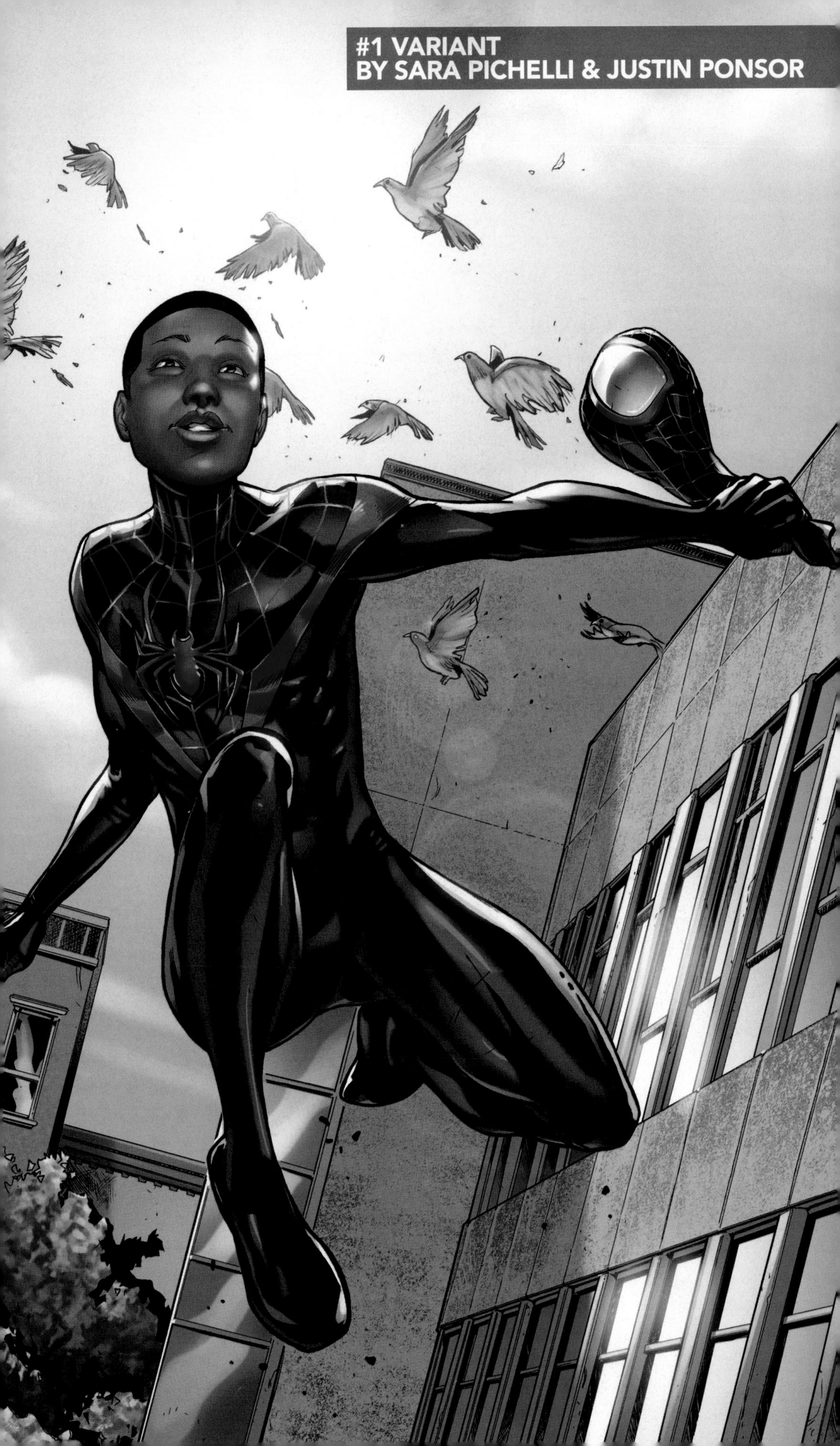

#1 VARIANT
BY SARA PICHELLI & JUSTIN PONSOR

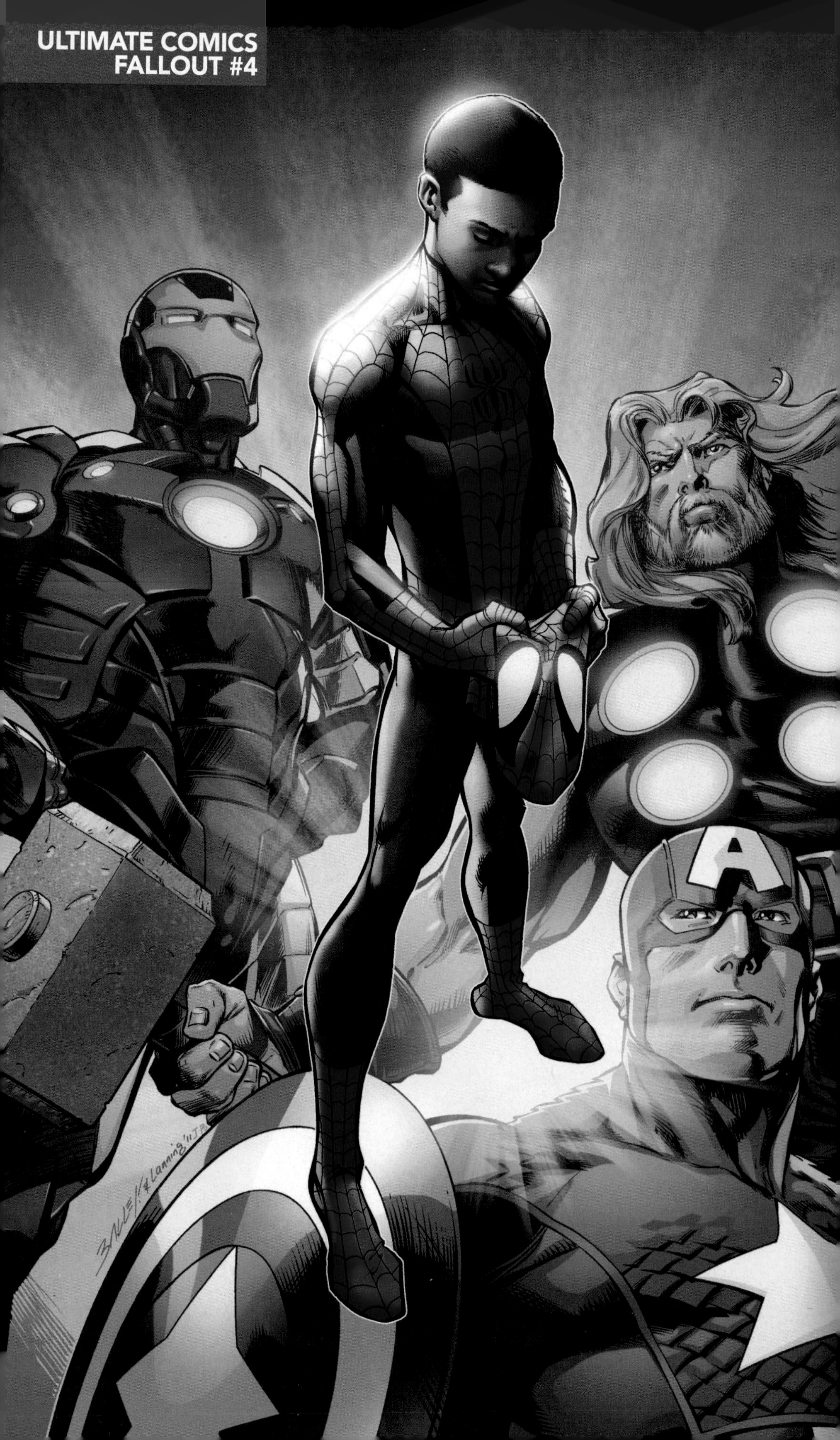
ULTIMATE COMICS
FALLOUT #4

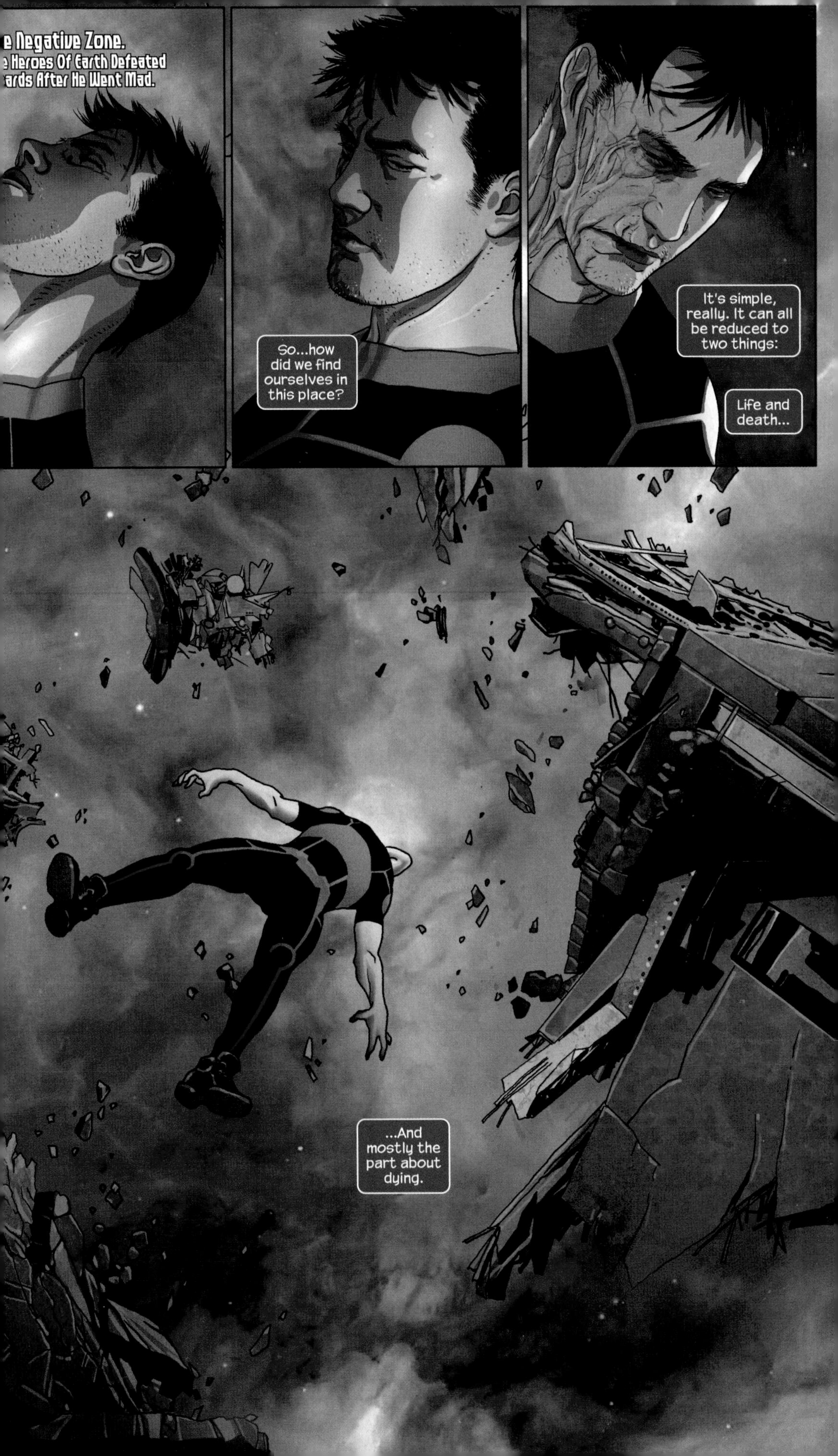
e Negative Zone.
e Heroes Of Earth Defeated
ards After He Went Mad.
So...how did we find ourselves in this place?
It's simple, really. It can all be reduced to two things:
Life and death...
...And mostly the part about dying.

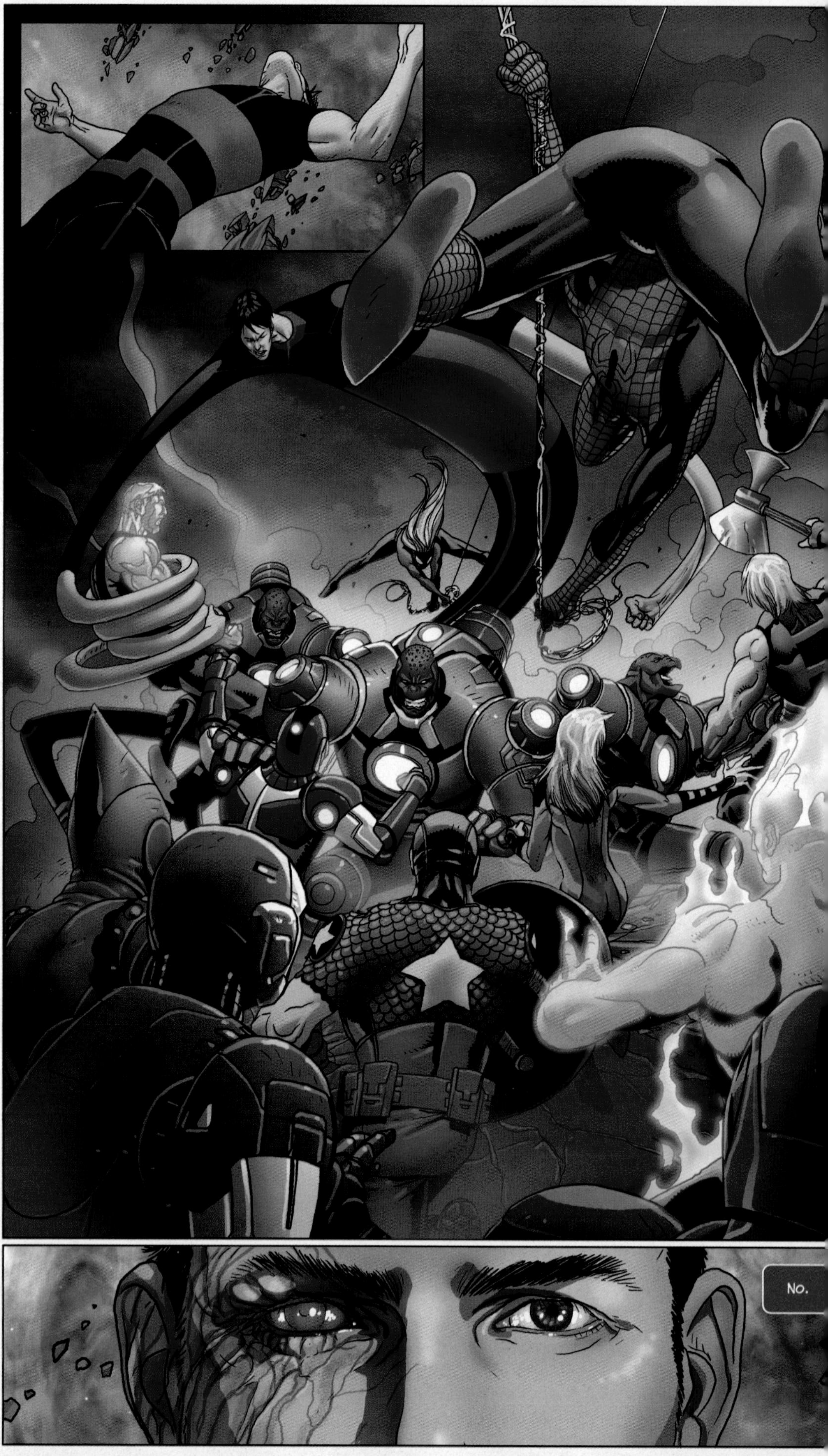
No.

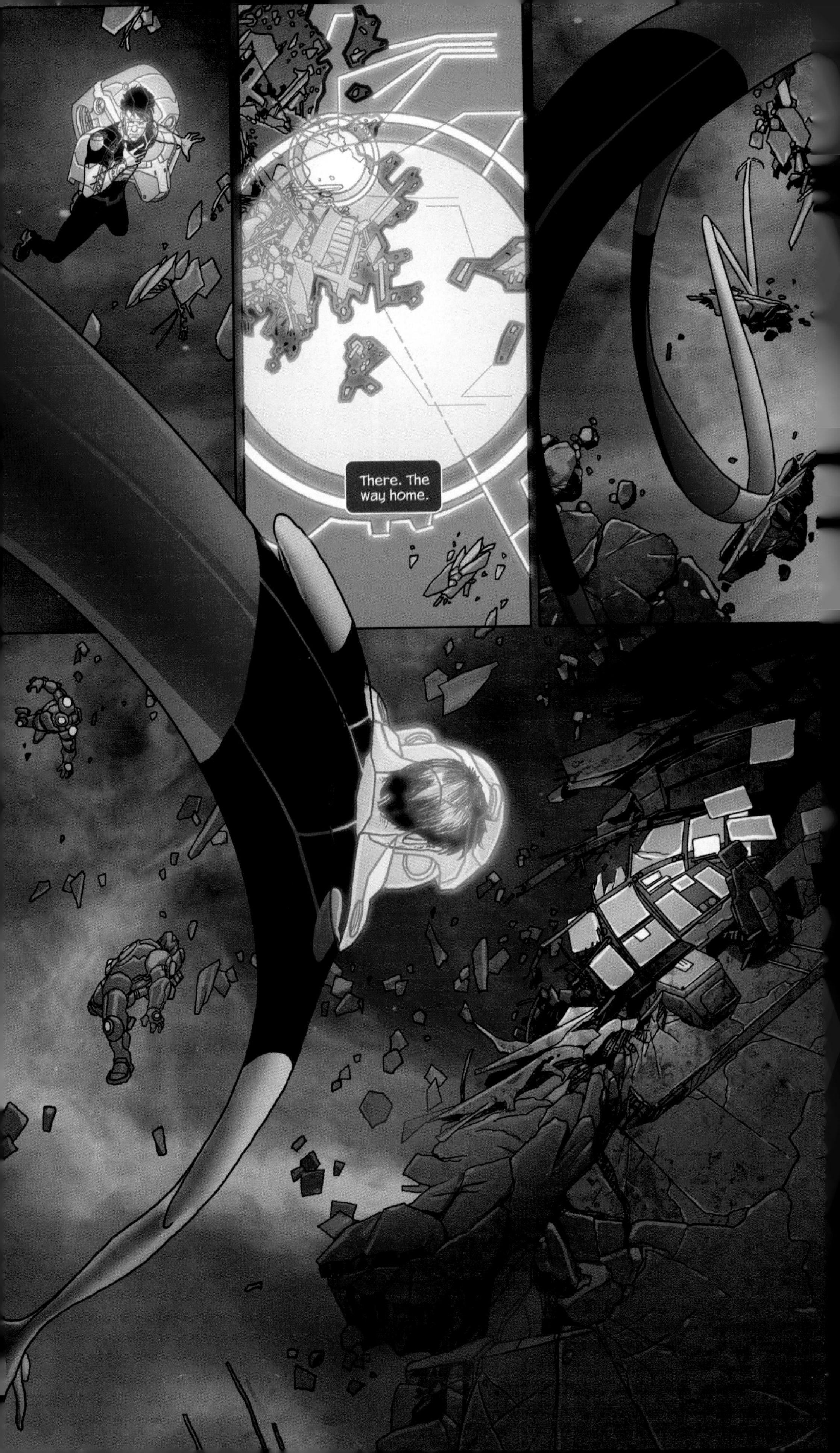
There. The way home.

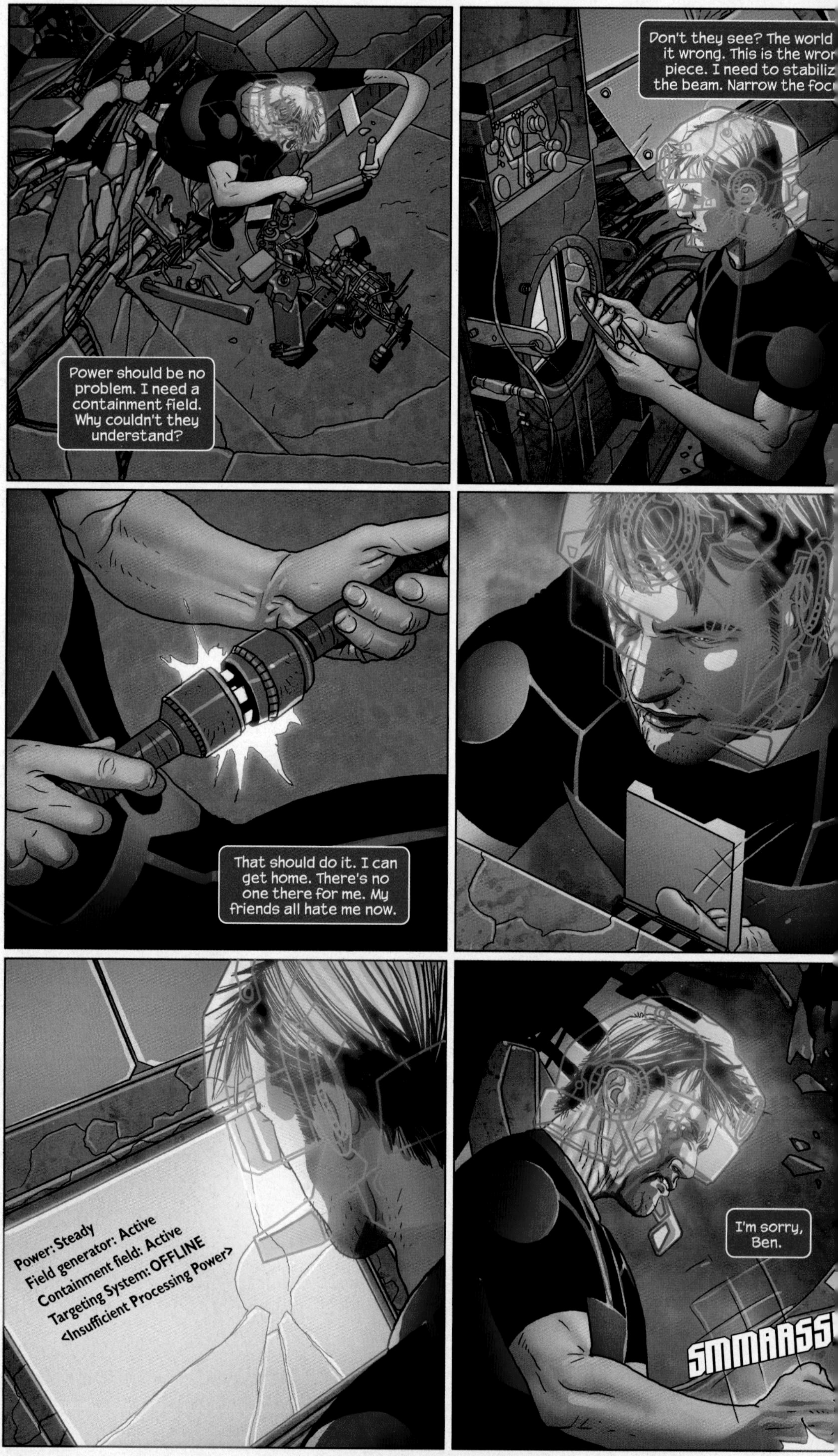

Power should be no problem. I need a containment field. Why couldn't they understand?
Don't they see? The world it wrong. This is the wror piece. I need to stabiliz the beam. Narrow the foc
That should do it. I can get home. There's no one there for me. My friends all hate me now.
Power: Steady
Field generator: Active
Containment field: Active
Targeting System: OFFLINE
<Insufficient Processing Power>
I'm sorry, Ben.
SMMAASS

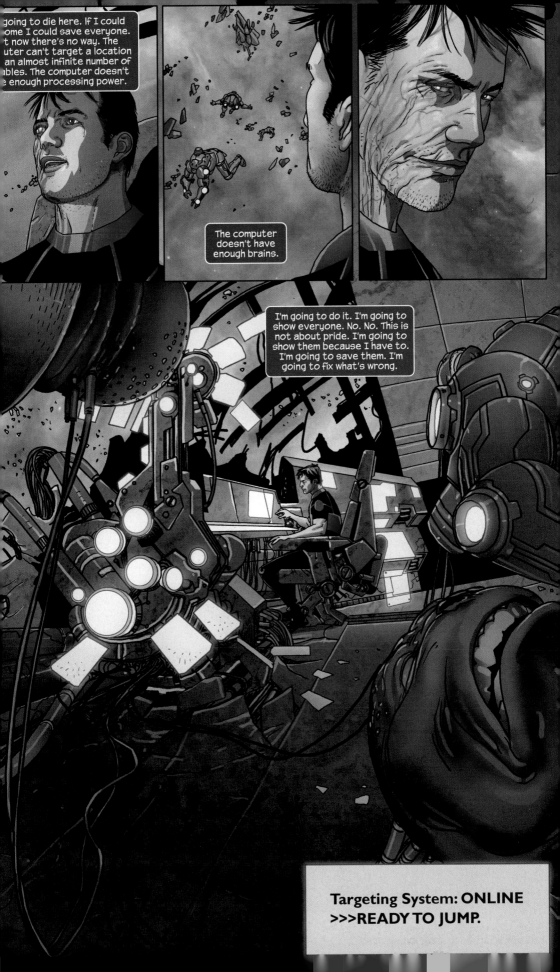

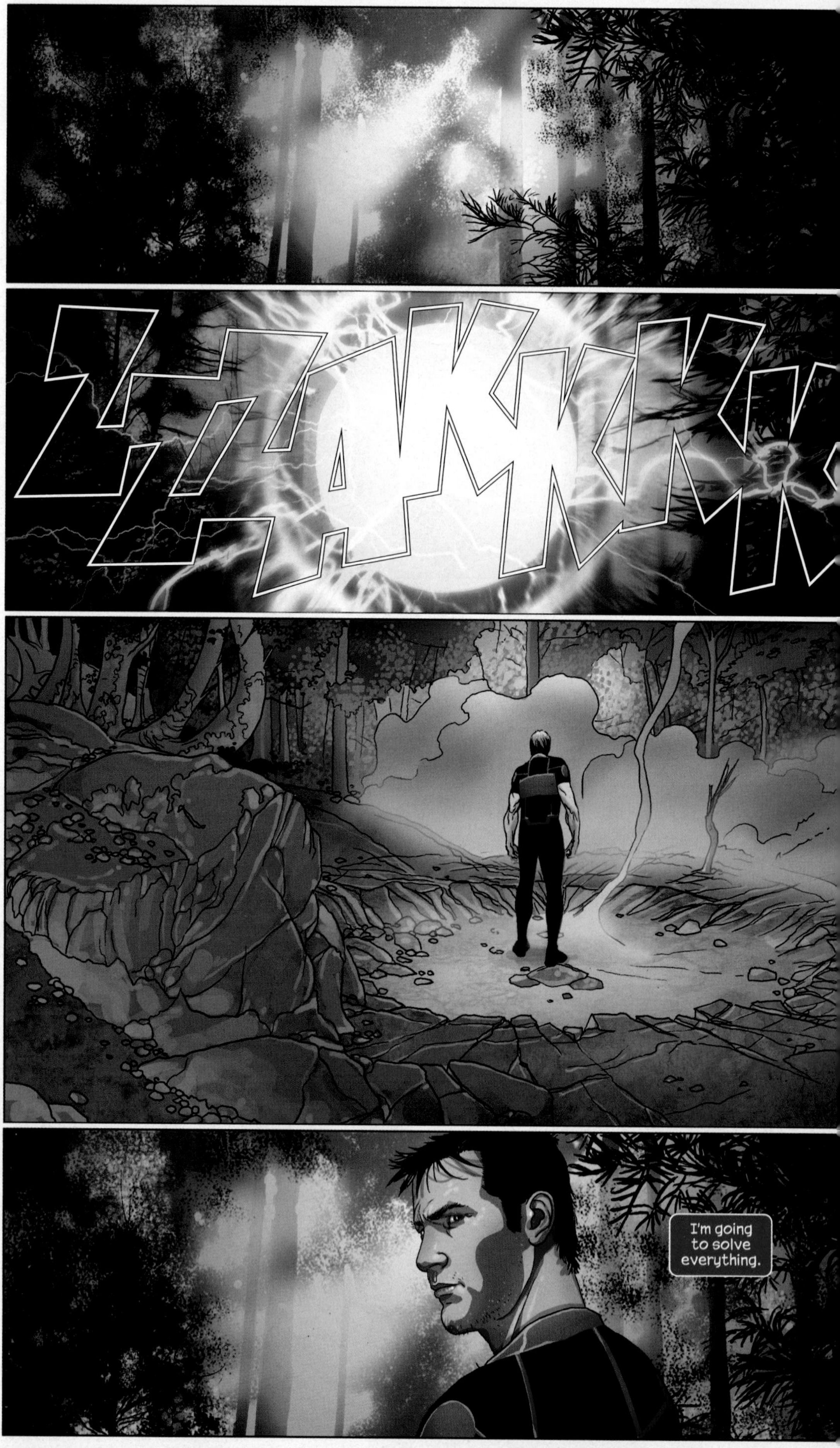
ZZAKKK
I'm going to solve everything.

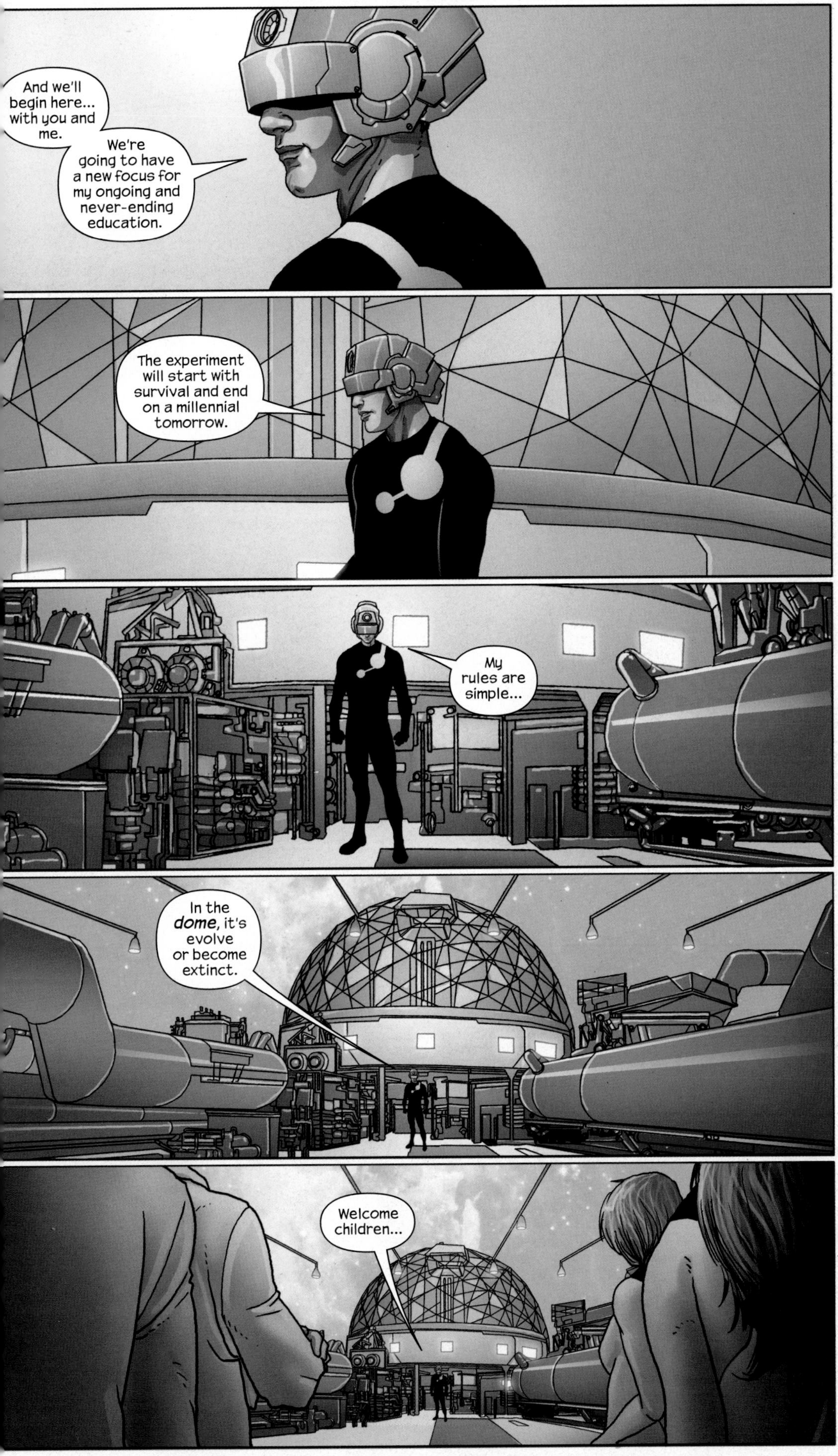

And we'll begin here... with you and me.
We're going to have a new focus for my ongoing and never-ending education.
The experiment will start with survival and end on a millennial tomorrow.
My rules are simple...
In the dome, it's evolve or become extinct.
Welcome children...

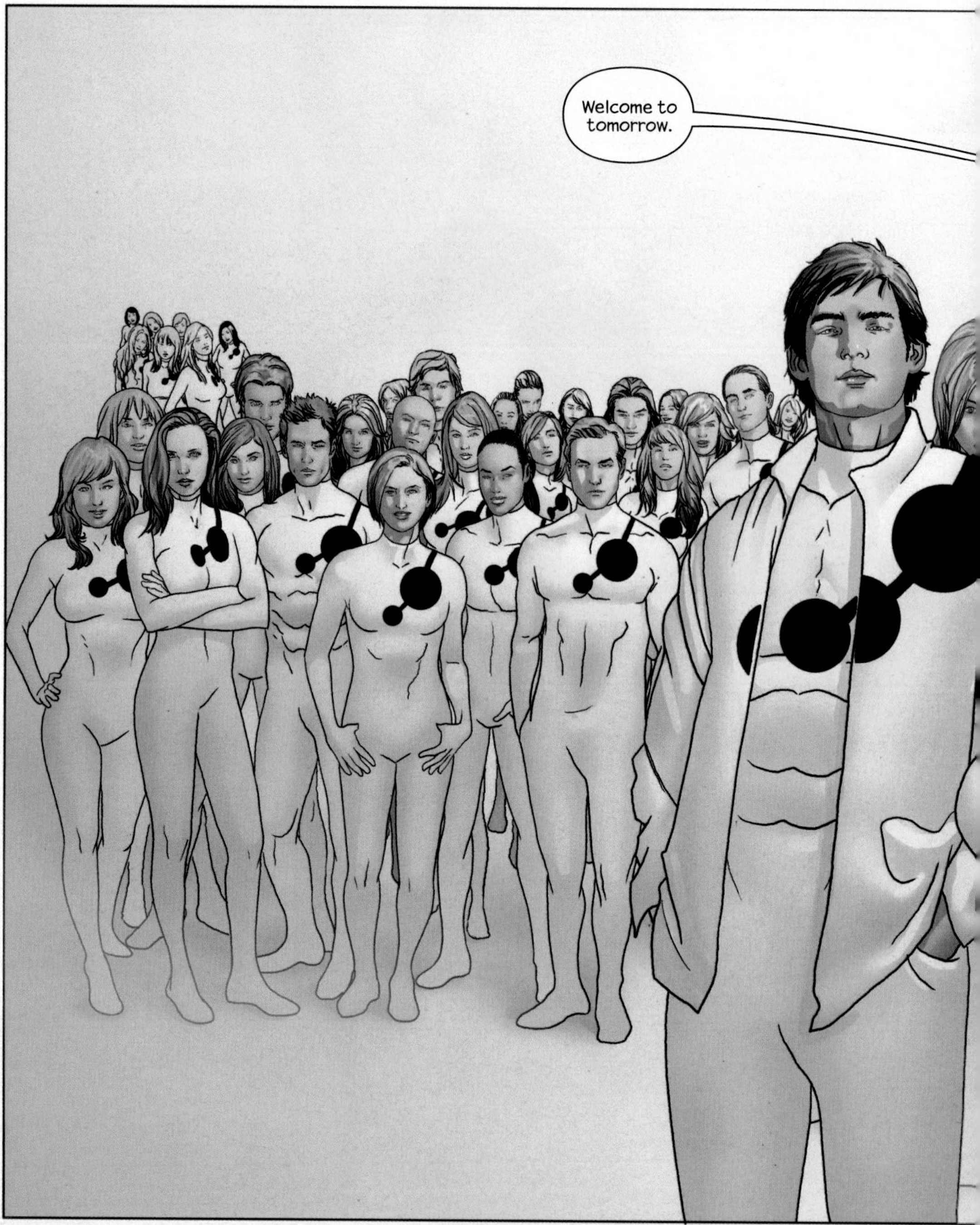

Welcome to tomorrow.

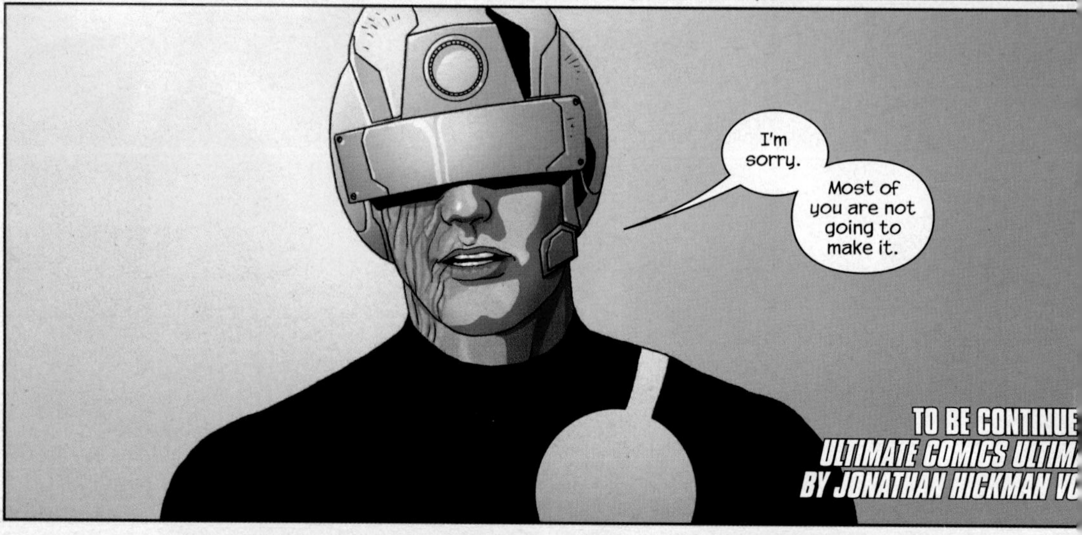

I'm sorry.
Most of you are not going to make it.
TO BE CONTINUE
ULTIMATE COMICS ULTIM
BY JONATHAN HICKMAN VO

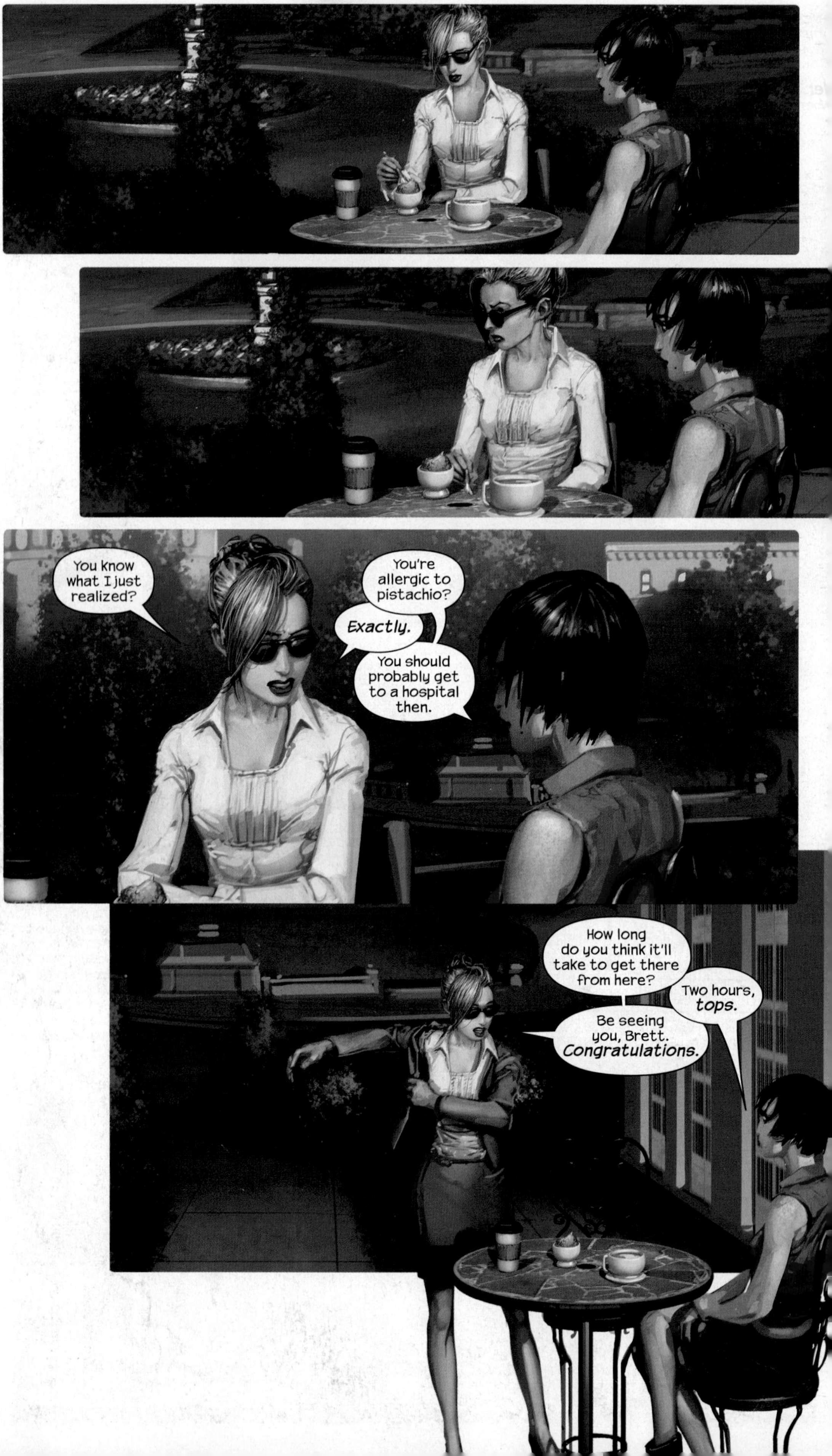

You know what I just realized?
You're allergic to pistachio?
Exactly.
You should probably get to a hospital then.
How long do you think it'll take to get there from here?
Two hours, *tops.*
Be seeing you, Brett. *Congratulations.*

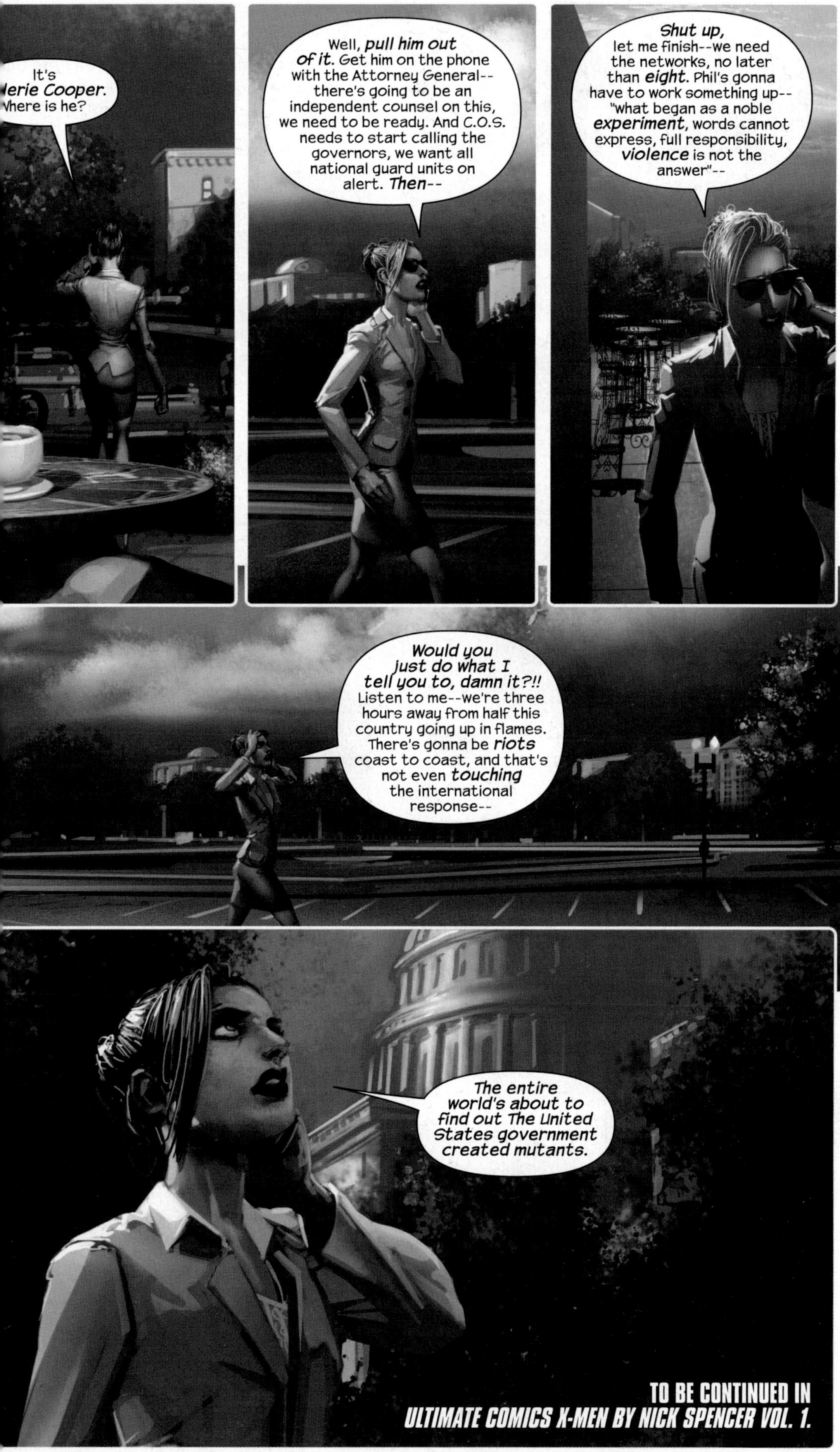
It's lerie Cooper. here is he?
Well, pull him out of it. Get him on the phone with the Attorney General--there's going to be an independent counsel on this, we need to be ready. And C.O.S. needs to start calling the governors, we want all national guard units on alert. Then--
Shut up, let me finish--we need the networks, no later than eight. Phil's gonna have to work something up--"what began as a noble experiment, words cannot express, full responsibility, violence is not the answer"--
Would you just do what I tell you to, damn it?!! Listen to me--we're three hours away from half this country going up in flames. There's gonna be riots coast to coast, and that's not even touching the international response--
The entire world's about to find out The United States government created mutants.
TO BE CONTINUED IN ULTIMATE COMICS X-MEN BY NICK SPENCER VOL. 1.

# ULTIMATE COMICS

**In the wake of Ultimatum,** the Ultimate Ur
was overhauled with comics top writers and
bringing a new energy to Ultimates characte

### ➤ Ultimate Comics Iron Man: Armor Wars HC/TP

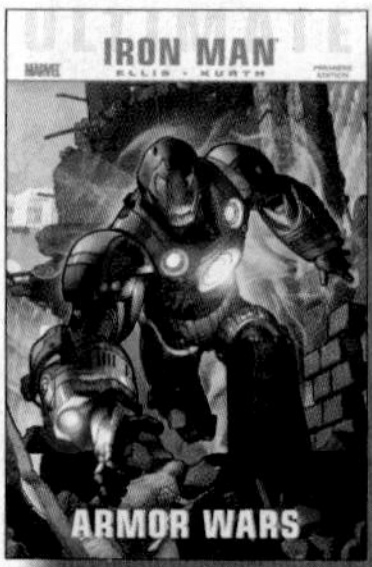
IRON MAN
ARMOR WARS

Collects *Ultimate Armor Wars* #1-4

By Warren Ellis and Steve Kurth

*Tony's armor falls into the wrong hands in the wake of Ultimatum!*

HC: JAN100637 • 978-0-7851-4250-8
TP: JUL100695 • 978-0-7851-4430-4

### ➤ Ultimate Comics Spider-Man Vol. 1: The World According to Peter Parker HC/TP

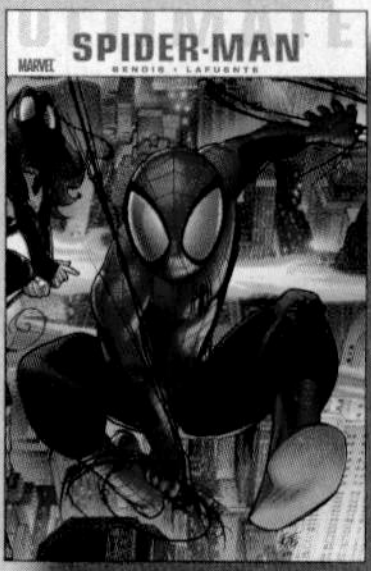
SPIDER-MAN

Collects *Ultimate Comics Spider-Man* #1-6

By Brian Michael Bendis and David Lafuente

*Six months after Ultimatum, Spidey picks up the pieces on a new life!*

HC: JAN100656 • 978-0-7851-4011-5
TP: APR100670 • 978-0-7851-4099-3

### ➤ Ultimate Comics Spider-Man Vol. 2: Chameleons HC/TP

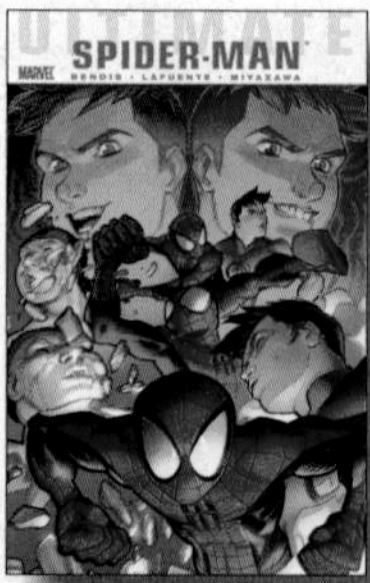
SPIDER-MAN

Collects *Ultimate Comics Spider-Man* #7-14

By Brian Michael Bendis, Takeshi Miyazawa and David Lafuente

*Rick Jones has some crazy new powers...and might just be crazy!*

HC: SEP100695 • 978-0-7851-4012-2
TP: MAR110801 • 978-0-7851-4100-6

### ➤ Ultimate Comics Avengers: Next Generation HC/TP

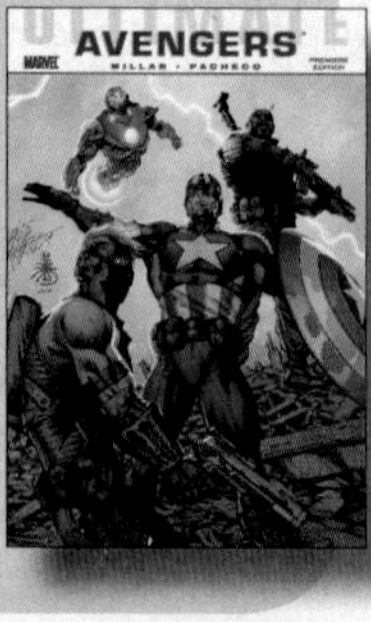
AVENGERS

Collects *Ultimate Avengers* #1-6

By Mark Millar and Carlos Pacheco

*Classified secrets threaten Captain America and only Nick Fury can help!*

HC: APR100654 • 978-0-7851-4010-8
TP: AUG100701 • 978-0-7851-4097-9

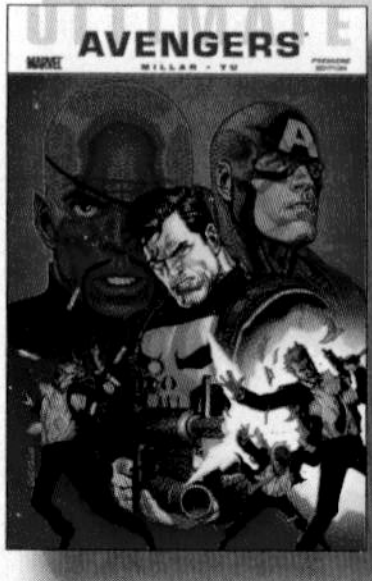
AVENGERS

### ➤ Ultimate Comics Ave
### Crime & Punishment H

Collects *Ultimate Avengers* .

By Mark Millar and Leinil Fra

*When the job is just too dirt*
*Fury calls in the Avengers!*

HC: AUG100688 • 978-0-785
TP: FEB110685 • 978-0-785

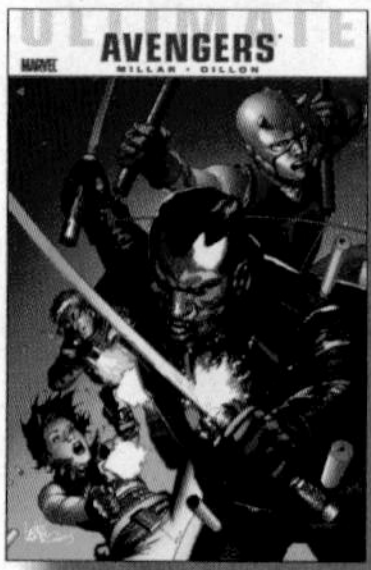
AVENGERS

### ➤ Ultimate Comics Ave
### Blade vs. Avengers HC/

Collects Ultimate Avengers

By Mark Millar and Steve D

*Blade is back in a bad way,*
*can only mean one thing: Va*

FEB110663 • 978-0-7851-

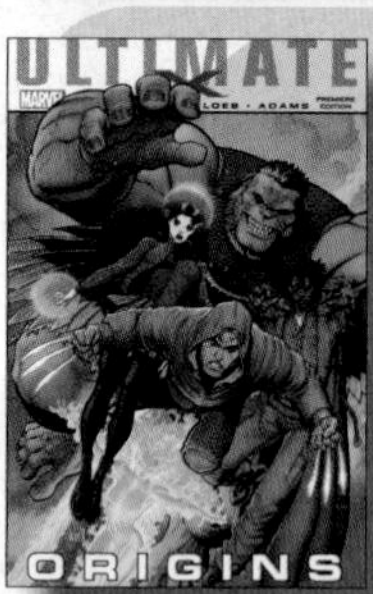
ULTIMATE
ORIGINS

### ➤ Ultimate Comics X: Origins HC

Collects *Ultimate Comics X*

By Jeph Loeb and Arthur A

*Who is Ultimate X? The cha*
*who will change the Ultimate*
*Universe forever!*

978-0-7851-4014-6

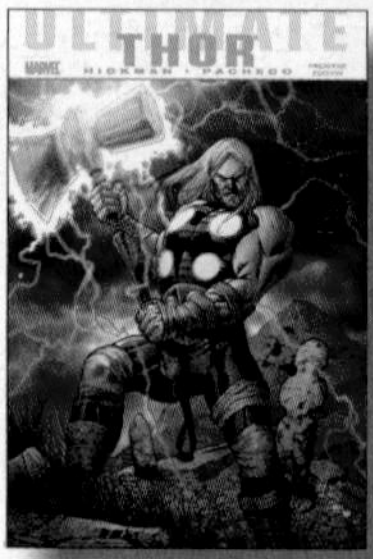
THOR

### ➤ Ultimate Comics Tho

Collects *Ultimate Comics Th*

By Jonathan Hickman and
Pacheco

*Origins revealed as Ultimate*
*back to the beginning of Tho*
*and Asgard!*

DEC100662 • 978-0-7851-

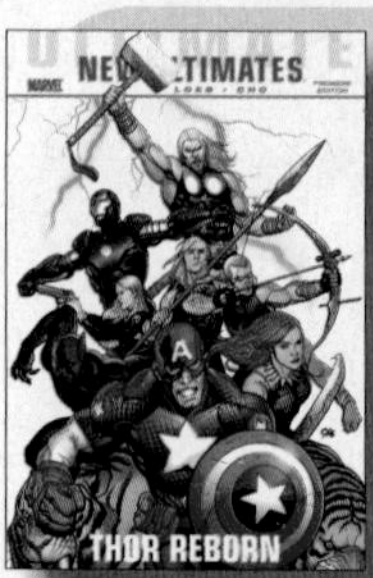
NEW ULTIMATES
THOR REBORN

### ➤ Ultimate Comics New
### Ultimates: Thor Reborn
### HC/TP

Collects *New Ultimates* #1-

By Jeph Loeb and Frank Ch

*Thor returns from the underw*
*ready to destroy Loki for goo*

JAN110838 • 978-0-7851-3

# Collected Editions

**Jltimate Comics Spider-Man Vol. 1: The World According o Peter Parker MPHC/TPB**

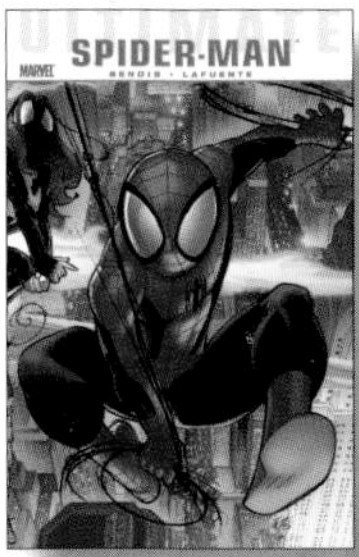
SPIDER-MAN
BENDIS • LAFUENTE

*Jltimate Comics Spider-Man 2009) #1-6*

Brian Michael Bendis & David .afuente

*Six months after Ultimatum, Spidey picks up the pieces of a new life!*

HC: JAN100656 • 978-0-7851-4011-5
TPB: APR100670 • 978-0-7851-4099-3

**Jltimate Comics Spider-Man Vol. 2: Chameleons MPHC/ TPB**

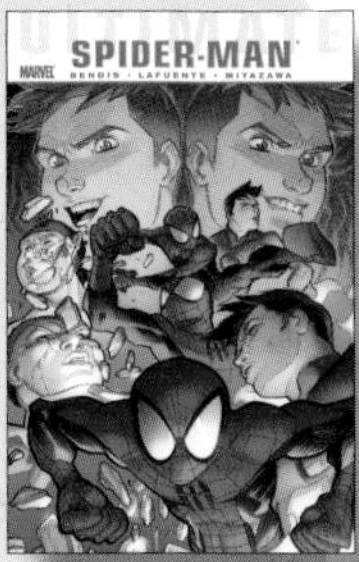
SPIDER-MAN
BENDIS • LAFUENTE • MIYAZAWA

*Jltimate Comics Spider-Man 2009) #7-14*

Brian Michael Bendis, Takeshi Miyazawa & David Lafuente

*Rick Jones has some crazy new powers...and might just be crazy!*

HC: SEP100695 • 978-0-7851-4012-2
TPB: MAR110801 • 978-0-7851-4100-6

**Ultimate Spider-Man Vol. 12 HC**

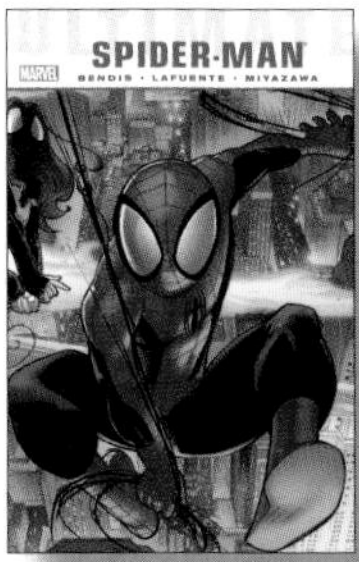
SPIDER-MAN
BENDIS • LAFUENTE • MIYAZAWA

*Ultimate Comics Spider-Man (2009) #1-14*

DEC110720 • 978-0-7851-6462-3

**Ultimate Comics Spider-Man Vol. 3: Death of Spider-Man Prelude MPHC/TPB**

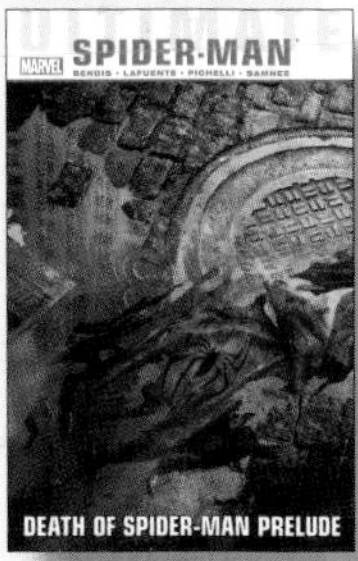
SPIDER-MAN
DEATH OF SPIDER-MAN PRELUDE

*Ultimate Comics Spider-Man (2009) #15 & #150-155*

Brian Michael Bendis, Sara Pichelli, Chris Samnee & others

*Spidey gets after-school super-hero training from the Ultimates!*

HC: APR110715 • 978-0-7851-4639-1
TPB: OCT110733 • 978-0-7851-4640-7

**Ultimate Comics Spider-Man Vol. 4: Death of Spider-Man MPHC/TPB**

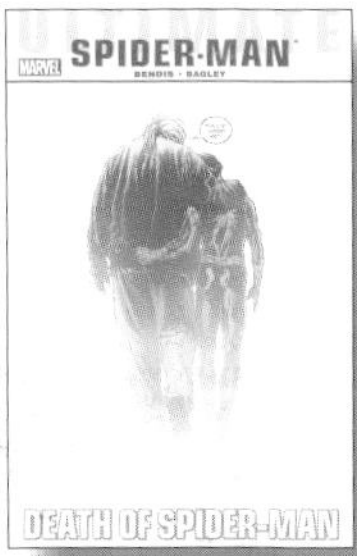
SPIDER-MAN
BENDIS • BAGLEY
DEATH OF SPIDER-MAN

*Ultimate Comics Spider-Man #156-160*

Brian Michael Bendis & Mark Bagley

*To save Aunt May and Mary Jane, can Peter make the ultimate sacrifice?*

HC: AUG110700 • 978-0-7851-5274-3
TPB: FEB120683 • 978-0-7851-5275-0

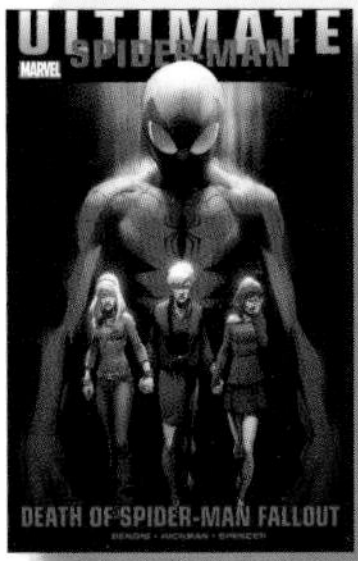
ULTIMATE
DEATH OF SPIDER-MAN FALLOUT

**Ultimate Comics: Death of Spider-Man Fallout MPHC/ TPB**

*Ultimate Comics Fallout #1-6*

Brian Michael Bendis, Jonathan Hickman, Mark Bagley & others

*The aftermath of Peter Parker's death.*

HC: SEP110655 • 978-0-7851-5912-4
TPB: MAR120684 • 978-0-7851-5913-1

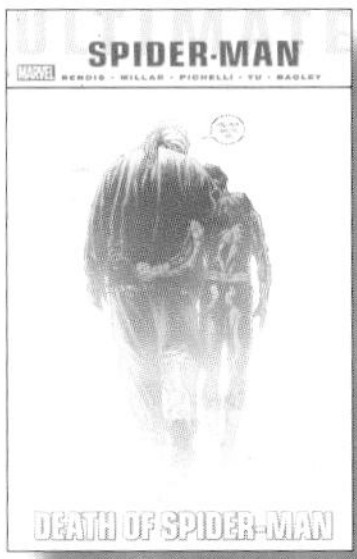
SPIDER-MAN
DEATH OF SPIDER-MAN

**Ultimate Comics Spider-Man: The Death of Spider-Man Omnibus HC**

*Ultimate Comics Spider-Man (2009) #15 & #150-160*

JUN120709 • 978-0-7851-6464-7

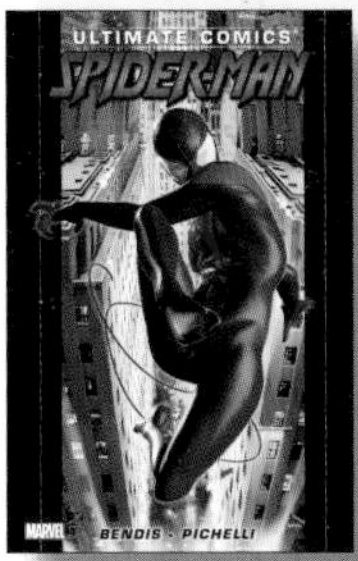
ULTIMATE COMICS
SPIDER-MAN
BENDIS • PICHELLI

**Ultimate Comics Spider-Man by Brian Michael Bendis Vol. 1 MPHC/TPB**

*Ultimate Comics Spider-Man (2011) #1-5*

Brian Michael Bendis, David Marquez & Sara Pichelli

*There's a new Ultimate Spider-Man, and it's Miles Morales!*

HC: DEC110727 • 978-0-7851-5712-0
TPB: MAY120769 • 978-0-7851-5713-7

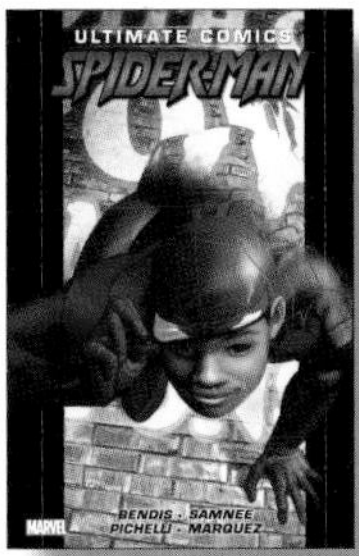
ULTIMATE COMICS
SPIDER-MAN

**Ultimate Comics Spider-Man by Brian Michael Bendis Vol. 2 MPHC/TPB**

*Ultimate Comics Spider-Man (2011) #6-10*

Brian Michael Bendis, Chris Samnee, David Marquez & Sara Pichelli

*Miles' Uncle Aaron – the Prowler – battles for his nephew's soul!*

HC: APR120712 • 978-0-7851-5714-4
TPB: AUG120710 • 978-0-7851-5715-1

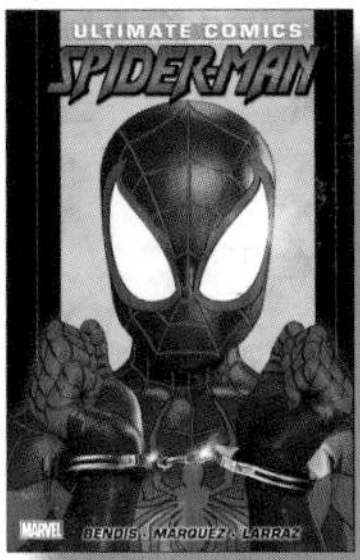
ULTIMATE COMICS
SPIDER-MAN

**Ultimate Comics Spider-Man by Brian Michael Bendis Vol. 3 MPHC**

*Ultimate Comics Spider-Man (2011) #11-15*

Brian Michael Bendis & David Marquez

*Spider-Man joins the Ultimates!*

HC: AUG120701 • 978-0-7851-6175-2
TPB: 978-0-7851-6176-9

# A NEW ERA OF ULTIMATE SPIDER-MAN STARTS HERE, IN THE EVENT THAT GRABBED WORLDWIDE HEADLINES!

"*Ultimate Spider-Man* is a relaunch done exactly right. A perfectly chosen creative team paired with a modern and forward thinking character to create a nearly perfect book that can work for longtime fans and new readers alike."
— Kelly Thompson, *ComicBookResources.com*

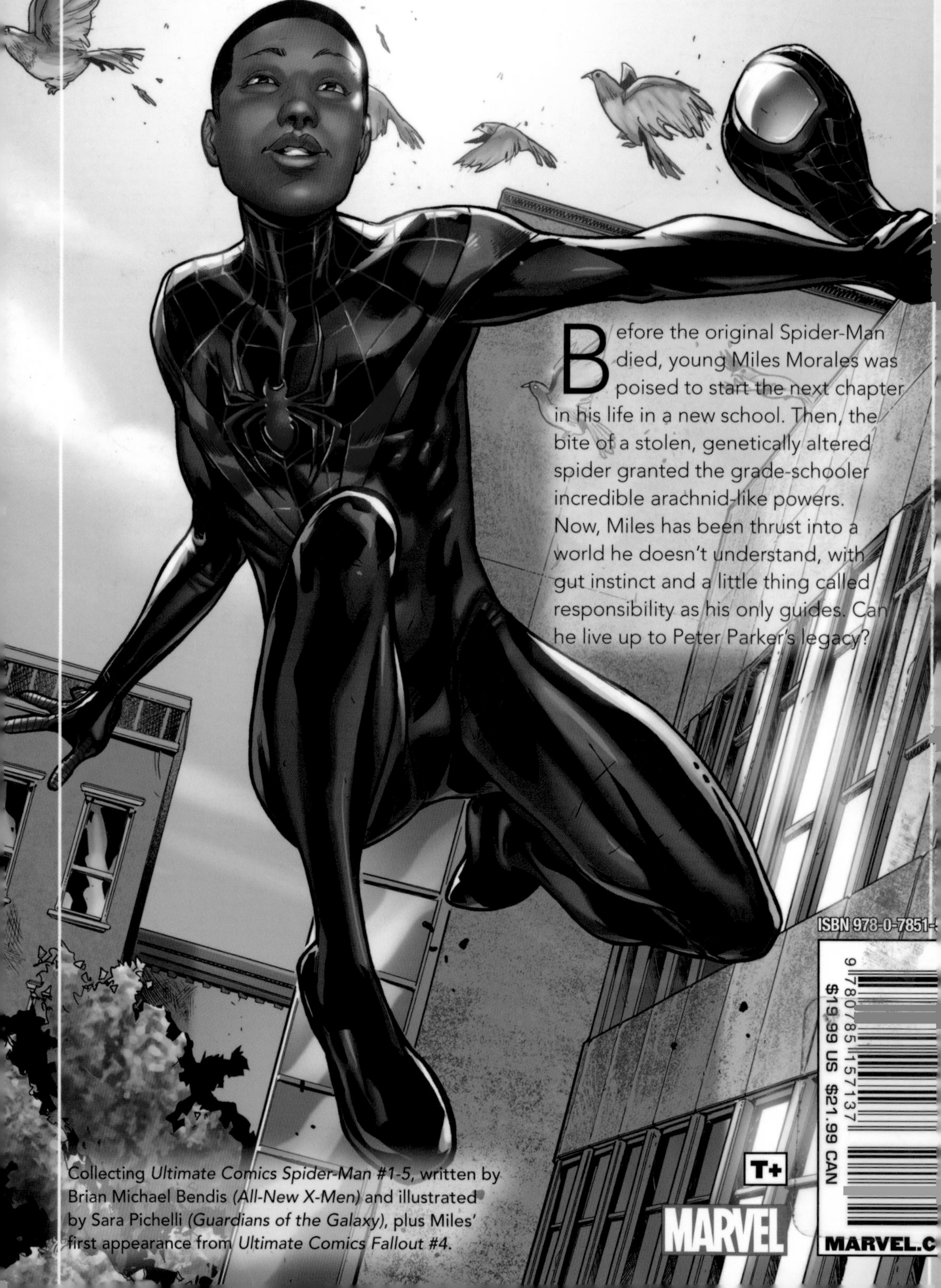

Before the original Spider-Man died, young Miles Morales was poised to start the next chapter in his life in a new school. Then, the bite of a stolen, genetically altered spider granted the grade-schooler incredible arachnid-like powers. Now, Miles has been thrust into a world he doesn't understand, with gut instinct and a little thing called responsibility as his only guides. Can he live up to Peter Parker's legacy?

Collecting *Ultimate Comics Spider-Man* #1-5, written by Brian Michael Bendis (*All-New X-Men*) and illustrated by Sara Pichelli (*Guardians of the Galaxy*), plus Miles' first appearance from *Ultimate Comics Fallout* #4.

T+

MARVEL

ISBN 978-0-7851-
9 780785 157137
$19.99 US $21.99 CAN
MARVEL.C